CRITICAL INFRASTRUCTURE PROTECTION II

IFIP – The International Federation for Information Processing

IFIP was founded in 1960 under the auspices of UNESCO, following the First World Computer Congress held in Paris the previous year. An umbrella organization for societies working in information processing, IFIP's aim is two-fold: to support information processing within its member countries and to encourage technology transfer to developing nations. As its mission statement clearly states,

> IFIP's mission is to be the leading, truly international, apolitical organization which encourages and assists in the development, exploitation and application of information technology for the benefit of all people.

IFIP is a non-profitmaking organization, run almost solely by 2500 volunteers. It operates through a number of technical committees, which organize events and publications. IFIP's events range from an international congress to local seminars, but the most important are:

• The IFIP World Computer Congress, held every second year;
• Open conferences;
• Working conferences.

The flagship event is the IFIP World Computer Congress, at which both invited and contributed papers are presented. Contributed papers are rigorously refereed and the rejection rate is high.

As with the Congress, participation in the open conferences is open to all and papers may be invited or submitted. Again, submitted papers are stringently refereed.

The working conferences are structured differently. They are usually run by a working group and attendance is small and by invitation only. Their purpose is to create an atmosphere conducive to innovation and development. Refereeing is less rigorous and papers are subjected to extensive group discussion.

Publications arising from IFIP events vary. The papers presented at the IFIP World Computer Congress and at open conferences are published as conference proceedings, while the results of the working conferences are often published as collections of selected and edited papers.

Any national society whose primary activity is in information may apply to become a full member of IFIP, although full membership is restricted to one society per country. Full members are entitled to vote at the annual General Assembly, National societies preferring a less committed involvement may apply for associate or corresponding membership. Associate members enjoy the same benefits as full members, but without voting rights. Corresponding members are not represented in IFIP bodies. Affiliated membership is open to non-national societies, and individual and honorary membership schemes are also offered.

CRITICAL INFRASTRUCTURE PROTECTION II

Edited by

MAURICIO PAPA

University of Tulsa
Tulsa, Oklahoma, USA

SUJEET SHENOI

University of Tulsa
Tulsa, Oklahoma, USA

 Springer

Critical Infrastructure Protection II

Edited by Mauricio Papa and Sujeet Shenoi

p. cm. (IFIP International Federation for Information Processing, a Springer Series in Computer Science)

ISSN: 1571-5736 / 1861-2288 (Internet)

ISBN: 978-1-4419-4695-9   e-ISBN: 978-0-387-88523-0

Printed on acid-free paper

9 8 7 6 5 4 3 2 1

springer.com

Contents

Contents

Contributing Authors

Anas Abou el Kalam is an Assistant Professor of Network Security at the National Polytechnic Institute, Toulouse, France. His research interests include security policies and models, intrusion detection, network security and embedded systems security.

Zahid Anwar is a Ph.D. candidate in Computer Science at the University of Illinois, Urbana-Champaign, Illinois. His research interests are in the areas of large-scale systems modeling, information assurance and control systems security.

Pierluigi Assogna is a Progam Manager at Theorematica SpA, Rome, Italy. His research interests include knowledge management, document management, manufacturing and control, and system interoperability.

Amine Baina is a Ph.D. student in Computer Security at LAAS-CNRS, Toulouse, France. His research interests include access control policies and models, collaboration technologies and critical infrastructure protection.

Carlo Bellettini is an Associate Professor of Computer Science at the University of Milan, Milan, Italy. His research interests include information security and the analysis, specification and design of real-time systems.

Glauco Bertocchi is a Professor of Information and Communications Technology Security at the Sapienza University of Rome, Rome, Italy, and is responsible for security at the Camera dei Deputati (Italian Congress), Rome, Italy. His research interests include systems security, infrastructure safety and security, and crisis management.

Joshua Blackwell is an M.A. student in Geography at the University of North Carolina at Charlotte, Charlotte, North Carolina. His research focuses on ontological approaches in critical infrastructure protection planning.

Sandro Bologna is a Senior Researcher at the Italian National Agency for New Technologies, Energy and the Environment (ENEA), Rome, Italy. His research interests include dependable computing and critical infrastructure protection.

Roy Campbell is the Sohaib and Sara Abbasi Professor of Computer Science at the University of Illinois, Urbana-Champaign, Illinois. His research interests include security, programming languages, software engineering, operating systems, distributed systems and networking.

Emiliano Casalicchio is a Computer Science Researcher at the University of Rome – Tor Vergata, Rome, Italy. His research interests include complex systems modeling and simulation, and distributed systems design, modeling and performance evaluation.

Rodrigo Chandia is a Ph.D. student in Computer Science at the University of Tulsa, Tulsa, Oklahoma. His research interests include SCADA security, computer security and open source software development methodologies.

Paul Craven is a Professor of Computer Science at Simpson College, Indianola, Iowa. His research interests are in the areas of information assurance and data communications for railroads.

Yves Deswarte is a Research Director at LAAS-CNRS, Toulouse, France. His research interests include distributed systems dependability and security, critical infrastructure protection and privacy-preserving authorization schemes.

Scott Dynes is a Senior Research Fellow at the Center for Digital Strategies, Tuck School of Business, Dartmouth College, Hanover, New Hampshire. His research interests include information risk management and the resilience of critical infrastructures to cyber disruptions.

Terry Fleury is a Research Programmer at the National Center for Supercomputing Applications, University of Illinois, Urbana-Champaign, Illinois. His research interests include grid computing security, computer-supported cooperative work and human-computer interaction.

Emanuele Galli is a Ph.D. student in Computer Science at the University of Rome – Tor Vergata, Rome, Italy. His research interests include critical infrastructure modeling and simulation, and agent-based modeling and simulation.

James Graham is the Henry Vogt Professor of Computer Science and Engineering at the University of Louisville, Louisville, Kentucky. His research interests include information security, digital forensics, critical infrastructure protection, high performance computing and intelligent systems.

Jeffrey Hieb is an Assistant Professor of Engineering Fundamentals at the University of Louisville, Louisville, Kentucky. His research interests include information security, honeypots, digital forensics, secure operating systems and engineering education.

Kenneth Hopkinson is an Assistant Professor of Computer Science at the Air Force Institute of Technology, Wright-Patterson Air Force Base, Ohio. His research interests include critical infrastructure modeling and simulation, and vulnerability analyses of power systems.

Jeffrey Hunker is a Professor of Technology and Public Policy at the Heinz School of Public Policy and Management at Carnegie Mellon University, Pittsburgh, Pennsylvania. He previously served as the Senior Director for Critical Infrastructure, National Security Council, The White House, Washington, DC. His research primarily focuses on information security and homeland security.

Robert Hutchinson is the Manager of the Networked Systems Survivability and Assurance Department and the Coordinator of Information Assurance Research at Sandia National Laboratories, Albuquerque, New Mexico. His research interests include hardware-based computer security, supply chain risk, and security through unpredictability.

Stig Johnsen is a Senior Research Scientist at SINTEF, Trondheim, Norway. His research interests include information security, SCADA systems, integrated oil and gas operations, and plant safety.

Wray Johnson is the Chief Software Architect for IntePoint LLC, Charlotte, North Carolina. His research focuses on extensible architectures for integrated modeling and simulation in support of system-of-systems analyses.

Mohamed Kaaniche is a Research Director at LAAS-CNRS, Toulouse, France. His research interests include the security and dependability of fault-tolerant computing systems and critical infrastructure protection.

Himanshu Khurana is a Principal Research Scientist at the Information Trust Institute, University of Illinois, Urbana-Champaign, Illinois. His research interests include access control, key management and critical infrastructure protection.

Marieke Klaver is a Senior Researcher at TNO Defence, Security and Safety, The Hague, The Netherlands. Her research interests include information assurance and critical infrastructure protection.

Seok-Won Lee is an Assistant Professor of Software and Information Systems at the University of North Carolina at Charlotte, Charlotte, North Carolina. His research areas include software engineering, machine learning and knowledge-based systems.

Rafal Leszczyna is a Scientific Officer at the Joint Research Center of the European Commission, Ispra, Italy, and a member of the Information Assurance Group at Gdansk University of Technology, Gdansk, Poland. His research interests include computer security, security protocols and software agents.

Eric Luiijf is a Principal Consultant at TNO Defence, Security and Safety, The Hague, The Netherlands. His research interests include information assurance and critical infrastructure protection.

Jonathan Margulies is a Senior Member of the Technical Staff at Sandia National Laboratories, Albuquerque, New Mexico. His research interests include secure system design and control systems security.

Marcelo Masera is a Scientific Officer at the Institute for the Protection and Security of the Citizen, Joint Research Center of the European Commission, Ispra, Italy. His research interests include the security of networked systems and systems-of-systems, risk governance, and control systems and communication systems security.

Vincenzo Masucci is a Senior Researcher with the CRIATE Consortium in Portici, Italy. His research interests include knowledge representation and knowledge management in the critical infrastructure domain.

Igor Nai Fovino is a Scientific Officer at the Institute for the Protection and Security of the Citizen, Joint Research Center of the European Commission, Ispra, Italy, and a Lecturer of Operating Systems at the University of Insubria, Varese, Italy. His research interests include system survivability, formal methods for security assessment, secure communication protocols and privacy-preserving data mining.

David Nicol is a Professor of Electrical and Computer Engineering at the University of Illinois, Urbana-Champaign, Illinois. His research interests are in the areas of high performance computing, performance analysis, simulation and modeling, and network security.

Albert Nieuwenhuijs is a Senior Researcher at TNO Defence, Security and Safety, The Hague, The Netherlands. His research interests include operational analysis and critical infrastructure protection.

Hamed Okhravi is a Ph.D. candidate in Electrical and Computer Engineering at the University of Illinois, Urbana-Champaign, Illinois. His research interests include cyber security, trusted computing, high assurance systems, cryptography and simulation.

Paul Oman is a Professor of Computer Science at the University of Idaho, Moscow, Idaho. His research interests include various aspects of information assurance, especially securing real-time systems used in critical infrastructures.

Alberto Paoluzzi is a Professor of Computer-Aided Design in the Department of Informatics and Automation at the Third University of Rome, Rome, Italy. His research interests include new methods for modeling complex systems, physically-based object representations using cell decompositions and algebraic topology methods.

Mauricio Papa is an Associate Professor of Computer Science at the University of Tulsa, Tulsa, Oklahoma. His research interests include distributed systems, information assurance, and network and SCADA systems security.

Brian Porter received his M.S. degree in Computer Science from the University of Tulsa, Tulsa, Oklahoma. His research interests include network security and SCADA systems security.

Richard Raines is a Professor of Electrical Engineering at the Air Force Institute of Technology, Wright-Patterson Air Force Base, Ohio. His research interests include computer and communications network security and vulnerability analysis.

Julian Rrushi is a Research Scholar in the Department of Computer Science, University of Illinois, Urbana-Champaign, Illinois, and a Ph.D. candidate in Computer Science at the University of Milan, Milan, Italy. His research interests are in the areas of computer and network security, and cryptology.

Andrew Schumpert is an M.A. student in Geography at the University of North Carolina at Charlotte, Charlotte, North Carolina. His research focuses on methodologies for critical infrastructure model development.

Giorgio Scorzelli is a Professor of Computer Graphics in the Department of Informatics and Automation at the Third University of Rome, Rome, Italy. His research interests include data analysis, topological methods for image segmentation, and progressive and multi-resolution techniques for scientific visualization.

Roberto Setola is the Director of the Complex Systems and Security Laboratory at University Campus Bio-Medico of Rome, Rome, Italy. His research interests include interdependent infrastructure modeling and analysis, control strategies for complex systems, non-linear estimation, mobile robots and biomedical systems.

Ryan Shayto received his Ph.D. degree in Computer Science from the University of Tulsa, Tulsa, Oklahoma. His research interests include information assurance and SCADA systems security.

Sujeet Shenoi, Chair, IFIP Working Group 11.10 on Critical Infrastructure Protection, is the F.P. Walter Professor of Computer Science at the University of Tulsa, Tulsa, Oklahoma. His research interests include information assurance, digital forensics, critical infrastructure protection and intelligent control.

Nils Svendsen is a Postdoctoral Research Fellow at the Norwegian Information Security Laboratory, Gjovik University College, Gjovik, Norway. His research interests include the modeling and simulation of critical infrastructures, graph theory, cryptography and coding theory.

William Tolone is an Associate Professor of Software and Information Systems at the University of North Carolina at Charlotte, Charlotte, North Carolina. His research interests include modeling and simulation, critical infrastructure protection, visual analytics, agent-based integration, collaborative systems, information environments and meta-level architectures.

Michele Vicentino is the Technical Director of TRS, Rome, Italy. His research interests include functional programming languages and their use in implementing complex, heterogeneous systems.

Von Welch is the Co-Director of Cyber Security at the National Center for Supercomputing Applications, University of Illinois, Urbana-Champaign, Illinois. His research interests include distributed and federated security architectures.

Dorsey Wilkin, a Captain in the U.S. Air Force, received his M.S. degree in Computer Science from the Air Force Institute of Technology, Wright-Patterson Air Force Base, Ohio. His research interests include information assurance and network security.

Paul Williams is a Major in the U.S. Air Force and an Assistant Professor of Computer Science at the Air Force Institute of Technology, Wright-Patterson Air Force Base, Ohio. His research interests include machine learning, data and information security, and computer hardware design.

Stephen Wolthusen is a Professor of Information Security at the Norwegian Information Security Laboratory, Gjovik University College, Gjovik, Norway, and a Lecturer in the Department of Mathematics at Royal Holloway, University of London, London, United Kingdom. His research interests include the modeling and simulation of critical infrastructures using combinatorial and graph-theoretic approaches as well as network and distributed systems security.

Wei-Ning Xiang is a Professor of Geography and Earth Sciences at the University of North Carolina at Charlotte, Charlotte, North Carolina. His research interests include geographic information science, multi-attribute assessment and evaluation, spatial simulation and modeling, and critical infrastructure protection.

Cody Yeager is an M.A. student in Geography at the University of North Carolina at Charlotte, Charlotte, North Carolina. His research focuses on the identification of intervention points during critical infrastructure disruptions.

Roberto Zollo is the Controller of Theorematica SpA, Rome, Italy and Chief Executive Officer of TRS, Rome Italy. His research interests include critical infrastructure protection, environmental control and crisis management.

Preface

The information infrastructure – comprising computers, embedded devices, networks and software systems – is vital to operations in every sector: information technology, telecommunications, energy, banking and finance, transportation systems, chemicals, agriculture and food, defense industrial base, public health and health care, national monuments and icons, drinking water and water treatment systems, commercial facilities, dams, emergency services, commercial nuclear reactors, materials and waste, postal and shipping, and government facilities. Global business and industry, governments, indeed society itself, cannot function if major components of the critical information infrastructure are degraded, disabled or destroyed.

This book, *Critical Infrastructure Protection II*, is the second volume in the annual series produced by IFIP Working Group 11.10 on Critical Infrastructure Protection, an active international community of scientists, engineers, practitioners and policy makers dedicated to advancing research, development and implementation efforts related to critical infrastructure protection. The book presents original research results and innovative applications in the area of infrastructure protection. Also, it highlights the importance of weaving science, technology and policy in crafting sophisticated, yet practical, solutions that will help secure information, computer and network assets in the various critical infrastructure sectors.

This volume contains twenty edited papers from the Second Annual IFIP Working Group 11.10 International Conference on Critical Infrastructure Protection, held at George Mason University, Arlington, Virginia, March 17–19, 2008. The papers were selected from forty-two submissions, which were refereed by members of IFIP Working Group 11.10 and other internationally-recognized experts in critical infrastructure protection.

The chapters are organized into six sections: themes and issues, infrastructure security, control systems security, security strategies, infrastructure interdependencies, and infrastructure modeling and simulation. The coverage of topics showcases the richness and vitality of the discipline, and offers promising avenues for future research in critical infrastructure protection.

This book is the result of the combined efforts of several individuals and organizations. In particular, we thank Rodrigo Chandia and Eric Goetz for their tireless work on behalf of IFIP Working Group 11.10. We gratefully acknowledge the Institute for Information Infrastructure Protection (I3P), managed by Dartmouth College, for nurturing IFIP Working Group 11.10 and sponsoring some of the research efforts whose results are described in this volume. We also thank the Department of Homeland Security and the National Security Agency for their support of IFIP Working Group 11.10 and its activities. Finally, we wish to note that all opinions, findings, conclusions and recommendations in the chapters of this book are those of the authors and do not necessarily reflect the views of their employers or funding agencies.

MAURICIO PAPA AND SUJEET SHENOI

I

THEMES AND ISSUES

Chapter 1

EMERGENT RISKS IN CRITICAL INFRASTRUCTURES

Scott Dynes

Abstract   Firms cannot function successfully without managing a host of internal and external organizational and process interdependencies. Part of this involves business continuity planning, which directly affects how resilient a firm and its business sector are in the face of disruptions. This paper presents the results of field studies related to information risk management practices in the health care and retail sectors. The studies explore information risk management coordinating signals within and across firms in these sectors as well as the potential effects of cyber disruptions on the firms as stand-alone entities and as part of a critical infrastructure. The health care case study investigates the impact of the Zotob worm on the ability to deliver medical care and treatment. The retail study examines the resilience of certain elements of the food supply chain to cyber disruptions.

Keywords: Information security, emergent risk, health care, grocery retail

1.   Introduction

> *No man is an island, entire of itself... John Donne (1572–1631)*

Donne wrote these words while contemplating the responsibilities of individuals in a shared society (*Devotions Upon Emergent Occasions, Meditation XVII*). His words are just as applicable today when contemplating the role of individual actors in critical infrastructures. A critical infrastructure is a composite of various entities (firms) that produce products and/or services. Several market forces are in play so that the ensemble acts in an apparently reliable fashion to provide a critical need. One can think of the resulting good or service as being a quasi-emergent property of the ensemble of firms acting individually to maximize their (economic) utility. These emergent properties are the result of a complex set of interactions involving explicit and implicit coordinating communications as well as the transfer of information and physical goods.

Please use the following format when citing this chapter:

Dynes, S., 2008, in IFIP International Federation for Information Processing, Volume 290; *Critical Infrastructure Protection II*, eds. Papa, M., Shenoi, S., (Boston: Springer), pp. 3–16.

Expanding on the theme of emergent risk requires looking beyond the risks of individual actors. The risk emerges at the level of the ensemble (infrastructure sector) due to a lack of understanding of the interdependencies and the consequences of various supply and information technology (IT) disruptions on the ability of the ensemble to produce the required good or service. Certain frameworks such as supply chain risk (e.g., [2, 7]) support the analysis of risk due to interdependencies. However, this paper focuses primarily on the risk to control mechanisms resulting from their use of the information infrastructure. The approach adopted is not to examine the resilience of the supply chain *per se*, but that of the communications used to coordinate the supply chain.

This paper examines the richness of coordinating signals relating to the resilience of the information infrastructure used to communicate information regarding business processes and the effect of the coordinating signals on business continuity. It investigates how information risk management (IRM) occurs among business participants to produce goods and services. The first hypothesis is that a correlation exists between an entity's dependence on IT and the level of IRM coordinating signals – entities more dependent on the information infrastructure take more steps to manage the risk due to cyber disruptions. The second hypothesis is that richer IRM coordinating signals result in more robust inter-entity business processes.

When examining critical infrastructure protection from an information security or risk perspective, it is also necessary to consider the emergent behavior of the ensemble. Much research has been devoted to IT risk management within individual firms. These firms are best viewed not as monoliths but as an integrated ensemble of agents whose activities are shaped by the economic forces driving the organization and its products. This view can explain why sophisticated organizations view information security as an exercise in IT risk management – appropriately reducing business risk means that the business will probably make more money.

To gain a deeper sense of the issue, it is instructive to view individual businesses and business sectors as a continuum of individual entities with differing levels of coordinating signals. At the highly coordinated end of the continuum is the individual corporation, which has separate departments for production, marketing, human resources, etc. Figure 1 shows a business as a set of individual entities (departments) with highly coordinated activities. Individual entities share information and/or physical goods with other entities in the business. These entities exchange a range of coordinating signals in order to optimize the production of goods and services. In some firms, the coordinating signals are explicitly mapped to enable them to better manage information risk. The emergent risk is reduced due to a decrease in the unknown response of the ensemble to specific disruptions.

At the the other end of the continuum are business sectors or supply chain networks, where the entity of interest is the firm and the coordinating signals are few (Figure 2). Interactions between entities in the sector are based on market forces or possible collaborations; their efforts are actively optimized for

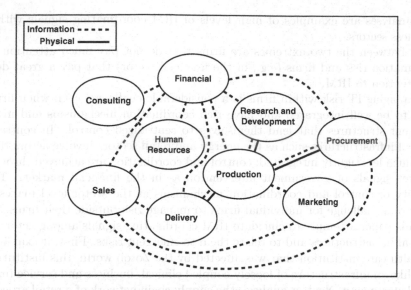

Figure 1. Business sector entities with highly coordinated activities.

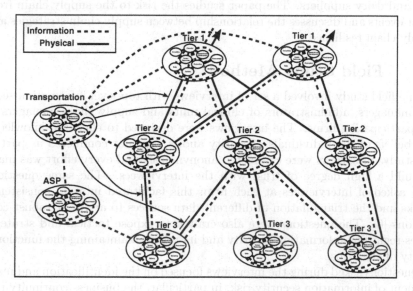

Figure 2. Business sector entities with loosely coordinated activities.

the good of the individual firms. In fact, interactions between entities may be limited to arms-length negotiations for goods and services, in which case IRM coordinating signals will be missing. Many firms are taking a more active approach in managing their referred risk (resulting from inadequate IRM practices at other firms) by requiring potential suppliers to fill out questionnaires about their information security practices [3]. Such assessments and follow-on gap analyses are examples of high levels of IRM coordinating signals within business sectors.

In between the two extremes are firms that do not pay much attention to information risk and firms (e.g., in the financial sector) that pay a great deal of attention to IRM.

Managing IT risk within firms is a considerable challenge, even when firms tend to be well integrated and have rich coordination mechanisms and management structures that lend themselves to centralized control. In contrast, critical infrastructures such as the energy and retail sectors involve actors that are much less tightly integrated; control and coordination are achieved through market signals or government intervention as in the financial market. The paucity of control and coordination mechanisms at the sector level makes it more of a challenge for individual firms to manage risk outside their firms.

This paper attempts to elucidate IRM coordinating signals among actors in critical infrastructures and to relate them to emergent risks. First, it examines a health care institution that was affected by the Zotob worm; this institution acts like an infrastructure of loosely coupled clinical, business and service (e.g., IT) departments. Next, it analyzes the supply chain network of a retail grocery chain, examining the information and physical supply chains of the retail grocery and dairy suppliers. The paper studies the risk to the supply chain from cyber events and discusses the relationship between supply chain strategies and supply chain resilience.

2.   Field Study Method

The field study involved a set of interviews with top-level information security managers, administrators of clinical units and supply chain managers at the participating firms. The interviews were designed to elicit the knowledge and beliefs of the individuals. Security audits were not conducted as part of the study. Interviews were conducted anonymously and every effort was made to build a high degree of trust with the interviewees. The same questions were asked of interviewees at each firm; this facilitated internal consistency checks and the triangulation of different data sources to arrive at robust conclusions [6]. The questions were also crafted to expose tactical and strategic issues regarding information security and its role in maintaining the functional ability of the firms.

Questions asked during the interviews focused on the identification and management of information security risk, in particular, the business continuity risk firms faced as a result of using IT to enable their services and supply chains. These open-ended questions elicited the impact that cyber events had on the ability of the interviewees' divisions to continue to operate. Another focus was determining the risk management culture within the division and the firm as a whole. The topics explored the perceived reliance on technology, the parties responsible for managing risk, and the development of contingency plans for cyber events. The results of these conversations were documented and serve as the basis for the conclusions presented in this paper.

The health care sector study interviewed eighteen individuals from two health care organizations (six clinical divisions, four administrative divisions and four information security (IS) divisions). The retail study interviewed twenty managers and directors from seven firms in the supply chain, ranging from suppliers of raw goods to a retail grocery chain.

3.   Field Study Results

This section presents the results of the field studies in the health care and retail sectors. The goals of the field study interviews were to determine the flows of information and physical goods within firms and with their immediate suppliers/customers, and to determine the impact of a loss of communication or local IT capability on their ability to produce goods and services.

The primary questions asked in the field studies were:

- What coordinating information flows exist between entities that might promote effective risk management?
- Is there a correlation between these information flows and the level of resilience in the critical infrastructures? Note that the focus was on the resilience to cyber disruptions, i.e., the ability of the infrastructure to provide goods or services in the face of cyber disruptions.
- What characteristics of individual entities and their coordinating activities lead to this level of resilience? In particular, are there strategies that lead to more robust ensembles? Entities within firms presumably have internal incentives to address the risk they face from relying on the IT infrastructure; it is not clear to what extent coordinating signals between entities at the sector level are driven by concerns about IT risk. As such, the emergent behavior of the sector is likely not optimized for resilience in the face of cyber disruptions.

Several other factors affect the ability of these infrastructures to operate, including the availability of the telephone system and transportation (trucking companies). Therefore, it is important not to lose sight of the profound interdependencies that exist between critical infrastructures.

3.1   Health Care Field Study

The health care organization consists of a main campus housing a hospital and multiple clinics. The organization also operates several hospitals and clinics throughout the geographic region. The main campus provides most of the administrative functions and serves as the ISP for these hospitals and clinics.

The health care organization has physicians on staff as well as independent, affiliated physicians who have admitting privileges. Staff physicians have access to assets such as digital patient records, laboratory results and the scheduling system via the internal network. Affiliated physicians have access through Internet-mediated (web-based) interfaces to these applications. Patients may access a limited amount of information via a web-based interface.

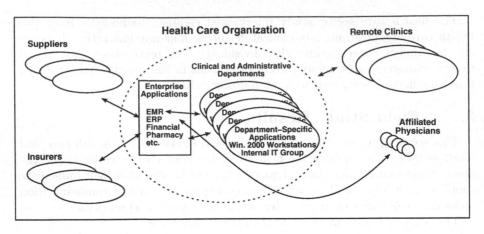

Figure 3.   Information structure in the health care organization.

Every department is dependent to some extent on IT. In general, departments use software applications for scheduling, patient tracking and other core functions. The hospital's electronic medical record (EMR) system is a collection of databases and information from many applications presented as a unified whole via an end-user interface. The EMR system contains patient information such as medical charts, radiological images and laboratory test results. Access to the records is available via the Internet for individuals located outside the main campus.

Figure 3 presents an overview of the information structure of the health care organization. Administrative and clinical units use enterprise-level applications, mainly the EMR system along with department-specific applications. Affiliated physicians access the EMR system over the Internet. Affiliated clinics also access enterprise applications over the Internet. The organization has several thousand workstations that primarily run Windows 2000. These are used to access the EMR system, scheduling and other applications that run on Unix machines, and other network-based applications that are internal or external to the hospital.

Information Risk Management Coordinating Signals. The IS and clinical units are loosely connected; many clinical departments have their own small IS units for developing and running applications. A formal liaison program exists between the hospital-level IS department and each individual clinical unit. However, the level of interaction is fairly low; in particular, the hospital-level IS department does not appear to have a substantive understanding of the IT needs of clinical units.

The perceived low level of IRM coordinating signals was reinforced during conversations with the hospital CIO and administrative directors of the various departments. The CIO was the first point of contact for the field study. At the first interview (conducted three months after the Zotob worm event), he mentioned that the impact of Zotob was felt almost entirely by the IS staff. He believed that few clinical or administrative personnel would recall the event and that its impact on the clinical and administrative departments were minimal. However, most of the clinical and administrative directors felt that the impact was significant. One clinical administrator declared, "All I can tell you is that it was living hell."

The IRM coordinating signals between the departments in the hospital appears to be very low. The response to IT reliability issues was primarily to develop a small departmental IS group rather than to coordinate with the hospital-level IS group. With respect to IRM planning, there is essentially no systemic risk management effort at the hospital level.

Resilience to the Zotob Event. Computing resources at the hospital were infected by the Zotob worm [9] in August 2005. Zotob targeted Windows 2000 machines, attempting to replicate itself by searching for other vulnerable machines on the network. The result was a flood of traffic on the hospital's intranet, resulting in denial-of-service attacks against the hospital's internal servers. The IS units were able to make the EMR system available about an hour into the event. However, most applications and the Internet were down for three days.

Zotob had a significant impact on business processes at the hospital, but there was little to no impact on the ability of the hospital to offer health care. The clinical and administrative units at the hospital were able to provide normal levels of service based on the volume of patients at the time. The principal exception was the radiology unit, which could take images but not deliver them via the intranet to physicians; consequently, the radiation oncology unit was also not operational. The interviewees universally agreed that the quality of care delivered was not affected by the event; however, they did feel that the event significantly increased the chances of providing substandard care.

This is not to say that providing medical care was easy. The Zotob worm had a great impact on operations – physicians did not know which patients they were to see and for what complaints; patients could not be scheduled; some medical procedures and services, especially those relying on radiology, were degraded (e.g., emergency room radiological images were viewed on the machines that took them). The hospital was able to function because of the dedication and flexibility of the staff. Many interviewees said that they simply had to make things happen – not providing medical care was not an option.

Is this resilience due to IRM coordinating signals between the various entities that make up the hospital? The evidence suggests not. Clearly, there was a lack of IRM coordinating signals among entities. The resilience was due to individual initiative and the ethic that medical care had to be provided.

3.2 Retail Grocery Field Study

The retail grocery environment is primarily a supply chain network, reaching from producers to retail grocery stores. The goal of the study was to determine

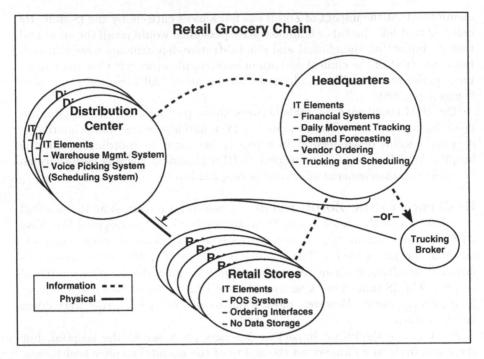

Figure 4. Schematic view of the retail grocery chain.

the resilience of the grocery supply chain to cyber disruptions. The method involved an analysis of the information and grocery supply chains, and the elucidation of IRM coordinating signals and reactions of entities to the signals. The retail grocery field study is different from the health care study in two key respects. First, the interactions of interest are between firms, not departments within the same firm. Second, the view of risk is evaluated proactively, not after a disruption as in the case of the health care field study. This section discusses the situation at the grocery retail chain as well as at a dairy supplier.

Retail Grocery Chain

The subject of the study is a U.S. regional grocery chain with more than 100 stores and in excess of 10,000 employees. The chain is wholly owned by a parent organization, which also owns and operates grocery chains in other regions of the country. The chain is fairly representative of others in the sector with respect to IT, stock replenishment and supply chain activities.

Figure 4 presents a schematic diagram of the retail grocery chain. It includes a headquarters, a distribution center and retail stores. The chain owns a fleet of trucks, but also contracts trucking firms. An important IT component is the scheduling system, a distributed system comprising servers located at the chain's headquarters and at distribution centers.

The use of IT is central to most of the business activities. At every store, point-of-sale data is used to track the movement of goods and create replenishment orders. Store managers of certain departments (e.g., produce) use wireless tablet devices to communicate their orders to headquarters. IT applications at each distribution center manage the inventory at the center. Wireless devices at the distribution centers assist workers in loading pallets; an algorithm optimizes pallet loads so that the heaviest items are placed at the bottom.

Practically all the IT systems are located at the chain's headquarters. There are no servers at store locations; the inventory systems used at the distribution centers are not located at the centers. When a customer swipes a credit or debit card to pay for a purchase at a store, the data is transmitted to the chain's headquarters. Applications that run the sales function contact a bank or clearing agent for approval, the approval is received by the application at the headquarters, which then sends the appropriate commands to the point-of-sale device at the store.

Communication with vendors is done primarily via electronic data interchange (EDI) or web-based applications. Examples include sending data about the daily movement of goods to vendors who manage their own inventories and to trucking firms that schedule deliveries to distribution centers and stores. Because of the dependence on IT, the grocery chain has invested in a backup data center that enables all data and applications to be quickly reconstituted after a disruption at the primary data center. The grocery chain also requires every store to have two ways of obtaining Internet connectivity to the applications running at its headquarters.

Information Risk Management Coordinating Signals. The grocery chain expends considerable effort to optimize its business processes. It has applications that optimize store replenishment orders based on the time of year and anticipated weather (e.g., hurricanes and snowstorms) and others that optimize the placement of products on shelves. There is a certain amount of pressure to automate business processes to "take the cost out of the business."

To support these efforts, the chain has a development group whose responsibility is to create and deploy applications that support business processes. The application development group works closely with the business side to define needs. Part of its task is to assess the levels of availability and redundancy of hardware, networks, disk storage, etc. to provide business continuity; these requirements are passed on to the infrastructure group.

The grocery chain clearly has a high level of IRM coordinating signals. Business managers interact with the application development group. The application development group works on a plan to manage the information risk, which is then made operational. Interviews with the head of the application development group indicated that he was very aware of the retail chain's dependence on the information infrastructure and that he was proactively taking steps to manage risk.

In contrast, there are few, if any, IRM coordinating signals between the grocery chain and its supply network. At the time the interviews were conducted, the grocery chain made no effort to determine IRM practices at its suppliers. Also, no examples of grocery chain and vendor contingency planning for cyber events emerged during the interviews.

Resilience to Cyber Events. Given these internal IRM coordinating signals, we examine the consequences of various cyber events.

- **Communications Events:** It is extremely important that stores can send their orders to the data canter. Each store has a leased line to the chain's headquarters along with a backup modem system that functions as a transparent failover. When a store does have a connectivity outage, a store manager writes the point-of-sale information on a CD or thumbdrive, takes it to a sister store, and uses the other store's resources to place its orders. In the event that the data center does not receive orders from a store, it uses the store's average order to replenish items at the store.

  Interviews with supply managers revealed that if the Internet were to go down, but the grocery chain's internal systems were up, and stores and distribution centers could access systems at the data center, orders to vendors that stocked the distribution centers could be replicated using telephone and fax communications. However, if the Internet outage were to be ongoing, the range of items ordered from vendors would be narrowed over time.

  According to the interviewees, an Internet outage that lasts a minute would pose no problem, nor would one that lasts an hour (no matter which hour). However, a daylong outage would impact purchase orders sent to vendors, the scheduling of deliveries at distribution centers, and orders from stores for perishable items. Orders for less perishable items and non perishable items would not be affected. Thus, the communications interruption would impact daily deliveries to stores; the impact to the business would not be serious.

  However, an outage that lasts two days would be problematic. Distribution centers would not be able to distribute goods or replenish their stocks; customers would certainly notice the difference. An outage lasting three days or longer would result in a chaotic situation, especially with regard to replenishing stocks at distribution centers and stores.

  If EDI transmissions to vendors were to be interrupted, operations would be manual (telephone and fax) for the first few days. If the interruption were to continue, triage would occur and fewer items would be ordered and shipped. The first priority is to ensure that products are on store shelves. Managers believe they could transmit orders to vendors via telephone or fax. However, the resources required for this would be so substantial that little else would be done in the way of business. In any case, it is not clear if vendors would be able to accept and process the blizzard of phone calls and faxes.

- **Hardware Events:** The grocery chain has two data centers, one located at its headquarters and the other, a backup center, located a few hours drive away. Each data center has a complete data set, but not a complete set of applications. Consequently, if the data center at headquarters were to have a major hardware failure, stores would be required to re-transmit their orders to the backup site.

Dairy Supplier

One goal of the study is to follow the supply chain of a staple food from a producer to the retail chain. The dairy supply chain is a good example. Diary products include milk, cream-based products (butter and cheese), dry milk products as well as casein, which is used in processed foods, adhesives and certain plastics. We primarily focus on liquid dairy products. The supply chain consists of dairy farms, dairy processors that process raw milk from dairy farms, and grocery stores that receive shipments of milk from dairy processors.

Coordinating Signals and Resilience. The grocery chain is the only entity in the dairy supply chain that exhibits IRM coordinating signals. In fact, our conclusion is that the grocery chain has a high level of internal IRM coordinating signals and acts on these signals. However, despite the lack of coordination signals, the evidence suggests that the diary supply chain would be resilient to cyber events, primarily because of its low level of reliance on technology. The dairy processor would suffer from a process control system outage, but many of the core functions can be performed manually.

4.   Discussion

What do the field studies say about the first hypotheses in the introduction? This hypothesis states that entities that are more dependent on the information infrastructure take more steps to manage the risk they face from cyber disruptions. The hospital and the retail grocery chain are very dependent on technology; cyber disruptions could severely impact their ability to function. This was seen at the hospital during the Zotob worm event. It is also clear that the grocery chain has much greater levels of IRM coordinating signals. This is evident in the efforts expended by the application development group to understand business needs and translate them to IT-based applications (and likely also review the applications that support business processes).

In contrast, the hospital IS organization made few, if any, attempts to understand the risk. Clearly, the hospital's IS group did take steps to ensure that certain applications would continue to run despite IT failures. This "local" view of their responsibility was evident from interviews with the CIO: the fact that applications were not accessible due to the Zotob infection was not as important to the CIO as the fact that they were running. The great majority of hospital departments believe information security to be the responsibility of the IS department. While it is not clear if the IS department feels that information security is its responsibility, it is evident that no IRM coordinating signals originate from the IS department. In fact, the only IRM coordinating signals observed at the hospital came from the materials acquisition department. This department developed a paper-based alternative to the usual web-based restocking application, which it distributed to other departments.

The other firms in the field studies are much less dependent on technology. One can argue that the dairy farm's dependence on electricity for refrigeration, automatic milking machines, etc. is a technical dependency. Diary farms are certainly very focused on managing this risk by maintaining redundant generators and storing fuel on site. Nevertheless, the conclusion is that the first hypothesis is false – no correlation exists between an entity's dependence on the information infrastructure and its IRM efforts.

Regarding the second hypothesis – Do increased IRM coordinating signals lead to more robust inter-entity business processes? – the results presented here and elsewhere [1, 4] indicate that the answer is not clear. The retail grocery chain did elect to take some action based on the observed information risk. However, there are several examples where increased coordinating signals have no impact on a firm's IRM efforts. A recent oil refinery study [5] specifically focused on developing IRM coordinating signals. This study utilized the RiskMAP process [8] to expose the refinery's business and IS leaders to the impact IT risk might have on their business. Despite the mapping of IT risk to business risk, the refinery chose not to invest in additional resources to reduce its risk (mainly because it did not perceive a significant threat). The conclusion is that, while IRM coordinating signals are required to increase the resilience of inter-entity business processes to cyber disruptions, they are not sufficient. The sticking point is that CISOs from major firms indicate that decisions regarding the acceptable level of risk are made on the basis of instinct. Therefore, increased IRM coordinating signals would lead to more robust inter-entity business processes only to the extent that a partner entity that makes a security investment sees a threat to its business.

Given the lack of IRM coordinating signals between firms in the field studies, is there emergent risk in these critical infrastructures? Despite the limited nature of the field studies, a recurring theme seen during the interviews was "the will to succeed." The main focus of all the hospital staff throughout the Zotob event was the continuity of patient care. The attitude of the clinical department managers was, "we can't stop, we just have to do what it takes to keep on going." The result was that even though some departments experienced major disruptions, patient care was delivered at normal levels. This is not to say that the worm event did not affect the delivered care. Interviewees indicated that while the care delivered was not compromised, the risk of substandard care was increased. The administrator of the perioperative unit was clear about this, saying "if we have to go backwards and do it (record notes, document procedures, phone for lab results) by hand, it sets us up for failure."

His concerns centered around the execution of operative procedures (worrying about waiting two to three times as long for lab results and wondering if nurses were going to pay attention to the computer screen to make sure an order for blood went through) and the documentation of what happened during the procedures (because of the staff's lack of experience using paper forms).

The will to succeed was also evident in the retail grocery field study. Despite the efforts at redundancy, distribution centers suffer from IT failures, which can have a significant impact on their ability to receive goods and build shipments for individual stores. Nevertheless, the interviews revealed that the distribution centers had not missed a shipment to a store in more than 40 years. The interviewees felt that, because they provide an essential service, they are duty bound to ensure that store shelves are well stocked. A fresh produce vendor also has the same will to succeed.

5. Conclusions

The field studies suggest that the degree of dependence on the information infrastructure within a firm and the steps taken by thse firm to manage information risk are not necessarily coordinated. Also, it is not clear if increased IRM coordinating signals lead to more robust inter-entity business processes. IRM coordinating signals are a requirement for increasing the resilience of inter-entity business processes to cyber disruptions, but they are not sufficient. Therefore, while there may be emergent information risk from poorly understood failure modes, the impact of the risk on the ability of infrastructures to operate would likely be less than expected.

Acknowledgements

This work was partially supported by the Institute for Information Infrastructure Protection (I3P) at Dartmouth College, Hanover, New Hampshire, under Award 2003-TK-TX-0003 from the U.S. Department of Homeland Security.

References

[1] Center for Digital Strategies, Security through Information Risk Management: A Workshop for Information Security Executives, Tuck School of Business, Dartmouth College, Hanover, New Hampshire (mba.tuck.dart mouth.edu/digital/Programs/CorporateEvents/CISO2007.html) 2007.

[2] M. Christopher and H. Peck, Building the resilient supply chain, *International Journal of Logistics Management*, vol. 15(2), pp. 1–14, 2004.

[3] S. Dynes, Information Security Investment Case Study: The Manufacturing Sector, Technical Report, Center for Digital Strategies, Tuck School of Business, Dartmouth College, Hanover, New Hampshire (mba.tuck.dartm outh.edu/digital/Research/ResearchProjects/InfoSecManufacturing.pdf), 2006.

[4] S. Dynes, E. Andrijcic and M. Johnson, Costs to the U.S. economy of information infrastructure failures: Estimates from field studies and economic data, presented at the *Workshop on the Economics of Information Security*, 2006.

[5] S. Dynes, E. Goetz and M. Freeman, Cyber security: Are economic incentives adequate? in *Critical Infrastructure Protection*, E. Goetz and S. Shenoi (Eds.), Springer, Boston, Massachusetts, pp. 15–27, 2007.

[6] J. Gubrium and J. Holstein, *Handbook of Interview Research: Context and Method*, Sage Publications, Thousand Oaks, California, 2001.

[7] A. Norrman and R. Lindroth, Categorization of supply chain risk management, in *Supply Chain Risk*, C. Brindley (Ed.), Ashgate, Aldershot, United Kingdom, pp. 14–27, 2004.

[8] C. Watters, Analyzing corporate risks with RiskMAP, presented at the *Second Annual I3P Process Control Systems Security Workshop*, 2006.

[9] Wikipedia, Zotob (computer worm) (en.wikipedia.org/wiki/Zotob), 2005.

Chapter 2

CYBERSPACE POLICY FOR CRITICAL INFRASTRUCTURES

Dorsey Wilkin, Richard Raines, Paul Williams and Kenneth Hopkinson

Abstract   The first step in preparing any battlespace is to define the domain for attack and maneuver. The various military service components have directed authority to focus their efforts in specific domains of operations (e.g., naval operations are mainly in the maritime domain). However, cyberspace operations pose challenges because they span multiple operational domains. This paper focuses on U.S. cyberspace policy related to defending and exploiting critical infrastructure assets. Also, it examines the issues involved in delineating responsibility for U.S. defensive and offensive operations related to critical infrastructures.

Keywords: Critical infrastructure, cyberspace operations, policy

1.   Introduction

Protecting and controlling cyberspace are daunting challenges. Cyberspace is pervasive and has no single owner or controller. Yet, practically every critical infrastructure component relies on cyberspace resources for its operation. Disruption of these resources can dramatically affect industry, government and the citizenry.

The U.S. Department of Defense (DoD) – like its counterparts in other countries – is responsible for providing the military forces needed to protect the nation's security. It is, therefore, critical to understand the DoD's roles and responsibilities associated with protecting critical infrastructure assets as well as exploiting those of an adversary in time of war.

This paper examines U.S. cyberspace policy related to defending and exploiting critical infrastructure assets. It traces the evolution of the definition of critical infrastructure from Executive Order 13010 in 1996 to Homeland Security Presidential Directive 7 in 2003. Also, it analyzes the issues involved in delineating responsibility for U.S. defensive and offensive operations focused on critical infrastructures.

Please use the following format when citing this chapter:

Wilkin, D., Raines, R., Williams, P. and Hopkinson, K., 2008, in IFIP International Federation for Information Processing, Volume 290; *Critical Infrastructure Protection II*, eds. Papa, M., Shenoi, S., (Boston: Springer), pp. 17–28.

2.   Defining Critical Infrastructure

Several definitions of "critical infrastructure" have been articulated. For example, Moteff and Parfomak [10] define it as:

> "[t]he framework of interdependent networks and systems comprising identifiable industries, institutions (including people and procedures), and distribution capabilities that provide a reliable flow of products and services essential to the defense and economic security of the [nation], the smooth functioning of government at all levels, and society as a whole."

However, in preparation for combat, it is imperative that the battlespace be well defined and scoped by the applicable authority. Furthermore, areas of responsibility must be explicitly delineated. To ensure proper coordination between government and the private sector in the area of critical infrastructure protection, nothing less than Presidential direction will suffice.

2.1   Executive Order 13010

Growing concerns about terrorism in the United States – largely due to the World Trade Center and Oklahoma City bombings in 1993 and 1995, respectively – led to serious efforts focused on protecting the nation's critical infrastructure assets. Meanwhile, the massive growth of the Internet during the 1990s changed the national defense focus from the physical realm to the cyber realm. To address these issues, President Clinton signed Executive Order (EO) 13010 on July 15, 1996 [6]. It emphasized that critical infrastructures "... are so vital that their incapacity or destruction would have a debilitating impact on the defense or economic security of the United States."

EO 13010 expounded on previous documents by categorizing threats as "physical threats," which are threats to tangible property, or "cyber threats," which are threats of electronic, radio frequency or computer-based attacks on the information and/or communications components that control critical infrastructures.

EO 13010 identified the following infrastructure sectors: telecommunications, electrical power systems, gas and oil storage and transportation, banking and finance, transportation, water supply systems, emergency services (including medical, police, fire and rescue) and continuity of government.

Finally, the order established the President's Commission on Critical Infrastructure Protection (PCCIP) that was tasked with assessing the scope and nature of the vulnerabilities and threats to U.S. critical infrastructures and recommending a comprehensive implementation strategy for critical infrastructure protection.

2.2   Presidential Decision Directive 63

In response to EO 13010, the PCCIP provided the following recommendations [13]:

Table 1. PDD 63 lead agency assignments.

Sector	Lead Agency
Information and Communications	Department of Commerce
Banking and Finance	Department of the Treasury
Water	Environmental Protection Agency
Aviation Highways Mass Transit Pipelines Rail Waterborne Commerce	Department of Transportation
Emergency Law Enforcement Services	Department of Justice/FBI
Emergency Fire Services Continuity of Government Services	Federal Emergency Management Agency
Public Health Services	Health and Human Services
Electric Power Oil and Gas Production and Storage	Department of Energy

- Conduct research and development in information assurance, monitoring and threat detection, vulnerability assessment and systems analysis, risk management and decision support, protection and mitigation, and incident response and recovery.

- Increase the federal investment in infrastructure assurance research to $500 million in FY99 and incrementally increase the investment over a five-year period to $1 billion in FY04.

- Establish a focal point for national infrastructure assurance research and development efforts and build a public/private-sector partnership to foster technology development and technology transfer.

Acting on the PCCIP recommendations, President Clinton signed Presidential Decision Directive (PDD) 63 on May 22, 1998, mandating law enforcement, foreign intelligence and defense preparedness to achieve and maintain critical infrastructure protection [7]. PDD 63 was the first document to assign lead agency responsibilities for critical infrastructure protection (Table 1). However, the DoD was not listed.

For three years, PDD 63 was the principal defining document for critical infrastructure protection. It was put to the test by the events of September 11, 2001.

2.3   Executive Orders 13228 and 13231

Responding to the lack of coordination before, during and after the terrorist attacks of September 11, 2001, President George W. Bush signed EO 13228 on October 8, 2001 that established the Office of Homeland Security [2]. The order gave the Office of Homeland Security the responsibility for coordinating the executive branch's efforts to detect, prepare, prevent, protect, respond and recover from terrorist attacks within the United States.

EO 13228 explicitly mentioned several critical infrastructure assets:

- Energy production, transmission and distribution services and critical facilities

- Other utilities

- Telecommunication systems

- Facilities that produce, use, store or dispose of nuclear material

- Public and privately owned information systems

- Special events of national significance

- Transportation systems, including railways, highways, shipping ports and waterways, airports and civilian aircraft

- Livestock, agriculture and systems for the provision of water and food for human use and consumption

EO 13228 designated many of the same critical infrastructure assets as PDD 63. However, it added nuclear sites, special events and agriculture.

On October 16, 2001, President Bush signed EO 13231 that created the President's Critical Infrastructure Protection Board (PCIPB) [3]. Like the PCCIP, the PCIPB was tasked with coordinating activities related to the protection of critical infrastructure assets and recovery from attacks. However, the PCIPB's primary function was to serve as the liaison between the President and the Office of Homeland Security. Interestingly, although EOs 13228 and 13231 stemmed from acts of terrorism launched by external enemies, the DoD was not mentioned in either executive order.

2.4   PATRIOT Act of 2001

The U.S. Congress passed the PATRIOT Act in 2001 that extended the capabilities of the newly created Office of Homeland Security. The act sought "[t]o deter and punish terrorist acts in the United States and around the world, to enhance law enforcement investigatory tools, and for other purposes" [17]. In Section 1016 of the PATRIOT Act, known as the Critical Infrastructure Protection Act of 2001, Congress updated the definition of critical infrastructure as follows:

"... systems and assets, whether physical or virtual, so vital to the United States that the incapacity or destruction of such systems and assets would have a debilitating impact on security, national economic security, national public health or safety, or any combination of those matters."

The act also appropriated $20 million to the DoD to ensure that any "physical or virtual disruption of the operation of the critical infrastructures of the United States [would] be rare, brief, geographically limited in effect, manageable, and minimally detrimental to the economy, human and government services, and national security of the United States."

The PATRIOT Act was the first document to give the DoD some responsibility for critical infrastructure protection. However, it did not give the DoD any authority or direction; these would eventually come from future documents.

2.5   National Strategy for Homeland Security

Executive Order 13228 created the Office of Homeland Security, the PATRIOT Act gave it broader authority and, on July 16, 2002, President George W. Bush signed the National Strategy for Homeland Security (NSHS) to organize and prioritize its efforts [11].

The NSHS used the same definition of critical infrastructure as the PATRIOT Act. However, it added chemical, postal and shipping services to the list of critical infrastructures identified by EO 13228 because they "help sustain our economy and touch the lives of Americans everyday." The NSHS specified eight major initiatives related to critical infrastructure protection:

- Unify America's infrastructure protection efforts in the Department of Homeland Security.

- Build and maintain a complete and accurate assessment of America's critical infrastructure and key assets.

- Enable effective partnerships with state and local governments and the private sector.

- Develop a national infrastructure protection plan.

- Secure cyberspace.

- Harness the best analytic and modeling tools to develop effective protective solutions.

- Guard America's critical infrastructure and key assets against "inside" threats.

- Partner with the international community to protect the transnational infrastructure.

The NSHS defined the lead agencies responsible for securing specific sectors of the U.S. critical infrastructure (Table 2). In particular, it modified the lead

Table 2.   NSHS lead agency assignments [11].

Sector	Lead Agency
Agriculture	Department of Agriculture
Meat and Poultry	Department of Agriculture
Other Food Products	Department of Health and Human Services
Water	Environmental Protection Agency
Public Health	Department of Health and Human Services
Emergency Services	Department of Homeland Security
Continuity of Government	Department of Homeland Security
Continuity of Operations	All Departments and Agencies
Defense Industrial Base	Department of Defense
Information and Telecommunications	Department of Homeland Security
Energy	Department of Energy
Transportation	Department of Homeland Security
Banking and Finance	Department of the Treasury
Chemical Industry and Hazardous Materials	Environmental Protection Agency
Postal and Shipping	Department of Homeland Security
National Monuments and Icons	Department of the Interior

agencies designated by PDD 63 for all but three sectors. Also, it required agencies to report directly to the newly-created Department of Homeland Security (DHS). Created by the Homeland Security Act of November 25, 2002, DHS is a cabinet-level department that united 22 distinct federal entities and absorbed the responsibilities of the Office of Homeland Security.

The NSHS designated the DoD as the lead authority for the defense industrial base. Also, it extended the scope of critical infrastructure to include transnational systems and identified cyberspace security as a primary initiative. However, the NSHS did not define the domain of cyberspace.

2.6   National Strategy to Secure Cyberspace

In February 2003, the PCIPB released the National Strategy to Secure Cyberspace (NSSC) [14]. Developed as an implementation component of the NSHS, the NSSC is intended to "engage and empower Americans to secure the portions of cyberspace that they own, operate, control, or with which they interact."

The NSSC specifically defines cyberspace as the "hundreds of thousands of interconnected computers, servers, routers, switches and fiber optic cables that make ... critical infrastructures work." Cyberspace is global in design and is, therefore, open to anyone, anywhere in the world. Under the NSSC, the primary strategic objective is to prevent cyber attacks against America's critical infrastructures. This is to be accomplished by delving deeper into the defense of critical infrastructures in order to detail cyber vulnerabilities and to develop strategies for mitigating attacks.

The NSSC is currently the highest-level document to identify digital control systems (DCSs) and supervisory control and data acquisition (SCADA) systems as vital to operations in the various critical infrastructure sectors. In its Security Threat and Vulnerability Reduction Program, the NSSC states that securing DCSs and SCADA systems is a national priority because "... the incapacity or destruction of [these] systems and assets would have a debilitating impact."

The NSSC is the first government document to mention offensive cyber operations as a response to cyber attacks. (Up to this point, government documents only focused on defensive operations related to critical infrastructure protection.) In particular, the NSSC states:

> "When a nation, terrorist group or other adversary attacks the United States through cyberspace, the U.S. response need not be limited to criminal prosecution. The United States reserves the right to respond in an appropriate manner. The United States will be prepared for such contingencies."

Finally, the NSSC lists the major risk factors involved in securing critical infrastructures from cyberspace attacks. It observes that cyberspace-related vulnerabilities persist because security implementations require investments that companies cannot afford, security features are not easily adapted to the space and/or power requirements of small systems, and security measures often reduce performance and impact the synchronization of large real-time processes.

2.7 Homeland Security Presidential Directive 7

On December 17, 2003, President George W. Bush signed the Homeland Security Presidential Directive (HSPD) 7 [4], which superseded PDD 63. HSPD-7 is the most up-to-date executive document on critical infrastructure identification, prioritization and protection. It uses the same definition for critical infrastructure as the PATRIOT Act and lists the same sectors and lead agencies as the NSHS.

HSPD-7 ordered all federal departments and agencies to develop plans for protecting the critical infrastructures that they own or operate by July 2004. These plans had to address the identification, prioritization, protection and contingency planning (including the recovery and reconstitution of essential capabilities) of all physical and cyber resources.

2.8 Defense Critical Infrastructure Program

In response to HSPD-7, DoD Directive 3020.40 [8] was issued on August 19, 2005 to update policy and assign responsibilities for the Defense Critical Infrastructure Program (DCIP). The directive defines the defense critical infrastructure as "DoD and non-DoD networked assets essential to project, support and sustain military forces and operations worldwide."

Table 3.   DCIP lead agency assignments.

Assignment	Lead Agency
Defense Industrial Base	Defense Contract Management Agency
Financial Services	Defense Finance and Accounting Service
Global Information Grid	Defense Information Systems Agency
Health Affairs	Assistant Secretary of Defense for Health Affairs
Intelligence, Surveillance and Reconnaissance	Defense Intelligence Agency
Logistics	Defense Logistics Agency
Personnel	DoD Human Resources Activity
Public Works	U.S. Army Corps of Engineers
Space	U.S. Strategic Command
Transportation	U.S. Transportation Command

The DCIP identifies ten critical sectors and the lead agencies responsible for the sectors (Table 3). It also requires the Secretary of every military department to designate an Office of Primary Responsibility (OPR) for identifying, prioritizing and protecting defense critical infrastructure assets.

3.   Offensive Cyber Operations Authority

While defensive measures can protect critical infrastructures, deterrence is not achieved purely by defensive means. History has shown that, in most cases, offensive operations achieve better results than adopting a completely defensive posture where attacks are simply endured. If military power is used, the Law of Proportionality may dictate that an offensive cyber capability be used "in kind". The NSSC states that when an "adversary attacks the [United States] through cyberspace ... [it] reserves the right to respond in an appropriate manner" [14]. The Commander of the U.S. Strategic Command (STRATCOM) has testified to Congress that "a purely defensive posture poses significant risks" and "the defense of the nation is better served by capabilities enabling [it] to take the fight to [its] adversaries" [5]. A computer network attack capability is necessary to ensure the defense of critical infrastructures. Cyberspace superiority is achieved by simultaneously exploiting the adversary's critical infrastructure assets.

3.1   Civilian Authority

In accordance with current law, HSPD-7 and the NSHS, the Department of Homeland Security (DHS) is the single accountable entity with the "responsibility for coordinating cyber and physical infrastructure protection efforts" [11]. DHS has created red teams for testing critical infrastructure defenses and training personnel in the private and public sectors [16]. Could DHS red teams be used to attack an adversary's critical infrastructure assets?

The technology exists for DHS red teams to conduct offensive operations well inside U.S. (or friendly) borders. However, important legal issues must be considered before civilians may conduct offensive cyber operations.

The Law of Armed Conflict comprises the Geneva Conventions, the Hague Conventions, various treaties and a vast body of case law. The law incorporates several rules that govern the use of civilians during times of war [12]. If a civilian uses software to infiltrate an adversary's critical infrastructure and negatively impact its citizens, the adversary can legally view the infiltration as an "attack" under Article 49.1. According to Article 52.2, software may be classified as a weapon when used in an attack on a critical infrastructure target because "[its] nature, location, purpose or use make [it] an effective contribution to military action." Also the civilian is a combatant under Article 51.3 because "civilians shall enjoy the protection afforded by [the Geneva Convention], unless and for such time as they take a direct part in hostilities."

Civilians who are designated as combatants can face serious problems if apprehended by an adversary. Under Articles 44.3 and 44.4, if a civilian combatant does not distinguish himself from the civilian population while engaged in an attack and if he is apprehended by the adversary while failing to distinguish himself, he would forfeit his right to be a prisoner of war. Of course, under Article 45.2, he would have the right to assert his entitlement to prisoner-of-war status before a judicial tribunal and to have that question adjudicated. The tribunal may then consider the civilian as a lawful combatant under Article 44.3 of Protocol I of the Geneva Convention [12] or as an unlawful combatant and label him a spy, mercenary or terrorist. An unlawful combatant is not a prisoner of war and can be tried and punished in accordance with local laws. He could be executed by firing squad like the mercenaries in Angola in 1976 [1].

3.2   Department of Defense Authority

Although EO 13010 raised the issue of using cyber operations to attack critical infrastructure assets as far back as 1996, it was not until 2001 that the Quadrennial Defense Review identified information operations (IO), which includes cyber operations, as a core capability of future military forces [15]. The concept was codified on May 3, 2002, when then Secretary of Defense Rumsfeld signed the classified Defense Planning Guidance (DPG 04) for the fiscal years 2004 through 2009 [15]. DPG 04 directed that "IO become a core military competency, fully integrated into deliberate and crisis action planning and capable of executing supported and supporting operations." Furthermore, it mandated that the Chairman of the Joint Chiefs of Staff develop an "IO Roadmap" that would address the full scope of IO as a core competency and include supporting studies focused on policy, plans, organization, education, career force, analytic support, psychological operations, operations security, electronic warfare, military deception and computer network operations.

The Unified Command Plan 02 (Change 2) was approved by the President on January 2, 2003. It identified six core IO capabilities: computer network attack (CNA), computer network defense (CND), electronic warfare (EW), operation security (OPSEC), psychological operations (PSYOPS) and military deception (MILDEC) [15]. Furthermore, it created the new office of the Under Secretary of Defense (Intelligence) within the Office of the Secretary of Defense for IO matters. STRATCOM was assigned as the combatant command responsible for "integrating and coordinating DoD IO that cross geographic areas of responsibility or across the IO core capabilities." Subsequently renamed as Offensive Cyber Operations, STRATCOM was responsible for "identifying desired characteristics and capabilities for CNA, conducting CNA in support of assigned missions and integrating CNA capabilities in support of other combatant commanders, as directed."

The IO Roadmap developed in response to DPF 04 was approved by Defense Secretary Rumsfeld October 30, 2003. It concluded that DoD must "fight the net" by improving CNA capability [15]. It recommended STRATCOM as the combatant command responsible for centralized IO planning, integration and analysis. Also, it specified that all the military services, including the Special Operations Command must organize, train and equip personnel for assignment to STRATCOM. Finally, it recommended that IO become "a dedicated military occupation specialty or career field" by designating service and joint IO billets.

Currently, the six IO core competencies are not universally defined, understood or applied. However, even if they were defined, each service would develop IO specialists that would meet its specific requirements. Also, the IO specialist communities within the services are relatively isolated. This results in a lack of knowledge for command-level IO planners and a gap between combatant command needs and what is provided by the services.

Entry-level IO personnel have limited, if any, experience in the discipline and require significant on-the-job training [15]. Unfortunately, none of the military services are mandated by Title 10 law to provide resources for IO training. Therefore, STRATCOM can request IO personnel from the services, but the services are not required by applicable law to expend their resources to train the IO personnel. For these reasons, the IO career force is progressing slower than desired.

3.3   U.S. Air Force Authority

On December 8, 2005, the Secretary of the Air Force and the Chief of Staff of the Air Force released a new mission statement that added cyberspace to the Air Force's core responsibilities. When asked why the Air Force was taking the lead for cyberspace, the Air Force Secretary stated that "the Air Force is a natural leader in the cyber world and we thought it would be best to recognize that talent" [9]. This statement may be true, but it does not recognize the lack of IO direction in the other services and the need for one service to take the lead in organizing, training and equipping an IO force. If IO is to become a new warfighting domain on par with land, sea and air, then the personnel and equipment ought to come from a single service. This follows from the service structure set forth by the Goldwater-Nichols Act of 1986. Also, when multiple services are responsible for the same mission, different techniques, tactics, procedures and equipment are developed that not interoperable. Numerous instances of these interoperability problems were encountered during the military efforts in Vietnam, Grenada, Panama and Iraq [18].

The Air Force has taken charge of the cyberspace domain without Title 10 authority or executive directive. In a September 6, 2006 memorandum to all the major Air Force commands, the Air Force Secretary and the Chief of Staff ordered the creation of a new operational command with the sole purpose of organizing, training and equipping cyberspace forces for combatant commanders and STRATCOM. The 8th Air Force created a provisional Cyberspace Command in September 2007. On par with the Air Combat Command and Space Command, this new major command is scheduled for permanency by October 1, 2008. But only time will tell if the Air Force's authority over the cyber realm will, in fact, endure.

4.   Conclusions

Legal and policy issues related to cyberspace operations are still not completely clear. However, what is clear is that military and civilian organizations must be afforded the resources commensurate with the importance of critical infrastructure protection. The strategic importance of offensive cyberspace operations cannot be overstated. The U.S. Department of Defense has recognized cyberspace as a domain for attack and maneuver and has begun to integrate it into wartime planning. Humankind is on the cusp of a new method of warfare and only time will reveal its viability.

References

[1] BBC News, On this Day (11 June 1976): Mercenaries trial begins in Angola, London, United Kingdom, (news.bbc.co.uk/onthisday/hi/dates/stor ies/june/11/newsid_2510000/2510947.stm).

[2] G. Bush, Executive Order 13228: Establishing the Office of Homeland Security and the Homeland Security Council, The White House, Washington, DC (fas.org/irp/offdocs/eo/eo-13228.htm), October 8, 2001.

[3] G. Bush, Executive Order 13231: Critical Infrastructure Protection in the Information Age, The White House, Washington, DC (fas.org/irp/offdocs /eo/eo-13231.htm), October 16, 2001.

[4] G. Bush, Homeland Security Presidential Directive (HSPD) 7, The White House, Washington, DC (www.whitehouse.gov/news/releases/2003/12/20 031217-5.html), December 17, 2003.

[5] J. Cartwright, Statement of General James E. Cartwright, Commander, United States Strategic Command on the United States Strategic Command, House Armed Services Committee, U.S. House of Representatives, Washington, DC (armedservices.house.gov/pdfs/FC032107 /Cartwright_Testimony032007.pdf), March 21, 2007.

[6] W. Clinton, Executive Order 13010: Critical Infrastructure Protection, The White House, Washington, DC (www.fas.org/irp/offdocs/eo13010.htm), July 15, 1996.

[7] W. Clinton, Presidential Decision Directive 63, The White House, Washington, DC (fas.org/irp/offdocs/pdd/pdd-63.htm), May 22, 1998.

[8] G. England, DoD Directive 3020.40, Defense Critical Infrastructure Program, Department of Defense, Washington, DC (www.dtic.mil/whs/dir ectives/corres/pdf/302040p.pdf), August 19, 2005.

[9] M. Gettle, Air Force releases new mission statement, Air Force Link, U.S. Air Force, Washington, DC (www.af.mil/news/story.asp?storyID= 123013440), December 8, 2005.

[10] J. Moteff and P. Parfomak, Critical Infrastructure and Key Assets: Definition and Identification, Congressional Research Service, The Library of Congress, Washington, DC (www.fas.org/sgp/crs/RL32631.pdf), 2004.

[11] Office of Homeland Security, National Strategy for Homeland Security, The White House, Washington, DC (www.whitehouse.gov/homeland/book /nat_strat_hls.pdf), 2002.

[12] Office of the United Nations High Commissioner for Human Rights, Protocol additional to the Geneva Conventions of 12 August 1949 and relating to the protection of victims of international armed conflicts (Protocol I), Geneva, Switzerland (www.unhchr.ch/html/menu3/b/93.htm), June 8, 1977.

[13] President's Commission on Critical Infrastructure Protection, Critical Foundations: Protecting America's Infrastructures, The White House, Washington, DC (chnm.gmu.edu/cipdigitalarchive/files/5_CriticalFound ationsPCCIP.pdf), 1997.

[14] President's Critical Infrastructure Protection Board, The National Strategy to Secure Cyberspace, The White House, Washington, DC (www .whitehouse.gov/pcipb/cyberspace_strategy.pdf), 2003.

[15] D. Rumsfeld, Information Operations Roadmap (declassfied in 2006), Department of Defense, Washington, DC (www.gwu.edu/~nsarchiv/NSAE BB/NSAEBB177/info_ops_roadmap.pdf), 2003.

[16] Sandia National Laboratories, Information Design Assurance Red Team (IDART), Albuquerque, New Mexico (www.idart.sandia.gov).

[17] U.S. Congress (107th Congress), Uniting and Strengthening America by Providing Appropriate Tools Required to Intercept and Obstruct Terrorism (USA PATRIOT) Act of 2001, Public Law 107-56, Government Printing Office, Washington, DC (frwebgate.access.gpo.gov/cgi-bin/get doc.cgi?dbname=107_cong_public_laws&docid=f:publ056.107.pdf), October 26, 2001.

[18] WGBH Educational Foundation, Frontline: Rumsfeld's War: The Military's Struggles and Evolution, Boston, Massachusetts (www.pbs.org /wgbh/pages/frontline/shows/pentagon/etc/cronagon.html), 2004.

II

INFRASTRUCTURE SECURITY

Chapter 3

SECURITY ASSESSMENT OF A TURBO-GAS POWER PLANT

Marcelo Masera, Igor Nai Fovino and Rafal Leszczyna

Abstract   Critical infrastructures are exposed to new threats due to the large number of vulnerabilities and architectural weaknesses introduced by the extensive use of information and communication technologies. This paper presents the results of an exhaustive security assessment for a turbo-gas power plant.

Keywords: Turbo-gas power plant, security assessment

1.   Introduction

Enterprise systems that employ information and communication technologies (ICT) are prone to vulnerabilities that can be exploited by malicious software and agents. Considering the massive use of ICT in national critical infrastructures, it is imperative to perform comprehensive risk assessments that evaluate the main threats and the effectiveness of countermeasures.

Several approaches have been proposed for conducting risk assessments of ICT infrastructures (see, e.g., [1, 4]). The InSAW methodology [4–9] is specifically tailored to analyzing the impact of ICT threats on critical infrastructure assets. Dondossola and colleagues [2] presented the first practical test of the InSAW methodology. They applied an embryonic version of InSAW to analyze the vulnerabilities of a simple, albeit not actually deployed, remote control station.

This paper discusses the results of an exhaustive InSAW security assessment of the ICT infrastructure of a turbo-gas power plant. It also presents a set of ICT attack scenarios that have been successfully implemented in a laboratory environment. This environment, which was developed in collaboration with a major energy company, reproduces the networks, SCADA systems and electromechanical devices used in the turbo-gas power plant.

Please use the following format when citing this chapter:

Masera, M., Fovino, I.N. and Leszczyna, R., 2008, in IFIP International Federation for Information Processing, Volume 290; *Critical Infrastructure Protection II*, eds. Papa, M., Shenoi, S., (Boston: Springer), pp. 31–40.

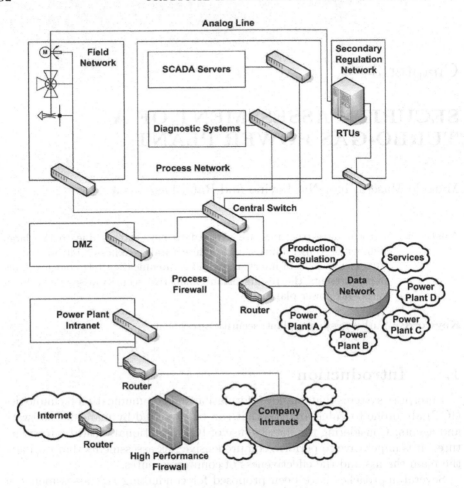

Figure 1. Power plant schematic.

2.   System Description

In order to conduct a security assessment, it is necessary to model a complex system in terms of functional blocks. Since the focus is on threats derived from the use of ICT in a turbo-gas power plant, we focus on the networking aspects of the power plant architecture.

2.1   Network Architecture

Figure 1 presents the high-level architecture of the turbo-gas power plant. Several major subsystems are relevant from the networking perspective:

- **Power Plant Backbone:** This subsystem contains all the network devices that allow the various power plant subnets to communicate. The principal devices include: (i) layer switches that manage traffic; (ii) process firewalls that separate and filter the traffic between the field network, process network and external entities; (iii) routers that interconnect various power plant subnets and the corporate intranet; and (iv) Internet firewalls that separate power plant company networks from the Internet.

- **Field Network:** This network interconnects the sensors and actuators that directly interact with power plant electromechanical devices.

- **Process Network:** This network hosts the SCADA systems used by operators to control power plant processes.

- **Demilitarized Zone (DMZ):** This area hosts data exchange servers that receive data from the process network and make it available to operators via the power plant intranet.

- **Secondary Regulation Network:** This network hosts remote terminal units (RTUs) that implement the secondary regulation protocol.

- **Power Plant Intranet:** This branch of the company network provides intranet services to plant operators. It is used for routine office activities as well as for remote plant control by providing access to the process network via a VPN through the DMZ.

- **Company Intranet:** This generic network, which typically uses Windows platforms, is used for all corporate activities. Note that "company" refers to the entity that owns and operates the power plant.

- **Data Network:** This high availability network is used to directly interconnect all company assets; it provides services such as DNS and antivirus software updates.

- **Internet:** This consists of all external computing assets.

2.2   Operational Flows and Dependencies

When analyzing a complex system, it is important to consider the operational flows generated by operator interactions with the system as well as the dependencies between the various subsystems. Due to a lack of space, it is not possible to discuss these in detail. Therefore, this section presents the operational flows and dependencies that are most relevant to the power plant attack scenarios considered in our work.

Field Network: The field network hosts all the devices (sensors and actuators) that are connected directly to the power plant hardware (e.g., gas turbine and steam system). The data flow uses dedicated communications protocols such as Modbus and Profibus. The field network devices are located on the "frontlines" of the ICT system; as such, they are vital to all power plant control operations. Thus, the device measurements and actions must be communicated to the higher control level (i.e., SCADA systems).

Process Network: The process network hosts the SCADA servers that interact with the field network. They analyze data received from the field network and present plant operators with summarized information about the state of the power plant. The operators use diagnostic systems, which exchange data with the SCADA servers, to investigate any anomalies that are observed. Based on the results of the analysis, an operator issues commands using the SCADA servers to devices in the field network to effect the appropriate changes to the state of the power plant.

Demilitarized Zone: The DMZ usually hosts a data exchange server. This server receives plant status data from the SCADA servers. Operators connected to the power plant intranet query the server to obtain high-level information about plant operations without having to access the process network. Remote access to the DMZ and to the process network is regulated by a properly-configured firewall, which also operates a point-to-point VPN (over Radius). Thus, only authorized operators can remotely access the DMZ and process network. Note, however, that traffic flow between the various servers is generally not authenticated.

Remote Terminal Unit Network: The RTU network receives power production data from the data network. The RTUs communicate directly with devices in the field network using a dedicated analog channel. Note that no mutual authentication is implemented between the RTUs and field network devices.

Intranet: The power plant intranet is typically a part of the company intranet. In our case study, the intranet uses Windows platforms with a strong set of security and access control policies. Operators connected to the intranet can establish VPN connections with the process firewall in order to access the process servers and DMZ servers. The operators can also access the Internet via the intranet.

Data Network: The data network connects all the power plant's process networks to facilitate fast data transfer over a private network. It also provides services such as DNS. Several flows exist between the process and data networks. The data network is also used by operators to send commands to the RTU network required for production operations and secondary regulation.

Internet: The Internet represents the external world, i.e., everything outside the company network. However, in our case study, public communication channels are used by remote operators to connect to power plant assets (e.g., for maintenance purposes). This uses Radius authentication over a site-to-site VPN network. Thus, remote operators appear virtually as "internal operators." Data flows between the intranet and Internet materialize whenever an internal operator conducts Internet-related activities. Note that Internet access policies are role-dependent: some operators are allowed to directly access the Internet while others have to pass through a set of proxy servers.

3. Vulnerability Analysis

Based on our security assessment methodology [8], we attempted to identify all relevant vulnerabilities before postulating attack scenarios. Our analysis identified several vulnerabilities, which we have organized into three classes:

- **Architectural Vulnerabilities:** These vulnerabilities directly derive from weaknesses in the network architecture. Example vulnerabilities include weak separation between the process and field networks; lack of authentication between active components (actuators and SCADA servers, actuators and RTUs, SCADA servers and data exchange servers, etc.); and the process firewall itself, which is a single point of failure.

- **Security Policy Vulnerabilities:** These vulnerabilities arise from weak security policies, especially related to users who remotely connect to the intranet (e.g., the machines used by remote users may not have the latest security patches and anti-virus protection). Other vulnerabilities are due to ambiguous traceability and access policies.

- **Software Vulnerabilities:** Several operating systems are used in the power plant: Linux, SCO Unix, Windows NT, Windows 2000 Server, Windows XP and Windows 2003 Server. Most of these systems did not have the latest patches and some unauthorized applications were installed. In all, we identified 240 software vulnerabilities that affected computers, servers, switches and routers. At least 100 of these vulnerabilities could be used to seize partial or complete control of the targeted machines. Moreover, more than 70 vulnerabilities could be exploited to block machines.

The results of the vulnerability analysis are not as dramatic as expected. In fact, very few of the identified vulnerabilities could be exploited to launch serious attacks. Nevertheless, the presence of these vulnerabilities highlights how the extensive use of ICT has significantly increased the number of possible "failure" scenarios.

4. Threat Analysis

The threat analysis component of the power plant study identified the potential threats starting from a list of typical hazards. The threats that were deemed to be the most effective were examined in greater detail. The results were then synthesized and the corresponding threat profiles and exposure indices developed. The following three phases were involved in the threat analysis:

- **Threat Hypothesis:** The threats are characterized according to their type (internal/external), agent (person/object), motivation (intentional, accidental, etc.), expertise and resources (required to manifest the threat), perceived value, plausibility and severity.

■ **Threat Verification:** The identified threats are screened according to the risks they might pose to the system.

■ **Threat Value:** The plausibility and severity values are qualitatively estimated for each threat.

Note that the "plausibility" of a threat is the likelihood of the existence of the menace that targets a certain vulnerability to produce damage to the system. The "severity" of a threat is the capacity to produce damage by exploiting a certain vulnerability.

No generally accepted definition of a threat exists. From the legal point of view, a threat by an agent is an unwanted (deliberate or accidental) expression of intent to execute an action that may result in harm to an asset. Therefore, a threat is the potential occurrence of a negative action, not its actual realization. The following is a generic list of threat agents that can jeopardize critical infrastructure assets [10]:

■ **Crackers, Malicious Hackers, Script Kiddies:** These individuals, who have varying levels of technical expertise, break into systems by subverting security mechanisms. They may launch attacks for the challenge or thrill of doing so, or for bragging rights in their communities.

■ **Insider Threat:** The disgruntled insider is a major threat. An insider may not have a great deal of knowledge about computer intrusions, but his knowledge of and access to the targeted system enables him to cause considerable damage.

■ **Malware Writers:** Malicious code writers produce software (viruses, worms or Trojan horses) designed specifically to damage or disrupt systems. This so-called malware can be specific (i.e., it targets particular systems or organizations) or it can be generic.

■ **Criminal Groups:** Criminal groups frequently attack systems for monetary gain. They may attempt to steal sensitive information for re-sale or for purposes of blackmail, extort money by threatening to attack computing assets, and commit various types of fraud (e.g., attempting to influence stocks) or forgery (e.g., changing payment information in invoices).

■ **Hacktivists:** Hacktivism refers to politically-motivated attacks on computing assets. Hacktivists may overload e-mail servers or hack into web sites to send political messages. Their actions against infrastructure assets are usually motivated by environmental, safety or nationalistic reasons.

Table 1. Principal threats.

Threat	Expertise	Resources	Value	Plausibility	Severity
Insider	Minimum	Limited	High	Medium	High
Int. Malware	Medium	Limited	Minimum	High	Low
Ext. Malware	High	High	Maximum	Low	Low
Hackers	Medium	Limited	Maximum	Medium	High
Criminals	High	Very High	Maximum	Medium	High

- **Terrorist Groups:** Terrorism is the unlawful use of force or violence against persons or property in order to intimidate or coerce a government or civilian population to further certain political or social objectives.

- **Information Warfare:** Several nations are aggressively developing information warfare doctrines, programs and capabilities. These capabilities can be used to disrupt the supply chain and inflict considerable damage to the various infrastructure sectors, ultimately affecting the economy and the residents of the targeted region or country.

The threats we have identified are presented in Table 1. The plausibility and severity values assigned to the threats were based on detailed analyses of power plant systems and on interviews conducted with plant operators and managers. For example, under normal conditions, the severity of an insider threat (disgruntled employee) is very high if the individual has direct access to the process network and to the SCADA systems. On the other hand, even if the plausibility of a malware infection is high, its impact on the power plant "core" (i.e., field network) is low. This is because the computing systems in the field network are less vulnerable to traditional viruses – they run dedicated services and use proprietary protocols; even if the systems are compromised, it is possible to bypass them and control the power plant manually. Of course, the evaluation scenario has to be modified if advanced viruses that specifically target power plant systems are introduced. Likewise, the severity of a hacking attack is high because a hacker (hypothetically) can seize control of critical systems. The same argument holds in the case of attacks launched by criminal groups.

5. Attack Scenarios

This section presents a high-level description of the attack scenarios that we identified and implemented. The purpose is to give an idea of the level of exposure faced by a typical power plant.

5.1   Radius Server Denial of Service

Denial-of-service attacks limit or block access to specific resources, making them, and possibly a larger system, unusable. In this scenario an attacker attempts to consume the bandwidth of a Radius server that is connected to the Internet.

The first step is to perform system fingerprinting, where information is collected about a target system. Since the Radius server is connected to the Internet, it is relatively easy to obtain information about it by analyzing the results of network scans, ICMP packet content, etc. Information about the targeted system can also be obtained using social engineering techniques on employees and other individuals familiar with the system and its configuration.

Bandwidth consumption is a simple task: an attacker directs large volumes of traffic to the targeted server. This is accomplished by compromising a sufficient number of machines connected to the network and using them to generate attack traffic. Our scenario involves a dedicated Trojan horse that propagates itself on networks and compromises machines, installing a backdoor in every compromised machine. The attacker uses the backdoors to seize control of the machines and proceeds to establish a "zombie network" for launching distributed denial-of-service attacks. Using the zombie network and the information gleaned from system fingerprinting and social engineering, the attacker blocks all external access to the company intranet and, thus, external access to the power plant network.

5.2   Intranet Virus Infection

In the virus infection scenario, the attacker gains control of a computer in the corporate intranet in order to impersonate a legitimate user. The infected computer is directed to perform malicious actions on critical plant networks, such as launching denial-of-service attacks on the process firewall or data exchange server, or corrupting diagnostic systems or SCADA subnets. Virus infections potentially affect all systems that are connected to an open network. Anti-virus software is the primary defensive mechanism, but even systems with the latest software are vulnerable to attack in the interval between the release of a new virus and the time the next patch is released.

The first step of the attack is to collect information about the target system (e.g., using system fingerprinting). Next, the attacker obtains a new virus that is tailored to the targeted system. It is assumed that the attacker has the expertise to write such a virus or is able to obtain the virus from the hacker community.

If the attacker has already gained access to the targeted machine, the virus can be directly installed on the machine. Alternatively, the attacker exploits a vulnerable service at an open port on the firewall or uses social engineering to convince a legitimate user to install software containing the virus.

If the virus has been designed with a backdoor, the attacker can gain control of the infected machine and impersonate a legitimate user, performing authorized actions as well as illegal actions that may be permitted by deficient security policies. Note that control of the compromised machine is easily maintained if the attacker is an insider. However, an external attacker would have to penetrate the firewall to reach the infected machine and perform the malicious actions. This poses an obstacle, but it is possible to create a virus that performs the malicious actions autonomously.

The virus attack can be used to cause damage to the data exchange server and the SCADA servers. Also, it could be used to steal credentials (user names and passwords) or deny service to the power plant firewall and other computing assets. Note that the virus infection scenario is developed for the intranet environment. A similar scenario may be devised for the data network, DMZ or process network. For example, if the infected machine is in the data network, which connects all power plant assets, it is possible to conduct a denial-of-service attack on the RTU network and disrupt the secondary regulation protocol.

5.3 Phishing Attack

In the phishing attack scenario, the attacker steals the credentials of an authorized user in order to target the power plant network. A phishing attack may send a fake e-mail message, display a seemingly legitimate link that actually connects to a malicious website, or poison the DNS server to make the victim connect to a malicious server.

In our scenario, the attacker has to replicate at least a portion of the system interfaces and infrastructure, e.g., by creating a fake domain and a data exchange server for data distribution. Information required to create the fake site that replicates system interfaces and infrastructure can be obtained via system fingerprinting. Once this is done, the attacker collects information on users and systems, including DNS data. This enables him to implement a DNS poisoning attack that re-routes users to the fake website instead of the data exchange server. The fake website provides false information about the state of the power plant and also captures their credentials, making it possible for the attacker to connect to the real data exchange server.

6. Conclusions

The security assessment of the operational power plant clearly demonstrates that ICT introduces a large number of vulnerabilities. Our experiments involving a laboratory testbed that reproduces much of the ICT infrastructure of the power plant verify that the ICT attack scenarios are feasible and can be very damaging. In particular, our use of a malware simulation framework [3] has enabled us to investigate the serious impact of virus infections on power plant safety and security.

Sophisticated analytic tools are required to identify and address the myriad security problems. Our use of the InSAW methodology in the analysis process has facilitated the identification of failure-prone relationships in power plant subsystems; this has helped discover weaknesses, create realistic attack scenarios and understand the potential cascading effects of failures. Still, our work is merely the first step in a systematic campaign to address the impact of ICT vulnerabilities on critical infrastructures. Our future research will investigate vulnerabilities in SCADA communication protocols and architectures with the goal of articulating effective security policies and countermeasures.

References

[1] C. Alberts and A. Dorofee, *Managing Information Security Risks: The OCTAVE (SM) Approach*, Addison-Wesley, Boston, Massachusetts, 2002.

[2] G. Dondossola, J. Szanto, M. Masera and I. Nai Fovino, Effects of intentional threats to power substation control systems, *International Journal of Critical Infrastructures*, vol. 4(1/2), pp. 129–143, 2008.

[3] R. Leszczyna, I. Nai Fovino and M. Masera, MalSim – Mobile agent malware simulator, *Proceedings of the First International Conference on Simulation Tools and Techniques for Communications, Networks and Systems*, 2008.

[4] M. Masera and I. Nai Fovino, A framework for the security assessment of remote control applications of critical infrastructures, *Proceedings of the Twenty-Ninth ESReDA Seminar*, 2005.

[5] M. Masera and I. Nai Fovino, Emergent disservices in interdependent systems and systems-of-systems, *Proceedings of the IEEE International Conference on Systems, Man and Cybernetics*, vol. 1, pp. 590–595, 2006.

[6] M. Masera and I. Nai Fovino, Models for security assessment and management, *Proceedings of the International Workshop on Complex Network and Infrastructure Protection*, 2006.

[7] M. Masera and I. Nai Fovino, Through the description of attacks: A multidimensional view, *Proceedings of the Twenty-Fifth International Conference on Computer Safety, Reliability and Security*, pp. 15–28, 2006.

[8] I. Nai Fovino and M. Masera, A service-oriented approach for assessing infrastructure security, in *Critical Infrastructure Protection*, E. Goetz and S. Shenoi (Eds.), Springer, Boston, Massachusetts, pp. 367–379, 2007.

[9] I. Nai Fovino, M. Masera and A. Decian, Integrating cyber attack within fault trees, *Proceedings of the European Safety and Reliability Conference*, 2007.

[10] United States General Accounting Office, Critical Infrastructure Protection: Challenges and Efforts to Secure Control Systems, Report GAO-04-354, Washington, DC (www.gao.gov/new.items/d04354.pdf), 2004.

Chapter 4

DETECTING CYBER ATTACKS ON NUCLEAR POWER PLANTS

Julian Rrushi and Roy Campbell

Abstract   This paper proposes an unconventional anomaly detection approach that provides digital instrumentation and control (I&C) systems in a nuclear power plant (NPP) with the capability to probabilistically discern between legitimate protocol frames and attack frames. The stochastic activity network (SAN) formalism is used to model the fusion of protocol activity in each digital I&C system and the operation of physical components of an NPP. SAN models are employed to analyze links between protocol frames as streams of bytes, their semantics in terms of NPP operations, control data as stored in the memory of I&C systems, the operations of I&C systems on NPP components, and NPP processes. Reward rates and impulse rewards are defined in the SAN models based on the activity-marking reward structure to estimate NPP operation profiles. These profiles are then used to probabilistically estimate the legitimacy of the semantics and payloads of protocol frames received by I&C systems.

Keywords: Nuclear plants, intrusion detection, stochastic activity networks

1.   Introduction

Digital instrumentation and control (I&C) systems are computer-based devices that monitor and control nuclear power plants (NPPs). Analog I&C systems have traditionally been used to perform monitoring and control functions in NPPs. However, Generation III+ and IV reactors are equipped with digital I&C systems; meanwhile, analog systems in older reactors are being replaced with digital systems. In general, NPP control networks communicate with SCADA systems to coordinate power production with transmission and distribution demands. The deployment of digital I&C systems and the connectivity between NPP control networks and external networks expose NPPs to cyber attacks whose consequences can include physical damage to reactors [3].

Please use the following format when citing this chapter:

Rrushi, J. and Campbell, R., 2008, in IFIP International Federation for Information Processing, Volume 290; *Critical Infrastructure Protection II*, eds. Papa, M., Shenoi, S., (Boston: Springer), pp. 41–54.

In addition, security exercises have underscored the threat of intrusions into NPP control networks.

This paper focuses on the problem of intrusion detection in NPP control networks. It addresses the following problem: Given a set of protocol data units (PDUs) received by a digital I&C system over an NPP control network, how could the digital I&C system assess if every PDU is legitimate and is not a component of attack traffic?

Digital I&C systems considered in this paper communicate via the Modbus protocol [8]. However, the intrusion detection approach is applicable to any industrial protocol. The approach falls in the category of protocol-based and anomaly-based intrusion detection strategies. Such an approach guards against attacks that use semantically regular PDUs to target an NPP as well as attacks that use irregular PDUs (e.g., memory corruption attacks).

The first set of attacks can take an NPP to abnormal conditions and initiate physical damage. NPPs are equipped with reactor protection systems that monitor operational variables and shut down systems if pre-defined thresholds are passed; this reduces the risk of physical damage. Nevertheless, the attacks impact availability because it takes several hours to restart an NPP. The second set of attacks, on the other hand, evade reactor protection systems and have the potential to cause physical damage, mainly because several NPP sensors are shared between I&C systems and reactor protection systems. Thus, attackers can initiate physical damage to an NPP as well as defeat reactor protection systems by passing them fake status data.

2.   Operation-Aware Intrusion Detection

This paper proposes operation-aware intrusion detection as an anomaly-based defensive capability for NPPs. Profiles of legitimate behavior of digital I&C applications are constructed by analyzing payloads of PDUs sent over control and/or fieldbus networks and the semantics of each PDU field in the context of NPP operations. Thus, PDUs are analyzed in terms of the bindings between streams of bits and tasks such as withdrawing control rods, changing the reactor feed pump rate or closing steamline isolation valves. This approach provides more visibility than model-based detection with regard to the potential of PDUs being legitimate or malicious. As a matter of fact, PDUs may be perfectly formatted according to the protocol specifications while having the potential to cause harm to an NPP.

For example, well-formatted PDUs that close the main turbine control valves when reactor power goes above 25% take the reactor to an anomalous state in which the reactor vessel pressure rises far beyond the maximum allowable value. A turbine bypass valve is supposed to provide for excess steam flow, but the flow capacity of the bypass valve is normally equivalent to 25% of steam flow. This flow capacity is insufficient to return the reactor vessel pressure to normal soon enough to maintain safe NPP conditions. Furthermore, several application-level attacks can be crafted that comply with protocol specifications. For example, memory addresses and shellcode injected as malicious PDUs in Modbus memory corruption attacks could be made to appear as valid coil and/or holding register values.

Modbus memory corruption attacks [1] highlight the need for operation-aware protocol-based intrusion detection. These attacks exploit faulty mappings between the addresses of data items defined by Modbus and the memory locations where the data items are actually stored. Register addresses and values used in such attacks are generally fully compliant with Modbus specifications. Nevertheless, it is unlikely that the attack PDUs will consistently have valid semantics in terms of NPP operation. These operational aspects of PDUs and the associated NPP states are leveraged by the intrusion detection approach described in this paper.

3. Modeling NPP Operations

The stochastic activity network (SAN) formalism [5, 11, 14] as implemented by the Möbius tool [2, 12] is used to model and analyze the operation of a boiling water reactor (a common type of NPP) along with its digital I&C systems that engage the Modbus protocol. The operation of Modbus applications in digital I&C systems, the control of digital I&C systems over NPP components and the interactions among NPP components as reflected by NPP operational variables are captured using atomic SAN models. Figure 1 presents an excerpt of an atomic model developed for a digital I&C system. Discrete inputs, coils, input registers and holding registers are modeled as SAN places, which we call "device places." The number of tokens in each device place represents the value of the Modbus data item that corresponds to the SAN place.

Depending on its configuration, a Modbus device may have as many as 65,536 data items; the corresponding atomic model would be extremely large. To address this issue, the information contained in PDU data fields is modeled as a set of SAN places, which we call "PDU places." The numbers of tokens in PDU places represent the values placed in the data fields of PDUs sent to digital I&C systems. PDU function codes are modeled as instantaneous activities, e.g., write coil, write multiple coils, write register and write multiple registers. Some of these instantaneous activities have several cases. The probability distributions of case selections for these instantaneous activities depend on the markings of the input places associated with the input gates of the instantaneous activity under consideration.

In general, case selections indicate the data items accessed from Modbus device memory. PDU places are fed with tokens by timed activities (not shown in Figure 1 due to space limitations) that model the behavior of a master device generating Modbus requests. The enabling predicates in the input gates in Figure 1 check whether the input places associated with the gates are not all zeroed, in which case the corresponding instantaneous activities are enabled. (A PDU that is not sent over the network is modeled using PDU places containing zero tokens.) Upon completion of an instantaneous activity, one of the associated activity cases is selected. In the case of instantaneous activities, when modeling a write function code of any kind, the output functions of out-

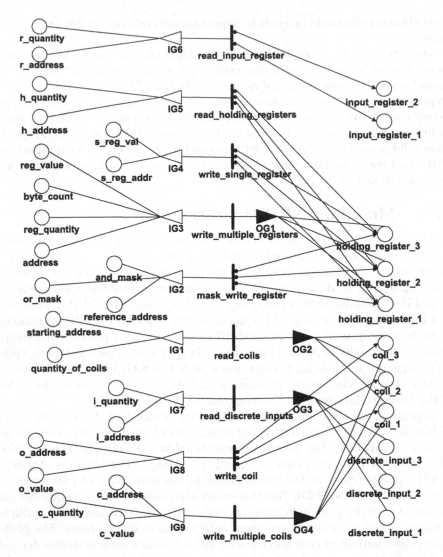

Figure 1. SAN model excerpt for a Modbus digital I&C system.

put gates associated with the selected activity case add a number of tokens to one or more device places.

The output functions zero the PDU places that enable the instantaneous activities modeling function codes associated with the output gates in question. In the case of instantaneous activities, when modeling a read function code, output functions act as identity functions on device places and add tokens to a set of places modeling variables for a master device (not shown in Figure 1 due to space limitations). The variables related to the operation of NPP physical components are also modeled as a set of places, which we call "NPP

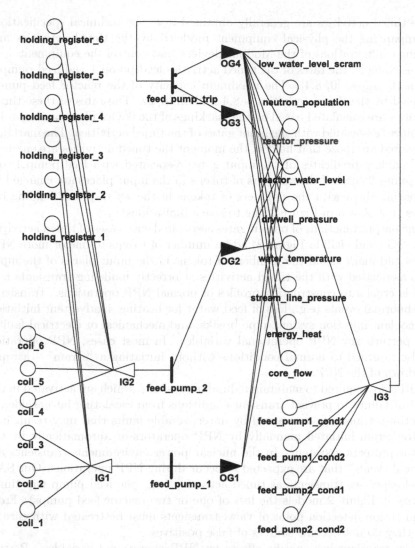

Figure 2. SAN model excerpt of a digital I&C system with two reactor feed pumps.

places." Examples include temperature and pressure of water and steam for a component such as the NPP moderator. The number of tokens in an NPP place represents the value of the NPP operational variable modeled by the place. For example, the fact that the reactor pressure is 900 psi is modeled as an NPP place (reactor pressure) that holds 900 tokens.

Figure 2 presents a SAN model excerpt of the operation of a digital I&C system that controls two reactor feed pumps. The mechanisms used to operate on the NPP are modeled as timed activities. The two reactor feed pumps are examples of these mechanisms, which, in terms of NPP operations, raise the pressure of the moderator to make it flow to the reactor vessel. The rates of these timed activities are generally obtained from the technical specifications accompanying the physical equipment modeled by the timed activities and specific configurations of the Modbus devices that control the equipment.

For example, the rates of the timed activities feed_pump_1 and feed_pump_2 are in the range [0, 8.4]. The maximum capacity of the reactor feed pumps modeled by the timed activities is 8.4 million lb/hr. The rates of these timed activities are calculated based on the markings of the device places acting as input places associated with the input gates of the timed activities. The markings considered are those that hold at the moment the timed activities are enabled. The enabling predicates of the input gates associated with feed_pump_1 and feed_pump_2 check if the numbers of tokens in the input places are changed by comparing them with the numbers of tokens in the set of places holding old values (not shown in Figure 2 due to space limitations).

The output functions of output gates associated with cases of timed activities (e.g., OG1 and OG2 in Figure 2) add a number of tokens to one or more NPP places and mark as old the numbers of tokens in the input places of the input gates associated with the timed activities. Correctly modeling transients in a SAN is crucial to constructing profiles of normal NPP operations. Transients are abnormal events (e.g., loss of feed water for heating, inadvertent initiation of a coolant injection system, pipe breaks, and mechanical or electrical faults) that perturb key NPP operational variables. In most cases, NPP operation can be returned to normal conditions without initiating a "scram" – a rapid shutdown of the NPP.

NPPs are required to maintain redundant systems, which are activated in the event of failure to prevent transient conditions from escalating into accidents. Sometimes transients are caused by unrecoverable faults that may result in a reactor scram initiated manually by NPP operators or automatically by the reactor protection system. In the nuclear power environment, transients are "normal events" that are expected to occur during NPP operations. Our SAN model expresses transients as timed activities (e.g., the feed_pump_trip timed activity in Figure 2 models the loss of one or two reactor feed pumps). From the intrusion detection point of view, transients must be treated with care so that they do not become sources of false positives.

Each transient has specific effects on NPP operational variables. Perturbations to NPP variables caused by a transient are reflected as changes to the values of data items stored in the memory of Modbus devices. However, there is always uncertainty whether drastic changes to data items during NPP operation are caused by transients or attacks. We employ the activity time distribution functions of timed activities that model possible transients to distinguish between transient effects and attack effects. Note that the estimation of the failure rates of physical NPP components is outside the scope of our work since it requires the consideration of electrical, chemical and mechanical properties of NPP components.

Condition data monitoring and aggregation techniques [4, 9] can be used to estimate the failure rates of most of the physical components of an NPP.

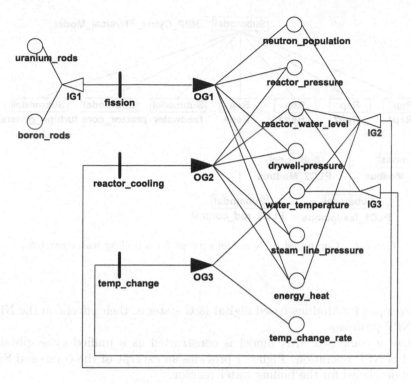

Figure 3. SAN model excerpt of NPP processes.

The time distribution functions of timed activities that model transients may be used to calculate the failure rates of physical components based on the numbers of tokens found at the moment of estimation in the SAN places used to model physical conditions. For example, the failure rate of feed_pump_trip in Figure 2 is computed based on the numbers of tokens in SAN places denoting various conditions of reactor feed pumps. The output functions of output gates associated with a timed activity that models a transient, in turn, models the perturbations to NPP operational variables by incrementing or decrementing the numbers of tokens in NPP places.

NPP operation modeling requires SAN models to be constructed for numerous reactor processes. Examples include nuclear fission, reactor cooling and the various physical relations between temperature, pressure, density, volume, etc. The rates of timed activities in these SAN models are provided in NPP technical manuals. The SAN models also incorporate timed activities that model NPP operation measures such as reactor period (time required for the reactor power to change by a factor of e, where e is the base of the natural logarithm) and reactivity (neutron population change with time). Figure 3 presents an excerpt of the SAN model developed for a set of reactor processes. The Join and Replicate operations of Möbius [6] are used to unify the atomic SAN mod-

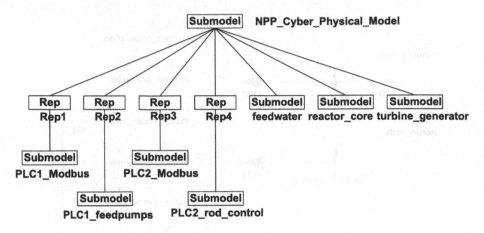

Figure 4. Composed SAN model excerpt for a boiling water reactor.

els developed for Modbus-based digital I&C systems, their effects on the NPP, and NPP processes.

Thus, a composed SAN model is constructed as a unified cyber-physical model of NPP operation. Figure 4 provides an excerpt of the composed SAN model developed for the boiling water reactor.

4.   Estimating NPP Operation Profiles

Let P denote the set of device places defined in the atomic SAN models developed for the boiling water reactor. The set of possible markings of P is the finite set of functions $F = \{f_n \mid f_n : P \to N, n \in N\}$. We assume that for each NPP power level l_m, where $m \in N$, P is marked according to a function η from a finite (in most cases small) set of functions Γ_m, where $\Gamma_m \subset F$, and that Γ_m can be estimated. The set of functions Γ_m for a power level l_m depends on the actual values of NPP operational variables during the interval of time that an NPP has that state and the tasks (e.g., inserting or withdrawing control rods, changing the rate of water pumps, opening or closing valves) are carried out on NPP components by digital I&C systems.

NPP operational variables (e.g., nuclear fission data estimated by a neutron monitoring system) are stored as Modbus data items in the memory of digital I&C systems. On the modeling side, the data values are reflected by the numbers of tokens in the corresponding device places, which we call "conditions device places." Further, the tasks carried out by digital I&C systems on NPP components are initiated via a series of writes to the memory locations designated for the corresponding Modbus data items. For example, the rate of a reactor feed pump for 100% NPP power can be set by writing a value of (say) 84 in the holding register of a digital I&C system; for 75% NPP power, the value of the holding register may be set to 63, and so on.

The correspondence existing between values of Modbus data items in the memory of digital I&C systems, operations or tasks carried out by digital I&C systems on NPP components, and NPP operational variables allows profiles of normal NPP operations to be estimated. Thus, given normal values of NPP operational variables associated with a power level l_m, we estimate the possible values of discrete inputs, coils, input registers and holding registers, which may be considered as legitimate.

We also assume that when an NPP transitions from a power level l_m to a power level $l_{m\pm\lambda}$, where $\lambda \in N$, the marking of P changes according to a finite set of marking transition flows, i.e., an ordered sequence of functions from Γ_m to $\Gamma_{m\pm\lambda}$. In general, throughout the operation of an NPP, a finite set of ordered sequences of functions from F exist that represent transitions of values of Modbus data items in digital I&C systems when the NPP is operated.

We leverage marking transition flows to construct NPP operation profiles. The normal operation of an NPP is simulated along with operational phenomena such as transients and the normal marking transition flows are estimated. Given an NPP at a power level l_m, the marking transition flow mechanism estimates if the semantics and payload of an arbitrary PDU received by a digital I&C system make sense in the Modbus configuration and will legitimately change the values of Modbus data items, respectively.

The set of functions Γ_m for each NPP power level l_m is constructed using reward models based on the activity-marking reward structure [13]. Each function in the finite set of functions F is assigned a rate of reward. A typical reward function for an element of F checks for a defined number of tokens in the conditions device places.

As mentioned above, NPP operational variables are reflected in Modbus data items in digital I&C systems that are modeled by conditions device places. The number of tokens in a SAN place represents a link between a power level l_m of an NPP and an element of F. In addition to these places, a reward function checks for the defined numbers of tokens in the remaining device places (i.e., device places that do not model NPP operational variables). In Möbius, the numbers of tokens in device places are parameterized using global variables. The composed SAN that models NPP operation is solved after all the global variables are assigned.

The following block of code implements a reward function:

```
double reward = 0;
if((PLC1_Modbus->holding_register_1->Mark()==reg_val_int1)&&
   (PLC1_Modbus->holding_register_2->Mark()==reg_val_int2) &&
   (PLC1_Modbus->holding_register_3->Mark()==reg_val_int3) &&
   (PLC1_Modbus->coil_1->Mark() == cval1) &&
   (PLC1_Modbus->discrete_input_1->Mark()==dval1) &&
   (PLC1_Modbus->input_register_1->Mark()==inp1))
{
   reward += 0.1;
}
return (reward);
```

The rates of reward fall in the interval-of-time category [13], where the total reward is accumulated during an interval of time covering all possible state transitions of an NPP. Solutions of the composed SAN model produce a reward for each element of F. The set of functions Γ_m for each power level l_m of an NPP consists of all the elements of F that map conditions device places to the numbers of tokens corresponding to values of NPP operational variables, in turn, identified by l_m, and whose accumulated reward is greater than 0.

Let S and V_m denote the set of conditions device places and the set of numbers of tokens that model values of NPP operational variables corresponding to power level l_m. Further, let R be a function that, for each element of F, returns the reward as estimated by composed SAN model solutions. Then, the set of functions Γ_m is $\{\mu \in F \mid \mu : S \rightarrow V_m, R(\mu) > 0\}$.

Marking transition flows are identified by incremental measurement time intervals in Möbius. For instance, if solutions of the composed SAN model produce non-zero rewards of, say, $r_{4,8}$, $r_{1,2,0}$ and $r_{1,6,0}$ for the functions $f_{4,8}$, $f_{1,2,0}$ and $f_{1,6,0}$, respectively, solving the composed model again while setting the measurement time interval to a value t close to zero may produce zero rewards for these functions. Setting the measurement time interval to $t + 1$, $t + 2$, etc. and then solving the composed SAN model may produce a reward of $r_{1,2,0}$ for function $f_{1,2,0}$. Incrementing the measurement time interval again and solving the composed SAN model again may produce rewards of $r_{1,2,0}$ and $r_{1,6,0}$ for the functions $f_{1,2,0}$ and $f_{1,6,0}$, respectively.

The measurement time interval may be further incremented until the solution of the composed SAN model produces rewards of $r_{4,8}$, $r_{1,2,0}$ and $r_{1,6,0}$ for the functions $f_{4,8}$, $f_{1,2,0}$ and $f_{1,6,0}$, respectively, leading to the identification of the marking transition flow $f_{1,2,0}$, $f_{1,6,0}$ and $f_{4,8}$. The frequency of marking transitions caused by events such as transients is quite relevant to the attribution of possible losses of equipment during NPP operation. The estimation of the frequency of these marking transitions is carried out by defining impulse rewards associated with completions of timed activities that model NPP transients. Like the rates of reward, the impulse rewards defined in our work belong to the interval-of-time category of the activity-marking reward structure [13].

5.   Deriving Intrusion Detection Rules

Our ultimate objective is to construct a set of practical intrusion detection rules. These rules scrutinize the values of Modbus data items and PDU fields to determine whether incoming PDUs are legitimate or malicious.

The SAN formalism is used to model regularities in Modbus data items and for marking transition flows so that the resulting SAN model is interpretable. The SAN model (Figure 5) is used to derive intrusion detection rules. The elements of P are modeled as SAN places. For each power level l_m of an NPP, the numbers of tokens in the SAN places are defined by elements of Γ_m. The activities in the SAN model capture individual memory writes carried out by Modbus requests.

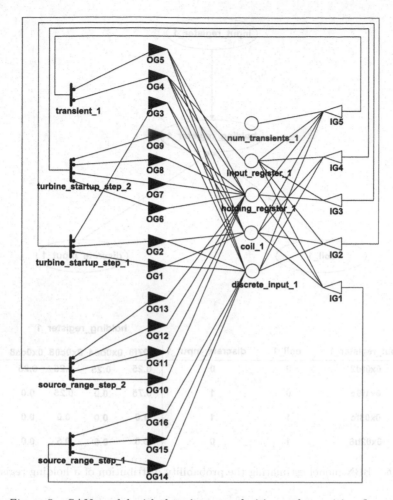

Figure 5. SAN model with data item regularities and transition flows.

For example, a PDU with function code 0x10 (write multiple registers) may write from 1 to 123 registers depending on the value in the registers field. Each of these memory writes is modeled by an activity in the SAN model. Thus, a marking transition is modeled as a set of activities. Activity cases model assignments of defined values to Modbus data items as a result of processing Modbus requests. The case distribution function of each activity models the probability distribution of a defined Modbus data item. Case distribution functions are constructed by analyzing the data provided by the set of functions Γ_m for each power level l_m, marking the transition flows and frequencies of marking transitions caused by transients.

These analyses are performed using the Bayesian belief network (BBN) formalism [10] as implemented by MSBNx [7]. Figure 6 illustrates the estimation of the probability distribution of a holding register using a BBN model. The

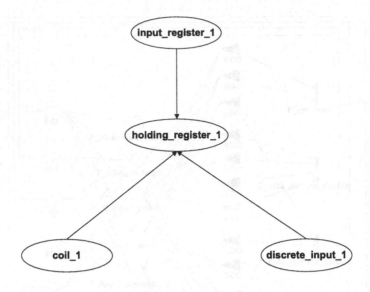

input_register_1	coil_1	discrete_input_1	holding_register_1			
			0x07f8	0x0be4	0x0c08	0x0ca8
0x0fd2	0	0	0.25	0.25	0.25	0.25
0x1f6c	0	1	0.75	0.0	0.25	0.0
0x03fc	1	1	1.0	0.0	0.0	0.0
0x02b6	1	0	0.0	0.5	0.5	0.0

Figure 6.   BBN model estimating the probability distribution of a holding register.

probability is 0.75 that holding_register_1 is assigned the value 2040 (0x07f8) while heading toward a legitimate marking according to a legitimate marking transition flow. Activities in Figure 5 complete in order and the probability distributions of the Modbus data items change as the markings of the elements of P change. During NPP operations, Modbus data items and the PDUs received over the network are required to follow a SAN model as shown in Figure 5 in order to be considered as legitimate traffic in NPP operations. Monitoring and control traffic is examined using the intrusion detection rules derived from the SAN model.

The enabling predicates in each input gate check if the current value of a Modbus data item allows for a memory write that modifies a Modbus data item in compliance with a defined set of functions and following a legitimate marking transition flow. In fact, under normal NPP operations, conditions exist under which the defined valves are never opened or closed, control rods are never inserted or withdrawn, etc. No matter what the modifying value is, the very action of modification may not comply with any NPP operation profile. Case distribution functions of activities and output functions (of output gates) are used to estimate the probabilities that legitimate values are assigned to Modbus data items. The following block of code consults the values of an input register, a coil and a discrete input, and returns a probability of 0.75 that 2040 (0x07f8) is assigned to the defined holding register in compliance with the operation profiles:

```
if((input_register_1->Mark() == 8044) && (coil_1->Mark()==0)
    && (discrete_input_1->Mark() == 1))
return(0.75);
holding_register_1->Mark() = 2040;
```

6. Conclusions

Operation-aware intrusion detection is a novel anomaly-based approach for detecting attacks on complex systems such as NPPs. Profiles of NPP operation as controlled and monitored by digital I&C systems are constructed using SAN models. The SAN formalism effectively models the interactions between a Modbus master and digital I&C systems, the operation of digital I&C systems on NPP components, and relevant NPP processes. The formalism also models and unifies NPP operation profiles estimated by the SAN model solutions. The resulting SAN model is interpretable as well as a valuable source of intrusion detection rules that can distinguish between legitimate protocol frames and attack frames.

Acknowledgements

The research of Julian Rrushi was partially supported by scholarships from the University of Milan and (ISC)².

References

[1] C. Bellettini and J. Rrushi, Vulnerability analysis of SCADA protocol binaries through detection of memory access taintedness, *Proceedings of the IEEE SMC Information Assurance and Security Workshop*, pp. 341–348, 2007.

[2] D. Deavours, G. Clark, T. Courtney, D. Daly, S. Derisavi, J. Doyle, W. Sanders and P. Webster, The Möbius framework and its implementation, *IEEE Transactions of Software Engineering*, vol. 20(10), pp. 956–969, 2002.

[3] R. Krutz, *Securing SCADA Systems*, Wiley, Indianapolis, Indiana, 2006.

[4] J. McCalley, Y. Jiang, V. Honavar, J. Pathak, M. Kezunovic, S. Natti, C. Singh and J. Panida, Automated Integration of Condition Monitoring with an Optimized Maintenance Scheduler for Circuit Breakers and Power Transformers, Final Project Report, Department of Computer Science, Iowa State University, Ames, Iowa, 2006.

[5] J. Meyer, A. Movaghar and W. Sanders, Stochastic activity networks: Structure, behavior and application, *Proceedings of the International Conference on Timed Petri Nets*, pp. 106–115, 1985.

[6] J. Meyer and W. Sanders, Specification and construction of performability models, *Proceedings of the Second International Workshop on Performability Modeling of Computer and Communication Systems*, 1993.

[7] Microsoft Research, MSBNx: Bayesian Network Editor and Tool Kit, Microsoft Corporation, Redmond, Washington (research.microsoft.com /adapt/MSBNx).

[8] Modbus IDA, MODBUS Application Protocol Specification v1.1a, North Grafton, Massachusetts (www.modbus.org/specs.php), 2004.

[9] J. Pathak, Y. Jiang, V. Honavar and J. McCalley, Condition data aggregation with application to failure rate calculation of power transformers, *Proceedings of the Thirty-Ninth Annual Hawaii International Conference on System Sciences*, p. 241a, 2005.

[10] J. Pearl, Bayesian networks: A model of self-activated memory for evidential reasoning, *Proceedings of the Seventh Conference of the Cognitive Science Society*, pp. 329–334, 1985.

[11] W. Sanders, Construction and Solution of Performability Models Based on Stochastic Activity Networks, Ph.D. Dissertation, Department of Electrical Engineering and Computer Science, University of Michigan, Ann Arbor, Michigan, 1988.

[12] W. Sanders, Integrated frameworks for multi-level and multi-formalism modeling, *Proceedings of the Eighth International Workshop on Petri Nets and Performance Models*, pp. 2–9, 1999.

[13] W. Sanders and J. Meyer, A unified approach for specifying measures of performance, dependability and performability, in *Dependable Computing for Critical Applications*, A. Avizienis and J. Laprie (Eds.), Springer-Verlag, Berlin-Heidelberg, Germany, pp. 215–237, 1991.

[14] W. Sanders and J. Meyer, Stochastic activity networks: Formal definitions and concepts, in *Lecture Notes in Computer Science, Volume 2090*, Springer, Berlin-Heidelberg, Germany, pp. 315–343, 2001.

III

CONTROL SYSTEMS SECURITY

Chapter 5

APPLYING TRUSTED NETWORK
TECHNOLOGY TO PROCESS
CONTROL SYSTEMS

Hamed Okhravi and David Nicol

Abstract   Interconnections between process control networks and enterprise networks expose instrumentation and control systems and the critical infrastructure components they operate to a variety of cyber attacks. Several architectural standards and security best practices have been proposed for industrial control systems. However, they are based on older architectures and do not leverage the latest hardware and software technologies. This paper describes new technologies that can be applied to the design of next generation security architectures for industrial control systems. The technologies are discussed along with their security benefits and design trade-offs.

Keywords: Process control systems, trusted networks, security architectures

1.   Introduction

The increased interconnectivity of industrial control networks and enterprise networks has resulted in the proliferation of standard communication protocols in industrial control systems. Legacy SCADA protocols are often encapsulated in TCP/IP packets for reasons of efficiency and cost, which blurs the network layer distinction between control traffic and enterprise traffic. The interconnection of industrial control networks and enterprise networks using commodity protocols exposes instrumentation and control systems and the critical infrastructure components they operate to a variety of cyber attacks.

Security surveys reveal significant increases in external attacks that target critical infrastructure assets [2] . The entry points in most of the incidents were corporate WANs, business networks, wireless access points, modems and the Internet.

Several government agencies and industry associations have proposed standards and security best practices for industrial control systems [11, 12, 17, 19].

Please use the following format when citing this chapter:

Okhravi, H. and Nicol, D., 2008, in IFIP International Federation for Information Processing, Volume 290; *Critical Infrastructure Protection II*, eds. Papa, M., Shenoi, S., (Boston: Springer), pp. 57–70.

However, these efforts are based on older technologies and security architectures that rely on the differentiation and separation of enterprise and control traffic. While the efforts are, no doubt, important, the underlying security philosophy exposes industrial control systems to attacks that exploit misconfigurations, out-of-band connectivity and blind trust in the identities of traffic sources.

However, new technologies are emerging that provide more pervasive security within networks [10]. These technologies push security from perimeter devices such as firewalls to the networked devices themselves. This paper reviews technologies that can be applied to designing the next generation of secure industrial control systems. The technologies are discussed along with their security benefits and design trade-offs.

2.   Control System Security Recommendations

Industrial control systems (ICSs) are highly distributed networks used for controlling operations in water distribution and treatment plants, electric power systems, oil and gas refineries, manufacturing facilities and chemical plants. ICSs include supervisory control and data acquisition (SCADA) systems and distributed control systems [19]. The main components of an ICS are the control server or master terminal unit (MTU), remote terminal units (RTUs), intelligent electronic devices (IEDs), programmable logic controllers (PLCs), operator consoles or human-machine interfaces (HMIs), and data historians. Generally, an ICS comprises two distinct networks: a process control network (PCN) containing controllers, switches, actuators and low-level control devices, and an enterprise network (EN) incorporating high-level supervisory nodes and corporate computers.

The National Institute of Standards and Technology (NIST), Institute of Electrical and Electronics Engineers (IEEE), Instrumentation Systems and Automation (ISA) Society, International Electrotechnical Commission (IEC) and Industrial Automation Open Networking Association (IAONA) have specified guidelines for securing ICSs (see, e.g., [11, 12, 19]). In fact, most security best practices recommend the segregation of PCNs and ENs.

Firewalls are often used to segregate PCNs and ENs [1, 18, 19]. A firewall can be configured to block unnecessary services, protocols and ports, thereby providing a higher degree of segregation between a PCN and EN. A router may be positioned in front of the firewall to perform simple packet filtering, leaving the firewall to perform more sophisticated tasks such as stateful filtering and acting as a proxy.

Using a single firewall between a PCN and EN has a serious drawback. This is because the firewall must allow the data historian to have a wide range of access to the PCN. Essentially, each service needs a "hole" in the firewall to operate correctly. Configuring too many holes in the firewall reduces PCN-EN segregation and opens the PCN to a slew of attacks. This problem is typically addressed by creating a "demilitarized zone" (DMZ) [1, 18, 19].

An architecture deploying a DMZ has three zones: an outside zone containing the EN, an inside zone containing the PCN, and a DMZ containing the data

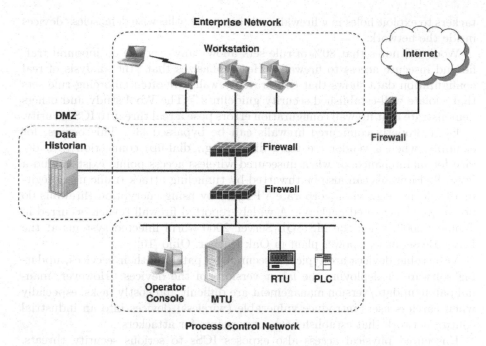

Figure 1. Paired firewall PCN architecture.

historian. Firewall rules are crafted to make the DMZ historian the sole point of contact between the PCN and EN. The historian can access PCN services that provide it data; in turn, the EN is allowed access to the historian. Firewall rules block PCN access by all other devices. Most attacks originating in (or passing through) the EN and targeting the historian will not affect the control systems; at worst, they would corrupt the historian's data (a redundant copy of this data is stored elsewhere).

A PCN architecture deploying paired firewalls separated by a DMZ [18, 19] is shown in Figure 1. It simplifies the firewall rules and achieves a clear separation of responsibility as the PCN-side firewall can be managed by the control group and the EN-side firewall by the IT group [18, 19]. This architecture is highly recommended for ICSs, and best practices have been identified for configuring the firewalls (see, e.g., [1, 11, 12, 19, 21]).

3.   Security Challenges

Firewall configuration errors can lead to security vulnerabilities. One problem is that firewalls often have large rule sets that are difficult to verify. According to a study by Wool [21], firewall rule sets may have as many as 2,600 rules with 5,800 objects, and a significant correlation exists between rule set complexity and the number of configuration errors. A second problem is that firewalls are usually the main line of defense. Configuration errors enable attackers to exploit holes in a firewall and target the otherwise defenseless devices inside the network.

Wool [21] notes that 80% of rule sets allow "any" service on inbound traffic and insecure access to firewalls. He emphasizes that "the analysis of real configuration data shows that corporate firewalls are often enforcing rule sets that violate well-established security guidelines." The Wool study and others demonstrate that firewall configuration errors pose a real threat to ICS security.

Even properly configured firewalls can be bypassed [3]. This occurs, for example, when a vendor creates a direct (e.g., dial-up) connection to a device for maintenance, or when unsecured wireless access points exist behind a firewall. Firewalls can also be thwarted by tunneling attack traffic using legitimate means (e.g., via a corporate VPN) or by using encryption (firewalls do not inspect encrypted packets). A widely-reported firewall breach occurred in January 2003, when the MS SQL Server 2000 worm infected systems at the Davis-Besse nuclear power plant in Oak Harbor, Ohio [16].

Vulnerable devices are typically secured by patching their services, updating software or deploying the latest versions of the devices. However, manual patch/update/version management are difficult and costly tasks, especially when careless users introduce vulnerable (wireless) devices into an industrial control network that establish new entry points for attackers.

Unsecured physical access also exposes ICSs to serious security threats. Open wireless access points and Ethernet ports on office walls enable attackers to enter ICS networks and target critical assets. Nothing in the traditional ICS architecture prevents suspect devices from connecting to the network; thus, serious threats are posed by devices whose hardware, operating systems, executables and/or configurations have been tampered with by attackers.

Many ICS vulnerabilities admit malware such as worms, viruses, Trojan horses and rootkits [15, 16]. ICS security trends reveal that external malware attacks are becoming increasingly common [2]. Finally, rogue users (insiders) are an ever-present threat to ICSs.

4. Trusted Process Control Networks

In a traditional network access control model, access is granted to a user without considering the security state of the user's machine. Likewise, firewall access control is agnostic about the security status of the device that sends traffic. A port on a machine is opened or not opened to traffic based entirely on the identity of the source.

A trusted network architecture uses information about the hardware and software states of devices in admission and access control decisions. When a device first "joins" the network, its hardware and software are checked; based on these checks, the appropriate access control rules are applied dynamically to the user, device and traffic. The same principle can be applied to process control architectures. This section discuss technologies that support this concept and their application to ICSs.

4.1 Trusted Networks

A trusted network (TN) architecture uses existing standards, protocols and hardware devices to implement "trust." TNs provide important security services such as user authentication, comprehensive network device admission control, end-device status checks, policy-based access control, traffic filtering, automated remediation of non-compliant devices and auditing.

The Trusted Computing Group (TCG) has promulgated industry standards for TNs [20]. Several commercial TN technologies have been developed, including Cisco TrustSec [6], Cisco CleanAccess [7] (formerly known as Cisco Network Admission Control (NAC) [5, 8]), and Microsoft Network Access Protection (NAP) [13]. Cisco NAC is interoperable with Microsoft NAP; details about their interoperation can be found in [9].

4.1.1 Trusted Network Components.
TN component vendors use a variety of names to describe their products. We use generic terms with a bias towards those adopted by Cisco CleanAccess.

A TN has the following components:

- **Client Device:** Every client device must be evaluated prior to admission to a TN.

- **Network Access Device:** All connectivity to a TN is implemented via a network access device (NAD), which enforces policy. NAD functionality may exist in devices such as switches, routers, VPN concentrators and wireless access points.

- **Authentication, Authorization and Access Control Server:** The authentication, authorization and access control (AAA) server maintains the policy and provides rules to NADs based on the results of authentication and posture validation.

- **Posture Validation Servers:** Posture validation servers (PVSs) evaluate the compliance of a client before it can join a TN. A PVS is typically a specialization for one client attribute (e.g., operating system version and patch or virus signature release).

- **Posture Remediation Servers:** These servers provide remediation options to a client device in case of non-compliance. For example, a server may maintain the latest virus signatures and require a non-compliant client device to load the signatures before joining a TN.

- **Directory Server:** This server authenticates client devices based on their identities or roles.

- **Other Servers:** These include trusted versions of Audit, DNS, DHCP and VPN servers [5, 7, 8].

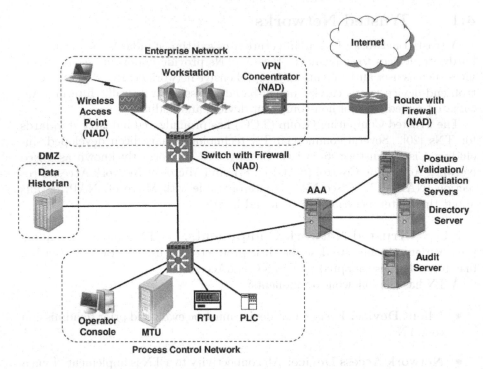

Figure 2. Trusted process control network.

4.1.2   Trusted Network Protocols.   TNs leverage existing standards and protocols to implement the required security functionality; this reduces the cost of building TNs. Protocols used in TNs include IPSec for hardening communications [7], EAP and 802.1x for authentication [5, 6], RADIUS/LDAP/Kerberos for directory services and authentication [5, 7], HCAP for compliance communication [5], and GAME for communications between AAA and audit servers [4].

4.2   TPCN Architecture

A trusted process control network (TPCN) architecture is presented in Figure 2. A client device intending to join the network communicates its request to the NAD. The NAD establishes the client device's identity using EAP over the 802.1x protocol and sends the results to the AAA server using the RADIUS protocol. The AAA server returns a list of posture validation requirements and the addresses of the appropriate PVSs.

The client then validates its posture with each of the PVSs. If the client is in compliance, the results are sent to the AAA server using the HCAP protocol. On the other hand, if the client lacks one or more requirements, the appropriate posture remediation servers suggest remediation actions to the client.

The directory server determines the client's group or role. Given all the results from the PVSs and the directory server, the AAA server determines the set of rules that apply to the client's access and traffic and sends them to the NAD for enforcement. From this point on, the client is permitted to communicate via the NAD and all its activities are monitored for policy compliance. Interested readers are referred to [5, 7, 8] for additional details.

The policy held by the AAA server is in the form of an authentication requirement and a list of posture validation requirements. For example, token-based authentication may be required and postures must be validated with the anti-virus server, patch management server and driver validation server. When a client device joins the network, a NAD communicates with an AAA server on behalf of the device. The AAA server authenticates the device and provides rules based on the device's security postures to the NAD. From this point on, the NAD enforces the policy on all ingress and egress traffic to/from the device. For example, an RTU with valid firmware is allowed to communicate with the historian; all other traffic is blocked. The two examples below further clarify the workings of a TPCN.

Example 1. Consider a scenario where an analyst on a workstation intends to connect wirelessly to the PCN to access historical data about plant operations. The workstation connects to a wireless access point (AP) in the enterprise network with NAD functionality. The AP applies the default policy, which is to block all traffic except what is needed to establish trust. The workstation then authenticates with the AP using EAP over the 802.1x protocol to send a stored certificate. The AP uses RADIUS to send the workstation's identity to the AAA server. The AAA server then sends the user's identity to the directory server, which knows the user's role ("analyst"). The AAA server uses RADIUS to send the workstation a list of posture requirements (anti-virus version number and OS patch history). The workstation uses a trusted platform module (TPM) chip to sign and send the posture values to the relevant PVSs, which proceed to validate these values. The patch management PVS discovers that the workstation OS has a missing patch and coordinates with the remediation server to have the appropriate patch sent to the workstation. The PVSs transmit the results back to the AAA server using the HCAP protocol. If the workstation is compliant, the AAA sends a rule set to the AP for enforcement. Since the user role is "analyst," the rule set allows TCP connections to the historian but blocks access to all other devices.

Example 2. Consider a scenario where an RTU intends to join the PCN. The RTU connects to a switch on the factory floor via a network cable; the switch has NAD functionality. The protocols used are the same as in Example 1, so we avoid repetition. The switch authenticates the RTU using the RTU's stored token. The AAA server requires the RTU to validate its configuration with a configuration management server. The RTU sends its configuration to the configuration management server, which returns the successful result to the

AAA server. The AAA server, in turn, sends the appropriate rule set for the compliant RTU to the switch for enforcement. The RTU may now communicate with other RTUs, the MTU and the historian; the switch blocks all other traffic.

4.3　TPCN Requirements

For added security and separation of duty, a TPCN requires at least two NADs (switches with firewalls) and a AAA server (Figure 2). An enterprise can add as many PVSs as required, e.g., an anti-virus validation server to ensure that devices have up-to-date virus protection, a patch management server to check that devices have the correct patches and a software validation server to verify the authenticity of embedded device firmware. Incorporating multiple PVSs adds to the cost of a TPCN, but enhances security.

All NADs (switches, routers, wireless access points, etc.) must support trusted network functionality. Many vendors offer products with trusted network functionality. Therefore, if an enterprise is already using new equipment, implementing a TPCN may be very cost-effective. Older systems would likely involve significant upgrades, which can be costly. Note that in a TPCN architecture the firewall functionality is integrated in NADs.

Client devices may need software and firmware upgrades to support trusted network functionality. A trusted network client is required for authentication with the AAA server and for sending posture values. For secure applications, TPM chips can be used to verify configurations and obtain posture signatures. Devices such as RTUs and PLCs do not usually have TPMs; however, as some RTUs already come with built-in web servers, adding TPM to these devices is feasible, especially if government regulations mandate the implementation of trusted ICS architectures.

The administrator applies system updates by imposing new requirements in the AAA and PVSs. The AAA server informs devices of the new policy. If the devices have the update, they verify this fact with a PVS and remain in the network. Otherwise, the appropriate server provides them with the required patches (or installs the patches automatically), upon which they can enter the network.

TPCNs have the same availability issues as traditional PCNs – applying patches can cause components to crash. Therefore, every patch or update must be tested thoroughly before being placed on the AAA server. Exact replicas of TPCN components should be used for testing. If concerns exist after testing, a backup device may be placed in the TPCN. In such a situation, the AAA server holds two different policies for the device. One policy is associated with the actual role and the other policy with the backup role. The backup policy does not enforce the new requirement on the backup device until the actual device is verified to function correctly with the patch. It is only then that the administrator applies the requirement to the backup device as well. Note that if the actual device is affected by the patch, the backup device can function correctly since it is not required by its policy to have the patch in order to connect to the network. TPCNs do not positively or negatively affect system availability; they merely enforce the requirements. It is the testing phase, before the specification of a requirement, that determines whether or not system availability is affected.

5.   TPCN Evaluation

The benefits of a TPCN are best seen in the light of how it addresses the security issues that impact traditional networks. A TPCN addresses the following security issues either partially or completely.

- **Firewall Configuration Errors (Partial):** A TPCN breaks the set of firewall rules into smaller rule sets associated with each access control group or role. These rule sets are sent by the AAA server to the NADs for enforcement upon completion of the authentication phase. According to Wool [21], the number of configuration errors decreases logarithmically as the rule set complexity decreases. Because a TPCN has smaller rule sets, the potential for firewall configuration errors is correspondingly lower. Moreover, access rules in a TPCN are defined based on groups or roles, not just IP addresses; this helps reduce confusion and, consequently, configuration errors. Note that configuration errors will never be completely eliminated; therefore, TPCN only provides a partial solution to the problem.

- **Bypassing Firewalls (Complete):** TPCNs explicitly address this issue by securing all NADs and requiring them to establish trust relationships with client devices before forwarding traffic (including wireless traffic and VPN traffic). Furthermore, the access control and traffic rules are applied at every access point. It is not possible to bypass the rules by hooking a line behind a firewall; this is because the line's switch (access point) enforces the rules.

- **Vulnerable Devices (Partial):** In a traditional network architecture, patch/update/version/configuration management is performed manually by the network administrator. This is an extremely difficult task for remote and mobile devices. As a result, it may be done less frequently than recommended or it may be simply ignored. In a TPCN, the state of a device is checked automatically before it can join the network. Moreover, its behavior is continuously monitored upon entry and status checks can be performed at the desired frequency. Consequently, a TPCN is less vulnerable to known attacks. Note, however, that a TPCN is still vulnerable to zero-day attacks.

- **Unsecured Physical Access (Complete):** TPCNs again address this problem by enforcing security policies on NAD ports. This is sometimes referred to as "port-based access control." Thus, a malicious or careless user cannot hook a device to an open Ethernet port and gain entry into the network. Note also that ports on TPCN switches and wireless access points do not forward traffic until trust relationships are established with the communicating entities.

- **Malware (Partial):** The compliance rules enforced on devices before and after joining a TPCN reduce the likelihood of infections by malware. A SCADA security study [2] notes that "the majority of worm events occurred months or years after the worm was widely known in IT world and patches were available." This implies that the majority of incidents can be prevented by enforcing compliance rules before a node joins a network. Since nearly 78% of the (external) SCADA security incidents are caused by malware [2], TPCN incidents are reduced dramatically. Nevertheless, a TPCN remains vulnerable to zero-day attacks.

- **Untrusted Devices (Complete):** TPCNs address this problem explicitly by verifying the signatures of the critical components of a device using the TPM chip and also checking the device status. Note that if the TPM chip is trusted, the device can attest its identity.

- **Untrusted Users (Partial):** By using stronger authentication methods and clearly defining user roles, TPCNs prevent attacks such as password cracking/stealing, access violations and impersonation. Also, by blocking all unnecessary accesses, TPCNs partially prevent accidents caused by careless insiders that account for more than 30% of all security incidents [2].

We employed the Common Attack Pattern Enumeration and Classification (CAPEC) database [14] to further compare the TPCN architecture with traditional PCN designs. CAPEC contains twelve attack categories along with their descriptions, prerequisites, methods, consequences and mitigation strategies. We consider nine attack categories (with 31 attack patterns), which we believe are meaningful in the ICS context and showcase the differences between TPCNs and traditional PCNs. For example, while buffer overflow attacks are effective against software applications, they are not relevant when evaluating network designs.

Tables 1 and 2 present the results of the comparison. The descriptor H (high) means that an attack is performed with little effort and cost; M (medium) implies that an attack is still possible but requires expert knowledge and is costly; L (low) indicates that an attack is highly unlikely or involves enormous effort, time and/or cost. The last column in Tables 1 and 2 shows the security controls provided by a TPCN to address the attack (if any).

Considering the 31 total attack patterns, a PCN is vulnerable to nineteen (61.3%) high, nine (29%) medium, and three (9.7%) low feasibility attacks. On the other hand, a TPCN is vulnerable to only two (6.5%) high feasibility attacks along with nine (29%) medium and twenty (64.5%) low feasibility attacks. Note that this is a qualitative comparison of the two architectures; the quantitative assessment of network architectures based on security metrics is an open research problem and is beyond the scope of this paper.

Table 1. Feasibility of attack patterns.

Category	Attack Pattern	PCN	TPCN	TPCN SC
Abuse of Functionality	Inducing Account Lockout	H	L	Strong Authentication
	Exploiting Password Recovery	H	L	Strong Authentication
	Trying Common Application Switches and Options	H	L	Configuration Verification
	Exploiting Incorrectly Configured SSL Security Levels	H	L	Configuration Verification
Spoofing	Faking the Data Source	M	L	Message Authentication
	Spoofing the Principal	H	L	Strong Authentication
	Man-in-the-Middle Attack	H	L	Device Authentication
	Creating a Malicious Client	M	L	Accounting
	External Entity Attack	H	L	VPN Access Control
Probabilistic Techniques	Brute Forcing Passwords	L	L	Strong Authentication
	Brute Forcing Encryption	L	L	N/A
	Rainbow Table Password Cracking	L	L	Strong Authentication
	Manipulating Opaque Client-Based Data Tokens	M	M	N/A
Exploiting Authentication	Exploiting Session Variables, Resource IDs and Other Credentials	M	M	Software Verification
	Reflection Attack on Authentication Protocol	H	H	N/A
	Bypassing Authentication	H	L	Port-Based Access Control

Table 2. Feasibility of attack patterns (continued).

Category	Attack Pattern	PCN	TPCN	TPCN SC
Resource Depletion	Denying Service via Resource Depletion	H	M	Compliance Verification
	Depleting Resource via Flooding	H	M	Traffic Filtering
Exploitation of Privilege or Trust	Lifting Credentials/Key Material Embedded in Client Distributions	M	L	Software Verification
	Lifting Cached, Sensitive Data Embedded in Client Distributions	M	L	Software Verification
	Accessing Functionality Improperly Constrained by ACLs	H	M	Small Rule Sets
	Exploiting Incorrectly Configured Access Control Security Levels	H	M	Role-Based Access Control
	Manipulating Writeable Configuration Files	H	L	Configuration Verification
Injection	LDAP Injection	H	H	N/A
	Sniffing Information on Public Networks	M	M	IPSec
	Manipulating User-Controlled Variables	H	L	Configuration Verification
	Manipulating Audit Log	H	L	Audit Verification
	Poisoning DNS Cache	H	L	Trusted DNS
Protocol Manipulation	Manipulating Inter-Component Protocol	M	M	N/A
	Manipulating Data Interchange Protocol	M	M	N/A
Time and State	Manipulating User State	H	L	Configuration Verification

6.   Conclusions

Trusted network technology can help address the challenges involved in securing industrial control systems that are vital to operating critical infrastructure assets. Adding trust to industrial control networks eliminates security problems posed by inadequate controls, non-compliant devices and malicious users. It dramatically reduces vulnerabilities to malware attacks that constitute the majority of external attacks. Also, the likelihood of internal attacks is reduced via compliance verification, port-based access control, device and user authentication, and role-based access control. Implementation and maintenance costs are major issues, especially when deploying security solutions for industrial control networks containing modern and legacy systems.

References

[1] E. Byres, B. Chauvin, J. Karsch, D. Hoffman and N. Kube, The special needs of SCADA/PCN firewalls: Architectures and test results, *Proceedings of the Tenth IEEE Conference on Emerging Technologies and Factory Automation*, 2005.

[2] E. Byres, D. Leversage and N. Kube, Security incident and trends in SCADA and process industries: A statistical review of the Industrial Security Incident Database (ISID), White Paper, Symantec Corporation, Cupertino, California, 2007.

[3] E. Byres and J. Lowe, The myths and facts behind cyber security risks for industrial control systems, *Proceedings of the VDE Congress*, pp. 213–218, 2004.

[4] D. Capite, *Self-Defending Networks: The Next Generation of Network Security*, Cisco Press, Indianapolis, Indiana, 2006.

[5] Cisco Systems, Implementing Network Admission Control – Phase One Configuration and Deployment, Version 1.1, San Jose, California, 2005.

[6] Cisco Systems, Cisco TrustSec: Enabling switch security services, San Jose, California (www.cisco.com/en/US/solutions/collateral/ns340/ns3 94/ns147/ns774/net_implementation_white_paper0900aecd80716abd.pdf), 2007.

[7] Cisco Systems, Cisco NAC Appliance – Clean Access Manager Installation and Configuration Guide, Release 4.1(3), San Jose, California (www .cisco.com/en/US/docs/security/nac/appliance/configuration_guide/413/ cam/cam413ug.pdf), 2008.

[8] Cisco Systems, Getting started with Cisco NAC network modules in Cisco access routers, San Jose, California (www.cisco.com/en/US/docs/security /nac/appliance/installation_guide/netmodule/nacnmgsg.pdf), 2008.

[9] Cisco Systems and Microsoft Corporation, Cisco Network Admission Control and Microsoft Network Access Protection Interoperability Architecture, Redmond, Washington (www.microsoft.com/presspass/events/ssc /docs/CiscoMSNACWP.pdf), 2006.

[10] M. Franz and D. Miller, Industrial Ethernet security: Threats and counter measures (www.threatmind.net/papers/franz-miller-industrial-ethernet-se c-03.pdf), 2003.

[11] Industrial Automation Open Networking Association, The IAONA Handbook for Network Security, Version 1.3, Magdeburg, Germany (www.iaona.org/pictures/files/1122888138-IAONA_HNS_1_3-reduced_050 725.pdf), 2005.

[12] Instrumentation, Systems and Automation Society, Integrating Electronic Security into the Manufacturing and Control Systems Environment, ANSI/ISA Technical Report TR99.00.02-2004, Research Triangle Park, North Carolina, 2004.

[13] Microsoft Corporation, Network access protection platform architecture, Redmond, Washington (www.microsoft.com/technet/network/nap/nap arch.mspx), 2004.

[14] MITRE Corporation, CAPEC: Common Attack Pattern Enumeration and Classification, Bedford, Massachusetts (capec mitre.org).

[15] North American Electric Reliability Council, SQL slammer worm lessons learned for consideration by the electricity sector, Princeton, New Jersey (www.esisac.com/publicdocs/SQL_Slammer_2003.pdf), 2003.

[16] Office of Nuclear Reactor Regulation, Potential vulnerability of plant computer network to worm infection, NRC Information Notice 2003-14, Nuclear Regulatory Commission, Washington, DC (www.nrc.gov/reading-rm/doc-collections/gen-comm/info-notices/2003/in200314.pdf), 2003.

[17] R. Ross, S. Katzke, A. Johnson, M. Swanson, G. Stoneburner and G. Rogers, Recommended Security Controls for Federal Information Systems, NIST Special Publication 800-53, National Institute of Standards and Technology, Gaithersburg, Maryland, 2005.

[18] M. Sopko and K. Winegardner, Process control network security concerns and remedies, *IEEE Cement Industry Technical Conference Record*, pp. 26–37, 2007.

[19] K. Stouffer, J. Falco and K. Scarfone, Guide to Industrial Control Systems Security, Second Public Draft, NIST Special Publication 800-82, National Institute of Standards and Technology, Gaithersburg, Maryland, 2007.

[20] Trusted Computing Group, Trusted network connect to ensure endpoint integrity, Beaverton, Oregon (www.trustedcomputinggroup.org/groups /network/TNC_NI_collateral_10_may.pdf), 2005.

[21] A. Wool, A quantitative study of firewall configuration errors, *IEEE Computer*, vol. 37(6), pp. 62–67, 2004.

Chapter 6

TOWARDS A TAXONOMY OF ATTACKS AGAINST ENERGY CONTROL SYSTEMS

Terry Fleury, Himanshu Khurana and Von Welch

Abstract   Control systems in the energy sector (e.g., supervisory control and data acquisition (SCADA) systems) involve a hierarchy of sensing, monitoring and control devices connected to centralized control stations or centers. The incorporation of commercial off-the-shelf technologies in energy control systems makes them vulnerable to cyber attacks. A taxonomy of cyber attacks against control systems can assist the energy sector in managing the cyber threat. This paper takes the first step towards a taxonomy by presenting a comprehensive model of attacks, vulnerabilities and damage related to control systems. The model is populated based on a survey of the technical literature from industry, academia and national laboratories.

Keywords: Energy sector, control systems, attack taxonomy

1.   Introduction

Energy control systems involve a hierarchy of sensing, monitoring and control devices connected to centralized control stations or centers. Within this hierarchy, control systems remotely monitor and control sensitive processes and physical functions. Supervisory control and data acquisition (SCADA) systems utilized to monitor power, oil and gas transmission systems are common instantiations of energy control systems. Owing to various commercial and external forces such as deregulation, asset owners are extending the connectivity of their control systems by adopting commercial off-the-shelf (COTS) components. Standard operating systems (e.g., Windows and UNIX) and communication technologies (e.g., public and private IP networks, public telephone networks and wireless networks) are being used more frequently in control systems.

Earlier control systems operated in isolated environments with proprietary technologies. Consequently, they faced little to no cyber security risk from

Please use the following format when citing this chapter:

Fleury, T., Khurana, H. and Welch, V., 2008, in IFIP International Federation for Information Processing, Volume 290; *Critical Infrastructure Protection II*, eds. Papa, M., Shenoi, S., (Boston: Springer), pp. 71–85.

external attackers. However, the adoption of commercial technologies causes process control systems in the energy sector to become increasingly connected and interdependent. This makes energy control systems attractive targets for attack. Along with the cost saving benefits of commercial technologies comes a multitude of vulnerabilities inherit in the technologies. This attracts a range of adversaries with the tools and capabilities to launch attacks from remote locations with significant consequences. Systems are attacked by hackers for glory and attention, by criminals for financial gain, by insiders for retribution, by industrial and government spies for intelligence gathering, and by botnet operators for inclusion in their bot armies. These adversaries may have significant resources at their disposal and use them to launch cyber attacks that exploit vulnerabilities and potentially cause harm.

Cyber attacks can have a significant impact on the operation of control systems. For example, denial-of-service attacks can disrupt the operation of control systems by delaying or blocking the flow of data through communication networks. Attacks that result in corruption of data can lead to propagation of false information to the control centers, which may result in unintended decisions and actions.

A large body of technical literature discusses security issues related to control systems, especially threats, attacks and vulnerabilities. Our survey has examined research efforts that address specific aspects of control systems security [1, 3, 4, 14, 16–18, 28] as well as work focused on broader security issues [5–8, 22, 24, 26, 29]. However, most of these efforts adopt *ad hoc* approaches to discuss and prioritize the various aspects of attacks. What is needed is an attack taxonomy that enables researchers and practitioners to have a comprehensive understanding of attacks against energy control systems. The taxonomy would help answer the following key questions:

- What are the different ways of perpetrating attacks against a control system?
- What kind of damage can these attacks cause?
- What are the challenges involved in defeating these attacks?
- What are the requirements for developing adequate defense mechanisms?

This paper takes the first major step towards the creation of a taxonomy by presenting a comprehensive attack model and populating the model based on an extensive survey of known attacks against control systems. This attack-vulnerability-damage (AVD) model places equal importance on how attacks take place, what vulnerabilities enable these attacks to be performed, and what damage these attacks can cause. The model is geared specifically towards control systems and serves as a basis for developing a comprehensive taxonomy of attacks against energy control systems.

2.   Energy Control Systems

Energy control systems include SCADA systems, distributed control systems (DCSs) and programmable logic controllers (PLCs). These systems are critical

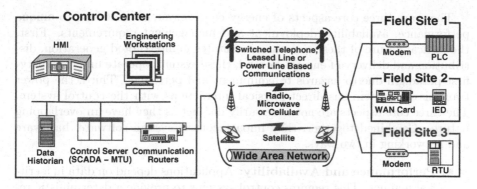

Figure 1. Sample SCADA system [27].

to the generation, distribution and delivery of energy across all sectors. SCADA systems provide centralized monitoring and control of field devices spread over large geographic areas. DCSs provide control of local processes that comprise integrated subsystems. PLCs are computer-based solid-state devices that are used in SCADA systems and DCSs as well as independently in small control systems.

This paper uses a SCADA system as a primary example of a complex control system employed in the energy sector. Figure 1 presents a typical SCADA system [27]. The SCADA system transmits operational data from field sites to control centers, and control information from control centers to field sites. Once field data reaches the control system, software systems provide capabilities to visualize and analyze the data. Based on automated or human-driven analysis, actions are performed as needed (e.g., recording data, processing alarms or sending control information back to the field sites). Data acquisition and supervisory control are undertaken by hardware and software systems connected by a multitude of networking technologies. The hardware includes PLCs, remote terminal units (RTUs), intelligent electronic devices (IEDs), relays, SCADA servers (master terminal units (MTUs)), communication routers, workstations and displays. These hardware systems run software for data input and output processing, data transfer and storage, state estimation, visualization, remote access, equipment control, and alarm processing and reporting. All these hardware and software systems are connected via local-area or wide-area networks depending on their proximity. Standard and proprietary communication protocols are used to transport information between the control center and field sites via telephone lines, cable, fiber, microwave and satellite links.

Due to the increased use of COTS hardware, software and networking components, control systems are beginning to look like traditional IT infrastructures. However, there are key differences between control and traditional IT systems that significantly impact design and management. This paper analyzes how these differences impact threat analysis and the development of an attack taxonomy.

There are three core aspects of energy control systems that lead to unique performance, availability, deployment and management requirements. First, the critical nature of these systems necessitates uninterrupted generation, distribution and delivery of energy. Second, these systems operate under a safety-first paradigm due to hazards to equipment and personnel. Third, the power transmission system has direct physical interactions with the control system. The three core aspects are not necessarily distinct as they have an overlapping nature. Combined together, they impact control system software, hardware and networking in two ways.

- **Performance and Availability:** Applications depend on data in a critical manner. This requires control systems to provide a deterministic response without delays or jitter in data delivery. In turn, the systems that generate and distribute data must be highly reliable and available, and the delivered data must have high integrity. Additionally, any (cyber) security mechanism, such as one that may provide integrity assurances, must be fail-safe. A failure of the security mechanism should not result in a failure of the underlying control system.

- **Deployment and Management:** Control systems must be tested extensively in "real" environments before they can be deployed. This is because they control physical systems over vast geographic areas and the deployed equipment typically has a long life (possibly one or two decades). Furthermore, downtime for system maintenance and upgrades (e.g., patch management) is unacceptable without significant advanced planning. In contrast, traditional IT systems are usually deployed without extensive testing. Their initial deployment phase often serves as a partial test environment. Also, IT systems have expected lifetimes of a few years and operate under the assumption that they may be taken down for maintenance and upgrades with relatively short notice.

3.   Methodology

A model for classifying cyber attacks against control systems must satisfy several goals.

- The model should be specific to cyber attacks on control systems. Several researchers have attempted to classify cyber threats to general computer systems (see, e.g., [11, 15]). Since the energy sector incorporates COTS technologies (e.g., TCP/IP), much of this research can be applied to energy control systems. However, as discussed above, control systems have unique features and requirements, and it is important that the model addresses these issues.

- The model should have a relatively high level of abstraction. Some classification schemes for cyber threats to general computer systems describe attacks in a detailed manner. For example, attack trees/graphs [3, 12, 23, 25] break down a single cyber attack into its constituent parts, tracing the attack from the source (attacker) through various system components to the target. Instead of enumerating every possible attack, the model should permit parts of specific attacks to be sorted into generalized categories.

■ The model should be easily expandable. New attacks are continually being developed. The model should accommodate instances of future attacks and grow and adapt as necessary.

■ The model should tolerate incompleteness. Incident reports often provide terse accounts of attacks for reasons of sensitivity. For example, a report may mention how an attack was carried out but omit its consequences. Alternatively, a report may describe a system vulnerability and how its exploitation may cause damage, but it may not discuss how attackers might conduct the exploit. The model should allow for such omissions while incorporating all the reported aspects of cyber threats.

With these goals in mind, we conducted an extensive survey of the technical literature. Nearly all the documents that were examined contained threat descriptions. Several papers (e.g., [2, 19]) described attacks and the associated vulnerabilities; others (e.g., [4, 10]) described attacks and their effects. One paper [8] discussed vulnerabilities and attack impact or damage. This clustering of descriptions led us to believe that cyber threats to energy control systems are best decomposed into three categories: attack, vulnerability and damage. These three categories form the basis of our attack-vulnerability-damage (AVD) model. The Howard-Longstaff approach [9] and the system-fault-risk (SFR) framework [30], in particular, matched our modeling goals and inspired the development of the AVD model.

4.   Attack-Vulnerability-Damage Model

This section describes the AVD model and populates it with examples of cyber attacks against energy control systems.

The AVD model (Table 1) classifies cyber threats based on three broad categories. The attack category includes "local" origins and "system" targets to identify physical control system components that may be the origin of the attack (e.g., compromised or exposed end device) and/or the target (e.g., unauthorized opening of a relay). The vulnerability category includes configuration and implementation errors in physical devices (e.g., malfunctioning device). The damage category considers the harm caused to computer systems as well as the physical control system (e.g., electric power relay). Given the time-critical nature of energy systems, the damage category also considers the performance effect and the severity of the attack.

Since control systems face threats that strongly overlap those that affect IT systems, several categories and descriptions in the AVD taxonomy are common to those encountered in attack taxonomies developed for IT systems. However, in this paper, we focus on example attacks that are specific to control systems in the energy sector.

Table 1. Attack-vulnerability-damage (AVD) model.

Attack

Origin	Action	Target
Local	Probe	Network
Remote	Scan	Process
	Flood	System
	Authenticate	Data
	Bypass	User
	Spoof	
	Eavesdrop	
	Misdirect	
	Read/Copy	
	Terminate	
	Execute	
	Modify	
	Delete	

Vulnerability

Configuration
Specification
Implementation

Damage

State Effect	Performance Effect	Severity
None	None	None
Availability	Timeliness	Low
Integrity	Precision	Medium
Confidentiality	Accuracy	High

4.1 Attacks

An attack has an origin, an action (taken by the attack) and a target (Table 2).

Attack Origin: The attack origin describes the location of the attacker with respect to the target.

- Local: A local attack originates from within the target. Such an attack occurs when the attacker has physical access to equipment [4, 13, 17] or when a malfunction occurs in a nearby piece of equipment [10].

- Remote: A remote attack originates outside the target site. Such an attack may involve a dial-up modem [4, 19], open wireless network [2, 4, 20, 29], private network and bridge [21] or a connection to a trusted third-party system [4].

Table 2.   Attack category examples.

Origin	
Local	*Remote*
Physical access to equipment	Dial-up modem
Malfunctioning PLC	Open wireless network
	Worm via private network and bridge
	Trusted third-party connection

Action	
Probe	*Scan*
Map available equipment	Perform simple vulnerability scan
Flood	*Authenticate*
Launch data storm	Guess/crack password
Launch denial-of-service attack	
Bypass	*Spoof*
Use different method to access process	Hijack session
Eavesdrop	*Misdirect*
Monitor wireless traffic	Alarm output not displayed
Read/Copy	*Terminate*
Download business reports	Shut down service
	Shut down SCADA system
Execute	*Modify*
Exploit MS-SQL vulnerability	Alter SCADA system metering data
	Change protection device settings
Delete	
Render data non-retrievable	

Target	
Network	*Process*
Deluge network with data	Disable safety monitoring
Wireless transmissions	Use computer resources to play games
System	*Data*
Digital circuit breaker	Business report
User	
Profile theft	

Attack Action: The attack action describes the activity that the attack performs on the target.

- Probe: A probe seeks to determine the characteristics of a particular system. For example, a probe may attempt to identify the make and model of a device or the software services (and versions) running on the device [8, 16].

- Scan: A scan attempts to access targets sequentially for the purpose of determining specific characteristics. An example is a network scan that identifies open ports [2].

- Flood: A flood repeatedly accesses a target, overloading it with traffic, possibly disabling it. Examples include data storms [10] and denial-of-service attacks [16].

- Authenticate: This involves unauthorized or illicit authentication as a valid user or process in order to access the target. An example is password cracking [16].

- Bypass: This involves the use of an alternative method to access the target (e.g., bypassing standard access protocols).

- Spoof: A spoofing attempt assumes the identity of a different user in order to access the target. An example is session hijacking [16].

- Eavesdrop: This involves the passive monitoring of a data stream to obtain information (e.g., sniffing unencrypted wireless traffic [29]).

- Misdirect: This involves intercepting communication channels and outputting bogus information. The recipients are unaware that the output is not genuine. An example is cross-site scripting where the input is redirected to a malicious site that outputs seemingly correct information.

- Read/Copy: This usually refers to a static data source, but could also refer to a dynamic data stream. In a "read" attack, the data is read by a human. A "copy" attack duplicates the original data source for later processing by a human or process. An example is downloading private business reports [2].

- Terminate: This involves stopping a running process. It could be as specific as shutting down a service (e.g., a monitoring or display system [13, 20]) or as broad as shutting down an entire SCADA system [17].

- Execute: This involves running a malicious process on the target. This behavior is typical of a virus or worm (e.g., Slammer worm that exploits an MS-SQL vulnerability [20]).

- Modify: This involves changing the contents of the target. Examples include modifying SCADA system data or device protection settings [17].

- Delete: This involves erasing data from the target or simply making the data non-retrievable.

Attack Target: The attack target describes the resource that is attacked.

- Network: A network comprises computers and networking equipment connected via wires or wirelessly. An attack on a network target typically involves disrupting communications between computers and network devices [10, 29].

Table 3. Vulnerability category examples.

Vulnerability	
Configuration	*Implementation*
Account management	Poor authentication
Unused services	Scripting/interface programming
Unpatched components	Malfunctioning devices
Perimeter protection	Poor logging/monitoring
Design/Specification	
Cleartext communications	
Poor coding practices	
Network addressing	
Web servers and clients	
Enumeration	

- Process: A process is a program running on a computing system. It consists of program code and data. Example attacks are disabling safety monitoring software [20] and using computer resources for entertainment (e.g., to play games) [17].

- System: A system comprises one or more connected components that perform computations. A system typically refers to a computer but could also describe a device such as a digital circuit breaker [19].

- Data: Data consists of information that is suitable for processing by humans and machines. Data can refer to a single resource such as a file stored on a hard drive or packets that are transmitted over a communications network. An example attack is the unauthorized access of data from a server [2].

- User: A user has authorization to access certain system resources. Attacks targeting users typically attempt to illicitly gain information for later use. An example is monitoring network traffic to discover user passwords [16].

4.2   Vulnerabilities

A vulnerability describes why a particular attack may be successful (Table 3). The vulnerability does not specify the actual target, but the weakness that can be exploited.

- Configuration: An improperly configured resource may enable an attacker to gain unauthorized access to a target. Examples include poor account management where certain unused accounts [8, 26, 28] and/or services [8] have high-level privileges; components with known flaws that are not

Table 4.   Damage category examples.

State Effect	
Availability	*Integrity*
Circuit breaker tripped	Corrupt data received
Recirculation pump failure	
Confidentiality	
Business reports downloaded	

Performance Effect	
Timeliness	*Accuracy*
Plant network slowdown	Missing alarm data
Precision	
Plant data cannot be viewed	

Severity	
None	*Low*
Attacker does not impact target	Attacker gains additional information
Medium	*High*
Attacker degrades performance	Attacker acts as a legitimate user
Attacker alters system state	Attacker gains admin rights
Loss of public confidence in services	Attacker disables process
	Attacker causes equipment damage
	Attacker spoofs displays via
	man-in-the-middle attack

properly patched [8, 21, 26]; weak or non-existent authentication (including unchanged passwords) [5, 28]; and misconfigured perimeter protection and/or access control policies [2, 8, 19, 26].

- Design/Specification: Design flaws in a process or component can be utilized in unintended ways to gain access to a target. Examples are insecure communication protocols used by processes and users [5, 8, 26, 29] and flawed code [8, 28].

- Implementation: Even when the design of a hardware or software system is correct, the implementation may be incorrect. This can lead to security holes [8, 20, 28] or malfunctions [10, 26].

4.3   Damage

The damage caused by an attack has three attributes: state effect, performance effect and severity (Table 4). State effects and performance effects describe the damage done to the system components. The severity attribute attempts to quantify the overall impact of the attack.

State Effect: A state effect describes the state change that occurs to the target because of the attack.

- Availability: The availability of an asset refers to its ability to service requests. A successful attack disables an asset or increases its response time. Example state effects include tripping a circuit breaker [19] and disrupting a recirculation pump [10].
- Integrity: Integrity refers to the correctness of an asset when meeting service requests. An example state effect is data corruption.
- Confidentiality: Confidentiality refers to authorized access to, or use of, an asset. An example state effect is the unauthorized access of business reports [2].

Performance Effect: A performance effect describes the performance degradation that occurs on the target because of the attack.

- Timeliness: This is a measure of time from data input to output. A timeliness performance effect has occurred when there is a sustained increase in this measure. An example is plant network slowdown [20].
- Precision: This is a measure of the amount of output generated by data input. A precision performance effect has occurred when the output is not 100% of the expected output. This may occur, for example, when a process is terminated before it completes its execution or when insufficient data output produces an "Unable to View Plant" error message [4].
- Accuracy: This is a measure of the correctness of the output generated by data input. For example, an accuracy performance effect has occurred when control messages or measurements are altered during transmission.

Severity: Severity seeks to quantify the level of impact of an attack.

- None: The attack may have been successful, but it has no noticeable impact on the target [8].
- Low: The attack typically gains information that may not be directly exploitable [2, 3, 8, 29]. An example is the discovery of user names but not the associated passwords.
- Medium: The attack degrades system performance [8, 13, 21] and/or alters the state of the system [3, 20]. State and/or performance effects may start to be seen. This may result in a loss of public confidence in system services [26].
- High: The attack enables the perpetrator to gain the privileges of a legitimate user [8], operator [4, 8] or administrator [3, 8] to disable processes [10, 19] or damage equipment [26].

Table 5.   Example attacks in the AVD model.

Attack	Origin		State Effect
	Action	Vulnerability	Performance Effect
	Target		Severity
Data Storm [10]	Local		Availability
	Flood	Specification	Precision
	Network		Medium
Slammer Worm	Remote		Integrity
(Remote) [20]	Copy	Implementation	Accuracy
	Process		Low
Slammer Worm	Local		Integrity
(Local) [20]	Execute	Specification	Accuracy
	System		High
Software Bug	Local		Integrity
XA/21 [21]	Terminate	Implementation	Timeliness
	Process		Medium
Dial-In	Remote		Any
Password [5]	Authenticate	Configuration	Any
	User		High
Component	Local		Integrity
Data Spoofing [5]	Modify	Specification	Accuracy
	Data		High

4.4   Example Attacks

Table 5 lists several complete attacks by name and shows how they fit into the AVD model.

5.   Conclusions

Energy control systems are vulnerable to cyber attacks. In order for the energy sector to deal effectively with these attacks, it is necessary to develop a taxonomy of attacks against control systems. The comprehensive model of attacks, vulnerabilities and damage presented in this paper is a first step to developing such a taxonomy.

Our future work on developing the taxonomy will expand the model by considering additional categories and sub-categories as well as analyzing a broader range of attack data. Categories for consideration include (i) attack sophistication, i.e., level of expertise required for an attack; (ii) fiscal impact, i.e., the financial loss incurred due to the attack; and (iii) protocol and operation system specifics, i.e., details of the attack in terms of the protocols and operating systems that are exploited.

Acknowledgements

This research was supported by the National Science Foundation under Grant No. CNS-0524695. The authors also wish to acknowledge the technical assistance provided by participants in the Trustworthy Cyber Infrastructure for the Power Grid Project.

References

[1] K. Birman, J. Chen, E. Hopkinson, R. Thomas, J. Thorp, R. van Rennesse and W. Vogels, Overcoming communications challenges in software for monitoring and controlling power systems, *Proceedings of the IEEE*, vol. 93(5), pp. 1028–1041, 2005.

[2] A. Brown, SCADA vs. the hackers, *Mechanical Engineering*, vol. 124(12), pp. 37–40, 2002.

[3] E. Byres, M. Franz and D. Miller, The use of attack trees in assessing vulnerabilities in SCADA systems, *Proceedings of the International Infrastructure Survivability Workshop*, 2004.

[4] E. Byres and J. Lowe, The myths and facts behind cyber security risks for industrial control systems, *Proceedings of the VDE Congress*, pp. 213–218, 2004.

[5] R. Carlson, Sandia SCADA Program: High-Security SCADA LDRD Final Report, Technical Report SAND2002-0729, Sandia National Laboratories, Albuquerque, New Mexico, 2002.

[6] J. Eisenhauer, P. Donnelly, M. Ellis and M. O'Brien, Roadmap to Secure Control Systems in the Energy Sector, Technical Report, Energetics Inc., Columbia, Maryland, 2006.

[7] J. Falco, J. Gilsinn and K. Stouffer, IT security for industrial control systems: Requirements specification and performance testing, presented at the *National Defense Industrial Association Homeland Security Conference and Exposition*, 2004.

[8] R. Fink, D. Spencer and R. Wells, Lessons Learned from Cyber Security Assessments of SCADA and Energy Management Systems, Technical Report INL/CON-06-11665, Idaho National Laboratory, Idaho Falls, Idaho, 2006.

[9] J. Howard and T. Longstaff, A Common Language for Computer Security Incidents, Technical Report SAND98-8667, Sandia National Laboratories, Livermore, California, 1998.

[10] R. Lemos, "Data storm" blamed for nuclear plant shutdown, *SecurityFocus*, May 18, 2007.

[11] U. Lindqvist and E. Jonsson, How to systematically classify computer security intrusions, *Proceedings of the IEEE Symposium on Security and Privacy*, pp. 154–163, 1997.

[12] R. Lippmann, K. Ingols, C. Scott, K. Piwowarski, K. Kratkiewicz, M. Artz and R. Cunningham, Validating and restoring defense in depth using attack graphs, *Proceedings of the Military Communications Conference*, pp. 1–10, 2006.

[13] R. McMillan, Admin faces prison for trying to axe California power grid, *PC World*, December 15, 2007.

[14] M. McQueen, W. Boyer, M. Flynn and G. Beitel, Quantitative cyber risk reduction estimation methodology for a small SCADA control system, *Proceedings of the Thirty-Ninth Annual Hawaii International Conference on System Sciences*, p. 226, 2006.

[15] J. Mirkovic and P. Reiher, A taxonomy of DDoS attack and DDoS defense mechanisms, *ACM SIGCOMM Computer Communication Review*, vol. 34(2), pp. 39–53, 2004.

[16] P. Oman, A. Risley, J. Roberts and E. Schweitzer, Attack and defend tools for remotely accessible control and protection equipment in electric power systems, presented at the *Fifty-Fifth Annual Conference for Protective Relay Engineers*, 2002.

[17] P. Oman, E. Schweitzer and J. Roberts, Protecting the grid from cyber attack, Part I: Recognizing our vulnerabilities, *Utility Automation & Engineering T&D*, vol. 6(7), pp. 16–22, 2001.

[18] P. Oman, E. Schweitzer and J. Roberts, Protecting the grid from cyber attack, Part II: Safeguarding IEDs, substations and SCADA systems, *Utility Automation & Engineering T&D*, vol. 7(1), pp. 25–32, 2002.

[19] K. Poulsen, Sparks over power grid cybersecurity, *SecurityFocus*, April 10, 2003.

[20] K. Poulsen, Slammer worm crashed Ohio nuke plant network, *SecurityFocus*, August 19, 2003.

[21] K. Poulsen, Software bug contributed to blackout, *SecurityFocus*, February 11, 2004.

[22] R. Schainker, J. Douglas and T. Kropp, Electric utility responses to grid security issues, *IEEE Power and Energy*, vol. 4(2), pp. 30–37, 2006.

[23] B. Schneier, Attack trees, *Dr. Dobb's Journal*, vol. 24(12), pp. 21–29, 1999.

[24] F. Sheldon, T. Potok, A. Loebl, A. Krings and P. Oman, Managing secure survivable critical infrastructures to avoid vulnerabilities, *Proceedings of the Eighth IEEE International Symposium on High Assurance Systems Engineering*, pp. 293–296, 2004.

[25] O. Sheyner, J. Haines, S. Jha, R. Lippmann and J. Wing, Automated generation and analysis of attack graphs, *Proceedings of the IEEE Symposium on Security and Privacy*, pp. 273–284, 2002.

[26] J. Stamp, J. Dillinger, W. Young and J. DePoy, Common Vulnerabilities in Critical Infrastructure Control Systems, Technical Report SAND2003-1772C, Sandia National Laboratories, Albuquerque, New Mexico, 2003.

[27] K. Stouffer, J. Falco and K. Scarfone, Guide to Industrial Control Systems Security, Second Public Draft, NIST Special Publication 800-82, National Institute of Standards and Technology, Gaithersburg, Maryland, 2007.

[28] C. Taylor, P. Oman and A. Krings, Assessing power substation network security and survivability: A work in progress report, *Proceedings of the International Conference on Security and Management*, pp. 281–287, 2003.

[29] D. Watts, Security and vulnerability in electric power systems, *Proceedings of the Thirty-Fifth North American Power Symposium*, pp. 559–566, 2003.

[30] N. Ye, C. Newman and T. Farley, A system-fault-risk framework for cyber attack classification, *Information-Knowledge-Systems Management*, vol. 5(2), pp. 135–151, 2005.

Chapter 7

ATTRIBUTION OF CYBER ATTACKS ON PROCESS CONTROL SYSTEMS

Jeffrey Hunker, Robert Hutchinson and Jonathan Margulies

Abstract   The attribution of cyber attacks is an important problem. Attribution gives critical infrastructure asset owners and operators legal recourse in the event of attacks and deters potential attacks. This paper discusses attribution techniques along with the associated legal and technical challenges. It presents a proposal for a voluntary network of attributable activity, an important first step towards a more complete attribution methodology for the control systems community.

Keywords: Process control systems, cyber attacks, attack attribution

1.   Introduction

United States Presidential Decision Directive NSC-63 (PDD 63) [1] listed the infrastructures that are critical to national security. The directive also stressed the need for public-private partnerships to identify and mitigate critical infrastructure (CI) vulnerabilities. Assessment and modeling efforts resulting from the recognition of vulnerability as outlined in PDD 63 have revealed significant interdependencies between infrastructures [4]. These efforts have also shown that CI protection is a global problem and that the global infrastructure depends on the proper operation of standardized, as well as specialized, information technology.

All the CIs are supported to varying degrees by the global information infrastructure, much of which is built on commodity technologies such as the TCP/IP protocol suite and backbone networks. Many CI assets, such as those responsible for energy production and distribution, require specialized control systems for safe and reliable operation. The growing convergence of specialized process control systems with general information and communication technologies (ICTs) is exposing control systems and the CI assets they manage to common operating system and Internet threats [5].

Please use the following format when citing this chapter:

Hunker, J., Hutchinson, R. and Margulies, J., 2008, in IFIP International Federation for Information Processing, Volume 290; *Critical Infrastructure Protection II*, eds. Papa, M., Shenoi, S., (Boston: Springer), pp. 87–99.

Attack attribution can provide new types of protection for CI assets. It gives asset owners and operators legal recourse in the event of attacks and deters malicious activities. The development and application of attribution techniques can drive law and policy, create incentives for cyber security, reduce threats and manage risk.

2.   Attack Attribution

Attribution is the determination of the identity or location of an attacker or an attacker's intermediary [6]. This paper focuses on attribution techniques for attacks launched over computer networks. Attribution is also important for physical attacks and social engineering attacks; however, these attacks are outside the scope of this paper. For the purposes of this paper, we consider attribution to be the identification of intermediaries who may or may not be willing participants in an attack. Note that determining motivation, particularly by technical means, is difficult at best. This problem is even more challenging when applied to intermediaries.

2.1   Importance of Attribution

The ability to identify the source of a cyber attack is the basis for taking action against the perpetrator. Legal and policy frameworks for responding to cyber attacks cannot work unless there is adequate attribution; these frameworks remain incomplete because there is insufficient basis (attribution) to actually use them. Attribution helps create a system of deterrence. Without the fear of being caught, convicted and punished, individuals and organizations will continue to use the Internet to conduct malicious activities.

Attribution also offers other benefits. Information gained during the process of attribution can be used to improve defensive techniques. Even partial attribution can provide the basis for interrupting attacks in progress and defending against future attacks and mitigating their effects.

While attribution is important, non-attribution can be just as vital to protecting radical ideas and minority views in oppressive regimes. The Internet has become a powerful medium for sharing opinions. For many users, the anonymity provided by the Internet – and the consequent freedom from retribution – makes it one of the only methods for freely expressing ideas. Mechanisms developed to facilitate attribution must enforce non-attribution for the purposes of sharing opinions and ideas. A well-crafted attribution mechanism should identify entities who engage in malicious behavior as defined by laws and/or policy. However, the mechanism should also make it impossible to attribute freely exchanged ideas, especially for purposes of retribution.

2.2   Attribution in Process Control Systems

Critical infrastructure owners and operators rely on standard ICTs to monitor and control physical processes. The adoption of these technologies in the global energy, chemical, transportation and service infrastructures injects ICT vulnerabilities into formerly stand-alone process control systems. This exposes CI assets to a slew of attacks by external entities, including exploits launched over the Internet. Infrastructure owners and operators are struggling to understand the new risks and incorporate appropriate risk mitigation techniques. ICT-based systems primarily rely on fortification mechanisms (e.g., firewalls, access control lists and physical access controls) to mitigate risk. Applying ICT security mechanisms and risk models to CI control systems is inadequate due to the major differences that exist between CI and ICT assets in terms of their physical layout, operating environments, security goals and threat space.

For reasons of complexity and cost, CI asset owners and operators have outsourced significant aspects of their operations. Control system hardware and software manufactured globally are customized to a particular operation, effectively incorporating vendors into the operational lifecycle. Control system vendors frequently provide onsite support and are often granted remote access to monitor system status and perform routine administration tasks. Given the number of entities – employees, equipment manufacturers, consultants and employees from partnering companies – that access CI assets, threats are better modeled as originating from malicious insiders than external attackers. Even so, CI assets are protected by fortification, a strategy that ignores insiders, which are a system's greatest threat.

Cyber attribution can help protect the essential command, control and communication functions of modern infrastructures. Attribution makes it possible to enforce existing laws and treaties and fine-tune law and policy to better protect CI assets. Coupled with the ability to detect malicious cyber activity, attribution and the prospect of penalties deter attackers, thereby reducing threats. Technology is a necessary component of cyber attribution, but it is insufficient by itself. To be successful and lasting, an attribution strategy must acknowledge the need for local and international cooperation while recognizing that the technical component must evolve with advances in technology.

2.3 Ideal Attribution

To provide a context for our work, it is necessary to define the ideal attribution system to which we aspire. As international law, policy and technology evolve, this definition must evolve as well.

Attribution should exist in a global context with overt support from all nation states and organized entities. Sufficient attribution of malicious cyber activity should be possible even when some entities do not cooperate fully. Attribution should only be sought for malicious activity.

An ideal attribution system should make it possible to detect all cyber attacks and determine the source and intent of each attack with sufficient precision. The results should be verifiable and specific enough to justify any response that has been agreed to in advance. The attribution system should generate threat data that informs the development and implementation of CI technologies and defensive strategies. Finally, the attribution system should enable new international agreements and pave the way toward comprehensive risk management.

3.　　Difficulty of Attribution

The Internet's architecture and its evolving administrative and governance systems make the attribution of cyber attacks extremely challenging.

3.1　　Internet Architecture

The Internet has no standard provisions for tracking or tracing. A sophisticated user can modify information in IP packets and, in particular, forge the source addresses of packets (which is very simple for one-way communication). Attacks often employ a series of stepping stones where compromised intermediate hosts are used to launder malicious packets. Packets can also be changed at hops between hosts; thus, attempting a traceback by correlating similar packets is ineffective when sophisticated attackers are involved.

3.2　　Administrative Issues

Internet attacks exploit an administrative system that was established when the Internet community was, in essence, a trusted commune, not the current global virtual city with consequent malefactors and little shared sense of community.

Internet attacks cross multiple administrative, jurisdictional and national boundaries with no common framework for cooperation, response or even trust across jurisdictions. The Internet Engineering Task Force (IETF) does not provide a global system policy and technical framework that the International Telecommunications Union (ITU) provides for the telephone system. According to Lipson [3]:

> "There are no universal technical standards or agreements for performing the monitoring and record keeping necessary to track and trace attacks. Moreover there are no universal laws or agreements as to what constitutes a cyber attack, and what punishments, economic sanctions, or liability should ensue. There are no universal international agreements for the monitoring, record keeping, and information sharing necessary to track and trace intruders. No existing privacy laws span the Internet as a whole. Existing international laws and agreements that might touch on these issues were not written for the Internet and need to be tested on cases involving Internet cyber-attacks."

3.3　　Limited Business Support

Businesses and government agencies routinely respond to malicious cyber activities by rebooting critical servers, restoring lost data and identifying and eliminating the vulnerabilities. The fundamental goal of IT professionals in industry and government is to maintain operations, and this is particularly true with regard to control systems. Because attribution is so difficult, few organizations are interested in investigating malicious Internet activity and moving them through the legal system. The current protection model, therefore, is primarily aimed at building improved fortifications and attempting to withstand constant attempts to overcome the fortifications.

3.4   Technical Impediments

Several technical impediments limit the effective attribution of attacks:

- Tunneling impedes tracking, but it is also very useful for creating virtual private networks (VPNs) that are important for security.

- Hackers often destroy logs and other audit data once they gain system access.

- Anonymizing services are valuable to Internet users (e.g., to facilitate political discourse in countries with repressive regimes). While anonymizers can be defeated in theory, there are numerous practical difficulties to achieving attribution when a sophisticated user desires anonymity.

- Even if an attack packet can be attributed to an IP address of a host computer, it is difficult to link the IP address to the actual perpetrator. A perpetrator can decouple his physical identity from an IP address by using cyber cafes, public Internet facilities (e.g., libraries) and prepaid Internet address cards that can be purchased from service providers without any personal identification.

- Short storage intervals on routers, especially those located at or near the high-speed core of the Internet, require forensic techniques to be extremely rapid (i.e., capture evidence before the router cache is overwritten). Alternatively, new capabilities have to be created to proactively preserve routing information.

- Sophisticated attacks that are extremely fast or extremely slow (that may execute over a period of months) are difficult to detect.

- Attribution techniques themselves have to be secured against attacks and subversion. Software used for authentication and data used for attribution must be protected. Moreover, attribution techniques should not create additional avenues for exploitation (e.g., a new DOS attack against the system).

3.5   Liability for Attributable Activities

Liability for the causes and consequences of cyber attacks is an undeveloped field within U.S. jurisprudence. All of the questions related to liability for domestic-only cyber attacks are equally applicable to attacks that traverse international boundaries. However, there are no clear answers to cyber attack liability questions, and relevant case law is sparse. This issue is of great concern to CI owners and operators because their losses due to cyber attacks can be extremely high.

Several important liability questions must be considered [3]: a major issue is the liability exposure for various entities – perpetrators; vendors whose software and/or hardware made the attack possible; owners, operators and administrators of intermediate (zombie or anonymizer) systems that participate in the attack or obscured the attack source; and service providers who did not block the attack when notified or did not help trace the attack in accordance with international agreements.

Another issue is whether certain kinds of waivers on liability exposure should be provided to entities who participate in tracking and tracing. Also, there is the issue of liability for the owners of systems that participate in attacks without the owners' knowledge, and entities that provide anonymizing services.

It is clear that liability will eventually form an important component in the policy framework for cyber security in general. This framework will affect the range of feasible options for effective attribution of cyber attacks.

3.6   Feasibility of Technical Solutions

Technology alone cannot provide attribution. To demonstrate this fact, we consider an ideal network with perfect attribution. The perfect attribution network (PAN) is designed and constructed so that all actions taken by a specific user on a particular machine are fully attributable to that machine and user.

The PAN foundation provides attribution services that cannot be altered or bypassed by any user or administrator. Any application installed on the PAN interfaces with the attribution foundation and adopts a complete set of attribution services. It is impossible for an application to bypass the attribution services or to alter the services in any way. Moreover, applications (e.g., process control system transaction management) installed on the PAN do not require modification to invoke the attribution services. The purpose of developing the PAN model in this way is to show that even perfect technical attribution services can be defeated.

Now consider an application installed on the PAN by a community of users wishing to engage in non-attributable actions within and outside of the community. Each instance of the non-attribution application (NAA) can communicate with every other instance of the NAA. While every point-to-point message processed by the NAA is fully attributable to source and destination users by the underlying PAN, the attribution scope is limited to the immediate source and destination of each message.

One strategy for achieving non-attribution is to remove the point-to-point context from all messages by applying an NAA overlay (NAAO). As a simple example, consider an NAAO configured in a logical ring topology. Messages in the ring topology flow clockwise and each NAA instance receives all of its incoming messages from a single NAA instance (the instance that is immediately counterclockwise) and transmits all outgoing messages to a different NAA instance (the instance that is immediately clockwise). The NAAO provides strong confidentiality of all messages, generates random messages to maintain roughly constant data flow bandwidth regardless of message content, and abstracts the actual message source and destination from the PAN. Direct PAN features cannot identify which messages are authentic, the real source and destination of messages or the real source of messages leaving the NAAO. Furthermore, constant bandwidth utilization in the ring topology makes traffic analysis very difficult (this is not a function of the PAN).

This simple example demonstrates that a purely technical attribution solution does not exist. It is possible to develop features that facilitate attribution such as unique communication keys, traceback and logging. However, these solutions may not provide sufficient attribution for most instances of malicious behavior. Essential to providing attribution services is a user base that is interested in supporting the services.

4.   Limitations of Current Solutions

Table 1 summarizes the technical solutions for attribution that are currently being employed, developed or considered. Details and drawbacks of these solutions are discussed extensively in [2].

The principal drawback is the lack of widespread adoption of new technologies. The record of Internet-wide adoption of new technologies has historically been poor. This is largely due to the new capabilities required of routers, but the problem is of a more general nature. Specific examples include IPv6, DNS security (DNSSec) extensions, and modifications to the Border Gateway Protocol (BGP).

These cases have two common issues. The first is that changes are effective only if they are adopted uniformly across the community. The second is that the costs and burden accrue to the individual entity, while the benefits of the changes are distributed and system-wide. Unlike the telecommunications sector where the ITU has an effective mechanism for creating and enforcing technical requirements, IETF's request for comment (RFC) process is essentially voluntary. Hence, a major policy issue is how to create incentives or a regulatory system that would ensure that system-wide changes are implemented.

5.   Attribution Steps

Several options are available for designing an attribution scheme.

- Design a scheme similar to that used in telephone systems where attribution is automatic – a call is traced back to the originating number. A user may turn this feature off, but this decision can be overridden by the courts.

- Design a system where users can opt in or opt out without any subsequent recovery ability by the system.

Table 1.   Technical solutions for attack attribution.

Technique	Description
Hash-Based IP Traceback	Routers store hash values of network packets. Attribution is done by tracing back hash values across network routers.
Ingress Filtering	All messages entering a network are required to have a source address in a valid range; this limits the range of possible attack sources.
ICMP Return to Sender	All packets destined for the victim are rejected and returned to their senders.
Overlay Network for IP Traceback	An overlay network links all ISP edge routers to a central tracking router; hop-by-hop approaches are used to find the source.
Trace Packet Generation (e.g., iTrace)	A router sends an ICMP traceback message periodically (e.g., every 1 in 20,000 packets) to the same destination address as the sample packet. The destination (or designated monitor) collects and correlates tracking information.
Probabilistic Packet Marking	A router randomly determines whether it should embed message route data in a message; this routing data is used to determine routes.
Hackback	Querying functionality is implemented in a host without the permission of the owner. If an attacker controls the host, this may not alert the attacker; thus, the information is more reliable.
Honeypots	Decoy systems capture information about attackers that can be used for attribution.
Watermarking	Files are branded as belonging to their rightful owners.

- Design multiple networks, each providing a different level of attribution; some networks may provide no attribution. Users are free to choose the networks from which they accept packets.

5.1   Implementing Clean Slate Approaches

The Internet was not designed for the purposes for which it is now used, nor for the security demands created by a user base without shared trust. A number of "clean slate" network projects are now underway, including the National Science Foundation's Future Internet Network Design (FIND) and the Department of Defense's Global Information Grid (GIG). The goal of these projects is to develop new networks of networks that address current and future needs.

The challenge faced by these projects is that network architectures are not just about technology – they also involve social, legal, administrative and economic infrastructures. Secure BGP and IPv6 have faced slow acceptance as much for technical reasons as for economic and administrative reasons.

No plans exist for the adoption of a clean slate network. Indeed, if some of the current clean slate work is successful, it would – in colloquial terms – be like the dog that chases the car finally catches it! This is not an academic question: technical designs that do not consider legal, social, economic and administrative issues definitely limit the utility of the new networks. Also, legal and/or administrative changes needed to promote the adoption of a new network architecture may take years.

However appealing it may be technically, the consideration of large-scale modifications to the Internet raises several interesting questions:

- What can we learn from other instances of transition from one large-scale infrastructure to another? The history of technological innovations provides a rich and varied set of case studies of adoption and failures. The transition from the telegraph to the telephone took decades; the adoption of HDTV required a carefully-crafted political process and major changes in spectrum policy; Sweden switched from driving on the left-hand side of the road to the right-hand side in a single day.

- What are the possible transition paths to a clean slate network? These could, for example, range from creating a DoD-only network to one that is adopted globally, with the current Internet rapidly phased out.

- How do the technical characteristics of clean slate networks match up with the suite of possible adoption paths? Identifying potential gaps can shape future research directions for clean slate networks.

- How do existing administrative structures and economic forces match with potential trajectories for clean slate network adoption? This question takes on even more relevance given the discussion of Internet governance at the World Summit on the Information Society.

It is important to note that we do not believe that widespread modifications to the existing Internet are inappropriate. Instead, our position is that the challenges to any modification are not just technical in nature, but involve a complex set of social, economic, legal and administrative issues that are poorly understood.

5.2   Technical Approach for Limited Attribution

It is possible to construct a logical overlay on the Internet that makes attribution possible within a subset of users, in this case, process control system operators. All relevant actions taken by an entity electing to join the attribution overlay can be fully attributed to that entity. This provides an online environment in which members are increasingly accountable for their actions.

For control system applications – where transaction accuracy is critical – the value of attribution is obvious. The control systems environment provides a unique opportunity to develop and demonstrate a limited attribution service because the drawbacks of attribution are minimal while the benefits are high. The ability to attribute control system activities promotes integrity as well as trust in operational decisions. Attribution also makes it possible to discover and discourage attempts at compromising process control systems, even those perpetrated by insiders.

Clearly, malicious actions taken by a non-member of an attribution network cannot necessarily be attributed to the offending party, but the attribution overlay can facilitate an investigation by proving that the action was generated outside of the membership community, protecting members from fraudulent transactions. Also, if an attributed action is repudiated by a member of the attribution overlay, that member's system can be segregated from the attribution overlay and examined for compromise.

The attribution overlay would provide control systems with greater transactional accuracy. Also, it would provide protection from Internet attacks originating outside the attribution overlay and protect machines inside the attribution overlay. The attribution overlay concept is not a defense against all forms of exploitation, but it is a step in the right direction. As is typical with security services, its implementation will inevitably introduce unanticipated complexities and vulnerabilities, and will, therefore, require continuous refinement.

One possible implementation of an attribution overlay is to use a root of trust made available to individual members by an attribution group management process. The trust root is responsible for authenticating the origin of inbound messages and sealing attribution data of outbound messages using a digital signature technique. Attribution data must include the member, machine, message content and context, and intended destination. The data may also include geo-location, source routing data, required responses and a two-way secure handshake. To avoid system compromise, the keys used for authenticating and sealing attribution data must be protected using a hardware device (e.g., trusted platform module (TPM) or smart card), which may serve as the root of trust.

This approach seeks to make it more difficult for malicious actors to exploit the system exclusively using software. Outbound messages that require attribution can be presented to the TPM or smart card to verify the message format and complete the digital signature. Inbound messages can be presented to the device to confirm origin, allowing each system an opportunity to ensure that all messages belong to the attribution overlay network before processing the messages. Note that this implementation would allow participants in the attribution overlay to restrict message processing to those messages that originate within the attribution overlay. Also, it allows operational security personnel to determine whether a compromise originated from within the attribution overlay or from an outside source. This simple distinction can help protect members of the attribution overlay from certain types of fraud.

In addition to using a root of trust at each end point, there is value to incorporating trust at multiple points within the network. These additional points of trust can attest (via a similar attribution process) to the existence of messages in the network at various times, providing investigators with the right information and strong confidence in the information. This would be similar to the process employed by physical investigators who often rely on recording devices: ATM cameras, traffic cameras, credit card records and DHCP data.

An attribution overlay must have a process to enroll and revoke members. This is a difficult problem that is currently being studied by digital identity management experts. Some approximate solutions for managing public key infrastructures can serve as the basis for an attribution overlay. However, as new methods for identity management emerge, the attribution overlay can be revised to take advantage of them. Although attribution overlay shares many challenges with digital identity management, attribution overlay has the advantage of uniform control. Specifically, attribution overlay can be constructed by a single entity (e.g., a control system working group) and managed according to a policy controlled by that entity. Under this model, control system operators and service providers can construct logical attribution overlays. Members may elect to join multiple attribution overlays, making all the actions relevant to that service provider attributable to the individual member. Note that it is also possible to use overlay technology to construct a non-attributable network for the free exchange of ideas.

Traditional attempts at creating network overlays require all the members to fully participate in the network overlay. Our approach does not require full participation and is intended to steadily gain acceptance for attribution services by providing value to the control systems community over time.

5.3 Reducing the Malicious Noise Floor

Malicious activity may be broadly divided into three categories: nuisance, criminal and politically-motivated (terrorist or nation-state) activities. The vast majority of reported activity falls in the first two categories; organizations such as the U.S. Computer Emergency Response Team (CERT) devote considerable resources to analyze malicious acts. This is possible because the methods used by actors to conduct nuisance activities and low-level crime are well understood by the computer security community. Because attribution is not currently possible, our approach is to measure and track these types of malicious activities. The effort expended to track them detracts from the ability to focus on high-level crime and politically-motivated activities such as terrorism. Therefore, low-level malicious activity has two undesirable results. First, it consumes valuable resources. Second, it raises the amount of malicious noise, making it difficult to detect more damaging types of activities.

Low-level malicious activity can be discouraged using low-grade attribution. It is not necessary to prosecute every low-level crime and resolve every low-level malicious activity to the computer and individual. All that is required is to increase the probability that an individual engaging in malicious activity can be identified, prosecuted and punished. Many interstate drivers know which jurisdictions tolerate speeding and which do not. They know where the risk of being caught is high and where the penalties are steep, and they tend to slow down in those jurisdictions. An example of an Internet "speed trap" is the Record Industry Association of America (RIAA) campaign to identify violations of copyright through Internet file sharing.

One technical approach for reducing the malicious noise floor is to implement features that make it easier for cooperating Internet service providers to trace individual packets and flows, which would make it possible to issue the equivalent of "Internet traffic tickets." The legal model of traffic ordinances, which stipulate penalties for violating the rules of proper conduct, may, thus, be extended to Internet activities. But, of course, attribution is key to enabling such an approach.

6.   Conclusions

Critical infrastructure protection is a global problem. The adoption of commodity information, computing and networking technologies in critical infrastructure assets increases the overall risk by growing the space of exploitable vulnerabilities and exposing systems to new threats. While new technologies should be developed to help reduce vulnerabilities, it is equally important to seek strategies that manage the threats. Cyber attribution supports threat management by identifying malicious actors and uncovering their motives and methods, in the process, informing vulnerability reduction efforts. Attribution gives critical infrastructure asset owners and operators legal recourse in the event of attacks and deters potential attacks. Technological advances alone will not solve the attribution problem. Effective and lasting attribution services require active user participation, and sustained legal and policy efforts.

Acknowledgements

This work was partially supported by the Institute for Information Infrastructure Protection (I3P) at Dartmouth College, Hanover, New Hampshire, under Award 2003-TK-TX-0003 from the U.S. Department of Homeland Security.

References

[1] W. Clinton, Presidential Decision Directive 63, The White House, Washington, DC (fas.org/irp/offdocs/pdd/pdd-63.htm), May 22, 1998.

[2] J. Hunker, R. Hutchinson and J. Margulies, Roles and Challenges for Sufficient Cyber Attack Attribution, Research Report, Institute for Information Infrastructure Protection, Dartmouth College, Hanover, New Hampshire, 2008.

[3] H. Lipson, Tracking and Tracing Cyber Attacks: Technical Challenges and Global Policy Issues, Special Report CMU/SEI-2002-SR-009, CERT Coordination Center, Software Engineering Institute, Carnegie Mellon University, Pittsburgh, Pennsylvania, 2002.

[4] P. Pederson, D. Dudenhoeffer, S. Hartley and M. Permann, Critical Infrastructure Interdependency Modeling: A Survey of U.S. and International Research, Report No. INL/EXT-06-11464, Critical Infrastructure Protection Division, Idaho National Laboratory, Idaho Falls, Idaho, 2006.

[5] T. Samad, P. McLaughlin and J. Lu, System architecture for process automation: Review and trends, *Journal of Process Control*, vol. 17(3), pp. 191–201, 2007.

[6] D. Wheeler and G. Larson, Techniques for Cyber Attack Attribution, IDA Paper P-3792, Institute for Defense Analyses, Alexandria, Virginia, 2003.

Chapter 8

MODELING AND DETECTING ANOMALIES IN SCADA SYSTEMS

Nils Svendsen and Stephen Wolthusen

Abstract   The detection of attacks and intrusions based on anomalies is hampered by the limits of specificity underlying the detection techniques. However, in the case of many critical infrastructure systems, domain-specific knowledge and models can impose constraints that potentially reduce error rates. At the same time, attackers can use their knowledge of system behavior to mask their manipulations, causing adverse effects to observed only after a significant period of time. This paper describes elementary statistical techniques that can be applied to detect anomalies in critical infrastructure networks. A SCADA system employed in liquefied natural gas (LNG) production is used as a case study.

Keywords: SCADA systems, anomaly detection, multivariate analysis

1.   Introduction

Supervisory control and data acquisition (SCADA) networks are a key component of the critical infrastructure. These systems are used by operators in modern industrial facilities to continuously monitor and control plant operations. SCADA systems have evolved in terms of the capabilities of their sensors and actuators as well as in their network topologies. SCADA network topologies have moved from simple point-to-point links to arbitrary mesh-type networks, including fixed and wireless links that support large numbers of nodes and overlapping networks.

Although the importance of SCADA systems has been recognized for some time [21], efforts investigating network security issues in SCADA environments have been relatively limited [3, 13]. Igure, et al. [13] identify several security challenges that have to be addressed for SCADA networks: access control, firewalls and intrusion detection systems, protocol vulnerability assessment, cryptography and key management, device and operating system security, and security management.

Please use the following format when citing this chapter:

Svendsen, N. and Wolthusen, S., 2008, in IFIP International Federation for Information Processing, Volume 290; *Critical Infrastructure Protection II*, eds. Papa, M., Shenoi, S., (Boston: Springer), pp. 101–113.

This paper is concerned with the question of whether the implementation of traditional security solutions in a SCADA network will provide adequate levels of security given the constraints and requirements imposed by the application area. The primary requirement is to maintain physical parameters within a set of quality and safety margins and to guarantee suitable reaction times. This is accomplished by gathering data from multiple (possibly hierarchical) sensors and subsystems, and verifying that the readings fall into acceptable ranges based on historical data. However, an attacker with the appropriate knowledge and access can alter correlated process variables to bring a system to a critical state, potentially causing degradation of service or even an outright failure. This paper employs applied statistical methods to detect anomalous behavior in SCADA networks. A case study involving a liquefied natural gas (LNG) production facility is used to demonstrate the utility of the statistical approach.

2.   Anomaly Detection in Control Systems

This section provides a brief overview of anomaly detection in control systems followed by an overview of applied statistical methods.

2.1   Anomaly Detection

A control system is a device or set of devices used to manage, command, direct and regulate the behavior of other devices or systems. It typically has four main components: sensors, analyzers, actuators and a communications infrastructure. Sensors determine the state of the controlled system, analyzers determine whether the system is stable or out of control, and actuators are used to maintain the system at (or restore it to) a stable state. Control systems incorporate feedback loops, which may be positive or negative, depending on the application.

Anomaly detection [2] involves establishing profiles of normal process behavior, comparing actual behavior with the established profiles, and identifying deviations from the normal. A profile or set of metrics is determined for each process. The metrics are measures of specific aspects of process behavior (e.g., pressure, temperature or composition).

Anomaly detection methods may be categorized as: statistical methods, rule-based methods, distance-based methods, profiling methods and model-based approaches. This paper focuses on statistical methods for anomaly detection. Denning [9] proposed four statistical models for determining whether an observation is abnormal with respect to previous observations. They are: (i) operational model (where abnormality is determined by comparing a new observation against fixed limits); mean and standard deviation model (where an observation is compared to a confidence interval based on historical observations); multivariate model (where correlations between two or more metrics are taken into account); and Markov process model (used in discrete systems where transaction frequencies between states and the probability of going from one state to another can be determined).

2.2   Univariate Quality Control Charts

Univariate quality control charts (see, e.g., [27]) can be used to determine if the performance of a process is at an acceptable level. A quality control chart consists of data plotted in time order and horizontal lines, called control limits, that indicate the amount of variation due to common causes. Control must be exerted on both the central tendency and variability, which are accomplished using an $\overline{X}$-chart and an S-chart, respectively.

Assume that the data consists of m samples of size n for which $S_1, S_2, \ldots, S_m$ are the sample standard deviations. The average values of the sample standard deviation $\overline{S}$ are computed along with the overall average $\overline{\overline{X}}$. The corresponding upper and lower control limits for the $\overline{X}$-chart to control the central tendency are:

$$UCL = \overline{\overline{X}} + A_3\overline{S} \qquad LCL = \overline{\overline{X}} - A_3\overline{S}$$

where $A_3 = 3/(c_4\sqrt{n})$ and

$$c_4 = \left(\frac{2}{n-1}\right)^{1/2} \frac{\Gamma(n/2)}{\Gamma[(n-1)/2]}$$

where $\Gamma(\cdot)$ is the gamma function. For the S-chart, we have:

$$UCL = B_6\sigma \qquad LCL = B_5\sigma$$

with $B_5 = c_4 - 3\sqrt{1 - c_4^2}$ and $B_5 = c_4 + 3\sqrt{1 - c_4^2}$. Given the control limits, the quality control charts are created by plotting the sample means (standard deviations) in time order in the same plot.

2.3   Multivariate Quality Control Charts

A multivariate approach is used when the data to be analyzed has multiple important characteristics. Such an approach may also be used when processes are assumed to be independent. The T^2-chart is commonly applied in these situations as it can be applied to a large number of variables. Given the mutually independent vectors $X_1, X_2, \ldots, X_n$ of length p where each X_j is distributed as $N_p(\mu_j, \Sigma)$, the control limits of the T^2-chart are set by assuming that $(X_j - \overline{X})'S^{-1}(X_j - \overline{X})$ has a chi-square distribution [14]. Note that S is the covariance matrix and $(X_j - \overline{X})'$ is the transpose of $(X_j - \overline{X})$. For the jth point, the T^2-statistic is computed as:

$$T_j^2 = (x_j - \overline{x})'S^{-1}(x_j - \overline{x})$$

and plotted on the time axis. The lower control limit (LCL) is zero while the upper control limit (UCL) is commonly set to $\chi_p^2(0.05)$.

3.   Liquefied Natural Gas Production

This section briefly describes the process for producing liquefied natural gas (LNG) [23].

Natural gas (NG) is retrieved from wells, each of which is controlled by a set of valves ("Xmas trees") that adapts the NG pressure from the well to the pressure in the pipeline system. At this point, monoethyleneglycol (MEG) is injected into the well-stream to inhibit the formation of hydrate, which could block the pipeline. MEG is distributed to the Xmas trees through a control distribution unit (CDU). The CDU also distributes electricity, control signals, hydraulic pressure and chemicals to the Xmas trees. The various well-streams are assembled at the pipeline end manifold (PLEM), were they gather into a single well-stream for transport through the main pipeline. The flow in the main pipeline has multiple phases: natural gas liquids (NG), condensate (light oil) and a mix of water and MEG.

The well-stream in the main pipeline often arrives in spurts, i.e., the gas and liquids separate and the gas arrives between slugs of liquid. A slug catcher is typically used to separate NG condensate and MEG. Carbon dioxide (CO_2) is then removed from the NG as it would freeze to dry ice during gas liquefaction, which could cause damage later in the process. The NG is already moist and the removal of CO_2 further augments its water content, which would form ice during the cooling process and cause damage. Therefore, the gas is dried before refrigeration. Another important pre-treatment process is the removal of very small quantities of mercury present in the heavier components. This is because mercury could cause corrosive damage to metal components and catalysts that come into contact with the gas stream.

At this point, the NG is ready for fractionation. This involves the separation of LNG from the heavier gas components, known as natural gas liquids (NGL), and the adjustment of the amounts of various hydrocarbons present in the gas. The gases that remain after NGL removal are passed to a "cold box" for cooling to LNG. This is a three-stage process that primarily employs heat exchangers. A byproduct of this phase is nitrogen, which is purified and released to the atmosphere. After NGL is separated from LNG, the NGL undergoes further fractionation to separate ethane and propane from the remaining condensate. Ethane and propane form liquefied petroleum gases (LPG).

LNG/LPG production is energy intensive. The energy requirement to bring the gas from high pressure and relatively high temperature to low pressure and very low temperature is tremendous as the pressure varies from 220 bar to 1 bar and the temperature from 90° C to −163°C. LNG/LPG plants tend to be self-sufficient with regard to energy since they operate gas-driven power plants; this largely eliminates the dependency on external power suppliers and the power grid.

4. LNG Process Attack Points

This section identifies possible LNG process attack points. The focus is on attacks that could halt or degrade LNG production. Outright terrorist acts and sabotage, such as blowing up a storage facility, are not included in the list of attack scenarios. Instead, the scenarios mainly involve subtle manipulations of process control systems and sensors. The scenarios assume that an attacker is knowledgeable about the system.

- **MEG Dosage:** MEG must be present in the well-stream to prevent the water component from freezing. An ice plug could cause a pipeline blockage, resulting in a lengthy shutdown of the plant. Also, the upstream pressure in the pipeline could rise to critical levels.

- **CO_2 Removal:** CO_2 can freeze into dry ice and cause a pipeline blockage, resulting in a lengthy shutdown. Pipeline pressure could also rise to critical levels.

- **Mercury Removal:** In this subtle scenario, the presence of mercury causes pipeline corrosion over the long term. In the best case, this increases maintenance costs; in the worst case, the pipeline could rupture.

The remainder of this paper focuses on how an attacker, by altering the moisture content readings for well-streams, could bring the MEG concentration to a critically low level without it being detected by sensors in the well-heads. The attack is carried out so that the moisture content at each well-head is within the control limit of the stream, meaning that it cannot be detected by univariate analysis. However, it can be detected by observing the correlation between the well-heads.

5. Model Description

This section presents two models, one for monitoring well-streams for unusual fluctuations in the volume flow of water and the other for relating the volume flow of water and the amount of MEG introduced.

5.1 Moisture Content in Well-Streams

Although it is a continuous phenomenon, the moisture content of a well-stream can be represented as a time series. We employ an elementary time series model that includes trend, seasonality and random noise [5]. Each observation X_t of a time series is of the form:

$$X_t = m_t + s_t + Y_t$$

where m_t is a slowly changing function (trend component), s_t is a periodic function of t with period d (seasonal effect), and Y_t is a zero-mean process (random noise and fluctuations). To capture the continuous properties of the moisture content, we use a random walk to represent fluctuations. For each well i, a well-stream X_{it} is defined. The volume flow from well i is given by Q_i. Thus, the volume flow of water at each time interval is given by the product $X_{it} \cdot Q_i$. Generally, Q_i can be made time-dependent, but we choose to keep it constant for the purpose of our analysis. The attack on the LNG production system is accomplished by introducing an extra constant term in the expression for X_{it} at time t_a during Δ_a iterations. Given the amplitude of the attack $A \in [0,1]$, the time series has the form:

$$X_t = \begin{cases} m_t + s_t + Y_t, & \text{if } x \notin [t_a, t_a + \Delta_a] \\ m_t + s_t + Y_t + Am_t, & \text{if } x \in [t_a, t_a + \Delta_a] \end{cases}$$

5.2   MEG Dosage

In order to create an elementary model that relates the volume flow of water in a well-stream and the quantity of MEG added, we assume that the well-streams are merged to one stream at the PLEM and that the sensors for measuring the water content in the individual well-streams and the joint well-stream are located at the PLEM. The main consequence is that a latency emerges between the time an attack is initiated (i.e., a change occurs in a well-stream) and the time when the attack is detected. The relationship between the MEG dosage and the water volume flow is given by $Q_{MEG}(t) = f(Q_{water}(t + \Delta_t))$ where $f(\cdot)$ is some function. Due to natural fluctuations in a well-stream, the MEG dosage is not adjusted based on an individual reading, but on a statistical test of whether the value of the current MEG dosage corresponds to the mean of the last k well-stream readings. The process is initiated with an expected water volume flow μ_0. For every water volume flow measurement, a test is performed to determine whether or not μ_0 is the mean of the last k readings. Assuming that the mean of the readings is μ, a one-sided test on a single sample can be performed using the hypothesis:

$$H_0 : \mu = \mu_0 \qquad H_1 : \mu \neq \mu_0.$$

If the H_0 hypothesis is rejected, $\mu_0 = \mu$ holds and the MEG flow is altered according to the function f.

6.   Simulation Results

Our simulation experiments consider a system with three well-streams. This section presents a reference simulation to demonstrate how a well-calibrated model is located within the control limits. Next, an attack is launched against all three well-streams and an attempt is made to detect the attack using quality control methods.

6.1   Three Wells with Seasonal Component

The following model is used to express the water content in the three wells:

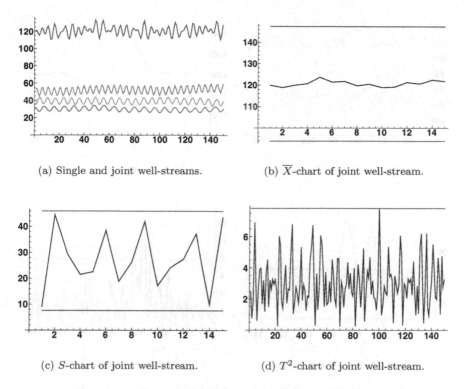

(a) Single and joint well-streams.

(b) $\overline{X}$-chart of joint well-stream.

(c) S-chart of joint well-stream.

(d) T^2-chart of joint well-stream.

Figure 1. Characteristic plots of a reference well-stream.

$$X_{1t} = 0.3 + 0.03\cos\left(\frac{i\pi}{100}\right) + 0.0005Y_{1t}$$

$$X_{2t} = 0.4 + 0.04\cos\left(\frac{i\pi}{80} + \frac{2\pi}{3}\right) + 0.0005Y_{2t}$$

$$X_{3t} = 0.5 + 0.03\cos\left(\frac{i\pi}{60} + \frac{4\pi}{3}\right) + 0.0005Y_{3t}$$

where $Y_{it} = Z_{i1} + Z_{i2} + \cdots + Z_{it}$, for $t = 1, 2, \ldots, 3750$ and $\{Z_{it}\}$ is independent and identically distributed random noise. The generated time series points are sampled at a rate of $1/25$. This is done to show that not every point for a continuous process can be sampled. The points are grouped in samples of fifteen elements before further analysis is performed. Figure 1 shows the characteristic plots of the well-streams and the control charts for the joint well-stream.

An attack is launched simultaneously against all three wells; the attack increases the water content of each well-stream by 15%. Note that in order for the attack to be successful, the attacker must have knowledge of the sampling strategy and the grouping of samples. The confidence limits for the $\overline{X}$-chart and S-chart are set based on historical observations of the process. A total of

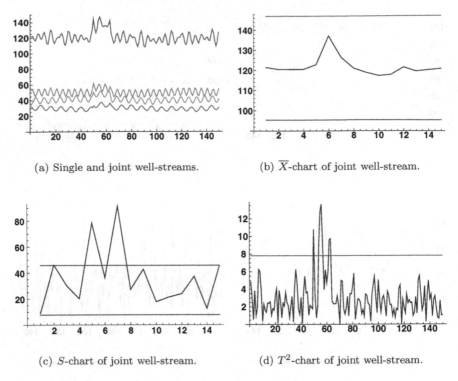

(a) Single and joint well-streams.   (b) $\overline{X}$-chart of joint well-stream.

(c) S-chart of joint well-stream.   (d) T^2-chart of joint well-stream.

Figure 2.   Characteristics plots of a well-stream being attacked.

25 runs of the reference process described above were carried out to determine the 95% upper and lower confidence intervals. Figure 2 shows the characteristic plots for the attack, which occurs between iterations 1250 and 1600. As seen in Figure 2(c), the attack can be detected by the change in variance.

Having assumed that the attacker has knowledge about the sampling strategy, we now examine the situation where the attack covers full samples. This means that the samples either contain points that are attack points or points that are not attack points. Thus, internal fluctuations in the samples are avoided. Figure 3 shows one such run where the attack produces no more variation than noise.

6.2   MEG Dosage

The water content is modeled using the series:

$$X_t = 0.3 + 0.03 \cos\left(\frac{i\pi}{100}\right) + 0.0005 Y_{1t}.$$

In the attack, a certain percentage of the expected flow is added to the well-stream. The duration of the attack corresponds to fourteen analyzed samples.

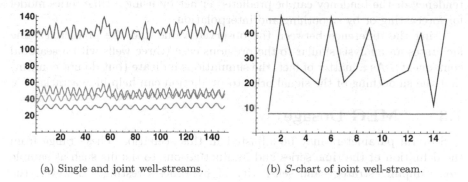

| (a) Single and joint well-streams. | (b) *S*-chart of joint well-stream. |

Figure 3.   Well-streams and *S*-chart of a well-stream being attacked.

Table 1.   Average number of samples before a change is detected.

Amplitude (%)	0	5	10	15	20	25	30
Samples to detect	14.6	6.8	4.1	3.6	2.1	2.3	1.6

Using the statistical analysis described above, we determine the average number of samples that must be considered before the change in the mean is detected (and the MEG quantity is adjusted). The results are presented in Table 1, which lists the average numbers of samples for expected flow percentages ranging from 0% to 30%.

7.   Analysis of Scenarios

This section analyzes the simulated scenarios and discusses how the statistical approach works in the case of time series with tendencies.

7.1   Three Wells with Seasonal Component

An examination of Figure 2 indicates that the attack is not detected by the $\overline{X}$-chart. Specifically, a peak in the sample mean is present, but it does not go over the confidence limits. We ran the attack 25 times and examined the fluctuations in the mean value for the joined well-stream. The attack was detected in 50% of the cases in the well-stream with the smallest volume flow (i.e., with the greatest sensitivity). This detection rate is only three times the false alarm rate in the stream due to random fluctuations. Note, however, that the T^2-chart detects the attack in all the cases.

7.2   Three Wells with Tendency

It is reasonable to assume that there is a tendency different from zero in the water content of a well-stream. Either there is a known model for the tendency or the tendency can be predicted either by using a time series model for forecasting or by smoothing and interpolation.

Using the difference between the observed value and the predicted value facilitates an analysis similar to the previous case (three wells with a seasonal component). As a matter of fact, the simulations indicate (but do not confirm) that the smoothing of the signal prior to prediction can help hide attacks.

7.3　MEG Dosage

Seeveral parameters may be adjusted in this scenario. These range from the definition of the time series and its fluctuations to details such as sample size, sampling strategy and sensitivity of hypothesis testing. However, the simulation results show that delays accumulate in large-scale systems where sensors and actuators are located in different physical locations and where the nature of the observed system is such that control actions cannot be performed based on single observations.

8.　Related Work

Early work on SCADA security focused almost exclusively on physical attacks [17]. However, intrusion detection in SCADA systems has become an important research area, especially as general-purpose network substrates are employed in control systems, and control networks are intentionally (and sometimes inadvertently) cross-linked with exposed networks. The risks to control networks posed by remote attacks were emphasized in a 1997 White House document [21]. However, much of the research related to SCADA security (see, e.g., [1, 13, 16, 18, 20]) has been driven by security-related incidents that occurred in 2001–2004 [11].

Considerable attention has focused on attacks against electrical power systems [26], although security issues related to other infrastructures have also been investigated [22]. The survivability of distributed control systems and their resilience to attacks, including subversion, is a major issue [4]. Chong, et al. [6] discuss the use of adaptive network security mechanisms for systems where service levels must be maintained during attacks. Significant work related to intrusion tolerance systems has been conducted under the MAFTIA Project [8, 24], which built on the results of the earlier Delta-4 project [10]. Lower-level *ad hoc* strategies have been discussed by Haji and co-workers [12]. Bigham, et al. [3] have investigated anomaly detection in SCADA environments based on invariant deduction as well as more commonly used *n*-gram techniques. A related approach is discussed by Coutinho, et al. [7].

SCADA systems employ multiple types of sensors that are often widely dispersed (especially in the case of the power grid and oil and gas pipelines). Kosut and Tong [15] discuss the application of data fusion techniques to sensors for which Byzantine behavior cannot be ignored. These security concerns apply to sensor data at rest and in transit as discussed by Subramanian, et al. [25]. Nguyen and Nahrstedt [19] have addressed the related issue of attack containment in large-scale industrial control environments using compartmentalization and trust groups.

9. Conclusions

Anomaly detection in SCADA systems has primarily focused on applying general network and host detection techniques. However, the characteristics of SCADA systems, the constraints imposed by real-time industrial environments, and the sophisticated models underlying industrial processes (e.g., state estimator models used for the electrical power grid) require high-level detection approaches as illustrated in this paper. A parallel threat results because attackers with knowledge about process models and SCADA systems can influence or fabricate sensor readings and actuator behavior so that they appear normal to operators. Such manipulations can degrade or disrupt vital industrial processes or force them to operate closer to the margins where a subsequent attack (e.g., a physical attack) could cause significant damage.

Statistical techniques, as decribed in this paper, are well suited to detecting anomalous behavior in SCADA systems (and critical infrastructure networks, in general). Simplified models and simulations were used in this work to illustrate the main concepts. Our future research will investigate the application of more elaborate hierarchical and composite models. We will also explore the use of multivariate analysis of variance techniques for detecting anomalies in systems with multiple dependent variables.

References

[1] M. Amanullah, A. Kalam and A. Zayegh, Network security vulnerabilities in SCADA and EMS, *Proceedings of the IEEE/PES Transmission and Distribution Conference and Exhibition: Asia and Pacific*, pp. 1–6, 2005.

[2] R Bace, *Intrusion Detection*, Sams, Indianapolis, Indiana, 2000.

[3] J. Bigham, D. Gamez and N. Lu, Safeguarding SCADA systems with anomaly detection, *Proceedings of the Second International Workshop on Mathematical Methods, Models and Architectures for Computer Network Security*, pp. 171–182, 2003.

[4] P. Bracken, *The Command and Control of Nuclear Forces*, Yale University Press, New Haven, Connecticut, 1985.

[5] P. Brockwell and R. Davis, *Introduction to Time Series and Forecasting*, Springer-Verlag, New York, 2002.

[6] J. Chong, P. Pal, M. Atigetchi, P. Rubel and F. Webber, Survivability architecture of a mission critical system: The DPASA example, *Proceedings of the Twenty-First Annual Computer Security Applications Conference*, pp. 495–504, 2005.

[7] M. Coutinho, G. Lambert-Torres, L. da Silva, E. Fonseca and H. Lazarek, A methodology to extract rules to identify attacks in power system critical infrastructure, *Proceedings of the IEEE Power Engineering Society General Meeting*, pp. 1–7, 2007.

[8] M. Dacier (Ed.), Design of an Intrusion-Tolerant Intrusion Detection System, MAFTIA Deliverable D10 (Version 4.3), IBM Zurich Research Laboratory, Zurich, Switzerland, 2002.

[9] D. Denning, An intrusion-detection model, *IEEE Transactions on Software Engineering*, vol. 13(2), pp. 222–232, 1987.

[10] Y. Deswarte, L. Blain and J. Fabre, Intrusion tolerance in distributed computing systems, *Proceedings of the IEEE Symposium on Research in Security and Privacy*, pp. 110–121, 1991.

[11] D. Dzung, M. Naedele, T. von Hoff and M. Crevatin, Security for industrial communication systems, *Proceedings of the IEEE*, vol. 93(6), pp. 1152–1177, 2005.

[12] F. Haji, L. Lindsay and S. Song, Practical security strategy for SCADA automation systems and networks, *Proceedings of the Canadian Conference on Electrical and Computer Engineering*, pp. 172–178, 2005.

[13] V. Igure, S. Laughter and R. Williams, Security issues in SCADA networks, *Computers and Security*, vol. 25(7), pp. 498–506, 2006.

[14] R. Johnson and D. Wichern, *Applied Multivariate Statistical Analysis*, Prentice Hall, Upper Saddle River, New Jersey, 2007.

[15] O. Kosut and L. Tong, Capacity of cooperative fusion in the presence of Byzantine sensors, *Proceedings of the Forty-Fourth Annual Allerton Conference on Communication, Control and Computation*, 2006.

[16] T. Kropp, System threats and vulnerabilities: Power system protection, *IEEE Power and Energy*, vol. 4(2), pp. 46–50, 2006.

[17] E. Murtoviita, J. Keronen, J. Suni and M. Bjork, Visual aids for substation monitoring and security control, *Proceedings of the Third International Conference on Power System Monitoring and Control*, pp. 225–227, 1991.

[18] M. Naedele, Addressing IT security for critical control systems, *Proceedings of the Fortieth Annual Hawaii International Conference on System Sciences*, p. 115, 2007.

[19] H. Nguyen and K. Nahrstedt, Attack containment framework for large-scale critical infrastructures, *Proceedings of the Sixteenth International Conference on Computer Communications and Networks*, pp. 442–449, 2007.

[20] P. Palensky and T. Sauter, Security considerations for FAN-Internet connections, *Proceedings of the IEEE International Workshop on Factory Communication Systems*, pp. 27–35, 2000.

[21] President's Commission on Critical Infrastructure Protection, Critical Foundations: Protecting America's Infrastructures, The White House, Washington, DC (chnm.gmu.edu/cipdigitalarchive/files/5_CriticalFound ationsPCCIP.pdf), 1997.

[22] G. Shafiullah, A. Gyasi-Agyei and P. Wolfs, Survey of wireless communications applications in the railway industry, *Proceedings of the Second International Conference on Wireless Broadband and Ultra Wideband Communications*, p. 65, 2007.

[23] StatoilHydro, The long road to LNG, Stavanger, Norway (www.statoilhyd ro.com/en/NewsAndMedia/Multimedia/features/SnohvitLNG/Pages/def ault.aspx), 2007.

[24] R. Stroud, I. Welch, J. Warne and P. Ryan, A qualitative analysis of the intrusion-tolerance capabilities of the MAFTIA architecture, *Proceedings of the International Conference on Dependable Systems and Networks*, pp. 453–461, 2004.

[25] N. Subramanian, C. Yang and W. Zhang, Securing distributed data storage and retrieval in sensor networks, *Proceedings of the Fifth Annual IEEE International Conference on Pervasive Computing and Communications*, pp. 191–200, 2007.

[26] Substations Committee of the IEEE Power Engineering Society, IEEE Recommended Practice for Network Communication in Electric Power Substations, IEEE Standard 1615-2007, IEEE, Piscataway, New Jersey, 2007.

[27] R. Walpole, R. Meyers and S. Meyers, *Probability and Statistics for Engineers and Scientists*, Prentice Hall, Upper Saddle River, New Jersey, 1998.

Chapter 9

ASSESSING THE INTEGRITY OF FIELD DEVICES IN MODBUS NETWORKS

Ryan Shayto, Brian Porter, Rodrigo Chandia, Mauricio Papa and Sujeet Shenoi

Abstract   Pipeline control systems often incorporate thousands of widely dispersed sensors and actuators, many of them in remote locations. Information about the operational aspects (functionality) and integrity (state) of these field devices is critical because they perform vital measurement and control functions.

This paper describes a distributed scanner for remotely verifying the functionality and state of field devices in Modbus networks. The scanner is designed for the Modbus protocol and, therefore, accommodates the delicate TCP/IP stacks of field devices. Furthermore, field device scanning and data storage and retrieval operations are scheduled so as not to impact normal pipeline control operations. Experimental results and simulations demonstrate that the distributed scanner is scalable, distributable and operates satisfactorily in low bandwidth networks.

Keywords: Modbus networks, distributed scanner, field devices, integrity

1.   Introduction

The oil and gas industry primarily uses distributed control systems implementing the Modbus protocol [6-8] for midstream and transport activities in pipeline operations. A typical midstream application may have 10,000 or more field devices dispersed over several thousand square miles, including offshore platforms and remote wells. On the other hand, a transport application may have 1,000 field devices located at various points along a 3,000 mile pipeline. Many of these devices are sensors that measure key process parameters such as pressure, temperature, flow and hydrogen sulfide content. Other field devices are actuators that perform various pipeline control actions.

Pipeline operators need accurate and timely information about the status and integrity of field devices [4, 5]. Operational and business decisions are

Please use the following format when citing this chapter:

Shayto, R., Porter, B., Chandia, R., Papa, M. and Shenoi, S., 2008, in IFIP International Federation for Information Processing, Volume 290; *Critical Infrastructure Protection II*, eds. Papa, M., Shenoi, S., (Boston: Springer), pp. 115–128.

adversely affected when large numbers of field devices are non-operational or corrupted; such a situation could also lead to an industrial accident. Most energy companies employ technicians whose only job is to travel to distant sites to verify the condition of field devices and service them. Field devices may be audited once a month, often just once a quarter.

This paper describes the design and implementation of a distributed scanner that remotely verifies the functionality and state of field devices in Modbus networks. The scanner accommodates the delicate TCP/IP stacks of field devices and scanning activities can be scheduled to minimize the impact on control operations. Tests on laboratory-scale and virtual environments indicate that the distributed scanner is scalable, distributable and operates satisfactorily in low bandwidth environments. These features make it an attractive tool for providing situational awareness in pipeline control networks, including those incorporating legacy systems.

2.   Modbus Protocol

The Modbus protocol is widely used in the oil and gas sector, especially for controlling natural gas and liquids pipelines. The original Modbus protocol [6] was designed in 1979 for serial communications between the control center (master unit) and field devices (slaves). The Modbus TCP protocol [7], which was published in 1999, extends its serial counterpart for use in IP-interconnected networks. The extended protocol enables a master to have multiple outstanding transactions, and a slave to engage in concurrent communications with multiple masters.

2.1   Modbus Serial Protocol

Modbus implements a strict request/response messaging system between a master unit and slave devices. The master uses unicast or broadcast messages to communicate with slave devices. In a unicast transaction, the master sends a request to a single slave device and waits for a response message from the slave. If a response message is not returned, the master assumes that the request has failed. In a broadcast transaction, the master sends a request to all the slave devices in the network; the slaves perform the requested action but do not send response messages to the master.

A Modbus message has three parts (Figure 1). The first is a header, which includes the slave's address and control information for the slave. The second part contains a protocol data unit (PDU), which specifies an application-level operation. PDUs have two fields: a function code describing the purpose of the message and function parameters associated with the request or reply aspect of the message. The third part of a Modbus message is used for error-checking.

The maximum length of a Modbus message is 256 bytes. The slave address and function code fields use one byte each and the error checking field uses two bytes; this leaves 252 bytes for the function parameters.

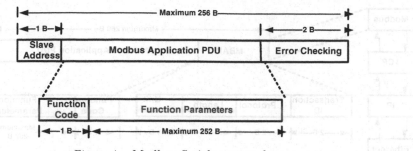

Figure 1. Modbus Serial message format.

Function codes are used by the master to perform diagnostic operations, configure slaves, perform control operations or obtain process data. Three types of function codes are defined in the Modbus protocol: public, user-defined and reserved codes. Public codes in the ranges [1, 64], [73, 99] and [111, 127] correspond to functions documented in the Modbus specification. Because there is no minimum set of function codes that is required to be implemented, vendors incorporate function codes in their products as needed. User-defined function codes in the ranges [65, 72] and [100, 110] are designated for vendors who wish to implement specialized functions. Reserved codes are used to support legacy systems; they overlap with public codes but cannot be used in new Modbus implementations.

Function codes in the [128, 255] range are used to denote error conditions. Specifically, if an error condition occurs for a function code $x \in [0, 127]$ in a request from a master to a slave, the corresponding error function code in the slave's response message is given by $y = x + 128$. Details about the error are indicated using an exception response in the data field of the message. Nine exception codes are specified: 1..6, 8 and 10..11. The exception codes 1..3 are useful when implementing Modbus network scanners. These codes are generated during the pre-processing of Modbus requests, i.e., before any action is taken by a slave to execute the master's request. Thus, malformed messages may be used by a Modbus scanner to obtain information about slave devices without affecting their state.

Table 1. Modbus memory table types.

Name	Data Size	Usage
Discrete Input	1 bit	Read-Only; Digital Input
Coil	1 bit	Read-Write; Digital Output
Input Register	16 bits	Read-Only; Analog Input
Holding Register	16 bits	Read-Write; Analog Output

Modbus devices store data in four types of tables: discrete inputs, coils, input registers and holding registers (Table 1). The maximum memory available for

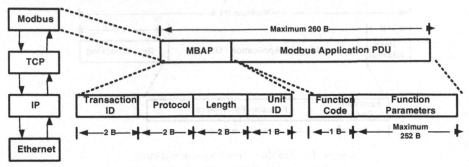

Figure 2.　Modbus TCP message format.

each table type is 65,536 addressable items. A device may implement the tables using separate or overlapping memory spaces.

2.2　Modbus TCP Protocol

Modbus TCP extends the serial version of the protocol by wrapping messages with TCP/IP headers. A master is defined as a "client" because it initiates a TCP connection while a slave device is a "server" that passively listens for a connection on port 502 (or other optional ports). The client and server roles cannot be changed after a TCP connection is established. However, a Modbus device can establish a new connection in which it may assume a different role.

A Modbus TCP message uses the Modbus application protocol (MBAP) header instead of the serial message header (Figure 2). The MBAP has four fields: transaction identifier (2 bytes), protocol identifier (2 bytes), length (2 bytes) and unit identifier (1 byte). Since the MBAP takes up seven bytes, the maximum size of a Modbus TCP packet is 260 bytes. This length restriction arises from legacy implementations of the serial protocol.

The transaction identifier uniquely marks each transaction to permit the matching of paired request and reply messages. The protocol identifier specifies the protocol used for the message (this is set to zero corresponding to the protocol identifier for Modbus). The length field gives the size of the remaining portion of the Modbus message, which includes the unit identifier and the PDU. The unit identifier is used for addressing a slave located behind a gateway that bridges an IP network and a legacy serial network. The PDU is largely unchanged from the serial version. It incorporates the function code and data fields; however, error-checking is provided by the TCP layer.

3.　Distributed Modbus Network Scanner

The distributed Modbus network scanner is designed to gather information about the functionality and state of field devices. It consists of a master scanner, remote sensors and a database, which stores data gathered during network scanning for further processing and applications support [10]. The master scanner controls the remote sensors that perform passive and/or active scans of local

Table 2.   Remote sensor actions.

Commands	Action
Configure Network Interface	Set network interface for listening to traffic
Configure Database	Set IP address, user name and password for accessing database
Start Passive Scanning	Open network interface; Process traffic
Stop Passive Scanning	Flush queue of packets; Close network interface
Start Active Scanning	Retrieve assigned records; Begin scanning
Stop Active Scanning	Finish current scan; Close connections

networks. In addition, the master scanner may passively or actively scan its own network.

3.1   Master Scanner

The master scanner controls remote sensors, schedules active scans, examines the network topology and reviews device records. These actions rely heavily on a relational database, which is ideally located on the same host or subnet as the master scanner.

The master scanner constantly listens for connections from remote sensors. After establishing a connection with a sensor, the master scanner sends commands to initiate passive or active scans or to update sensor configuration.

3.2   Remote Sensors

Remote sensors deployed at field sites serve as collectors and filters of Modbus messages. Upon receiving the appropriate command from the master scanner, a remote sensor may configure its network interface or database connection, start/stop passive scanning or start/stop active scanning. Table 2 summarizes the actions performed by remote sensors upon receiving commands from the master scanner.

3.3   Database

A relational database is used to maintain data gathered by the master scanner and remote sensors, and to store system status information. The database contains tables that model field devices, and store data about device fingerprints and the status of active scans.

Three tables are used to hold information about Modbus field devices. The primary table, *Modbus Device*, stores identifying information about Modbus devices. The other two tables, *Function Codes* and *Memory Contents*, hold information about the functionality and state of field devices. In particular, *Function Codes* maintains records of the implemented function codes and *Memory Contents* stores the memory maps of field devices.

The *Device Fingerprint* table stores known fingerprints, including the components that define the signature. A device signature is based on the implemented function codes (device functionality) and the memory map (device state). This data enables the comparison of field devices against known fingerprints. The comparison is done using SQL commands, which offload processing from the scanner to the database.

The *Active Scan State* table stores the scanning status of each field device. An active scan involves several steps and may be performed over several days to conserve network bandwidth. The *Active Scan State* table provides information about the progress of a scan and enables scanning to resume in the event of sensor interruption or failure.

4.   Modbus Network Scanning

This section describes the passive and active scanning modes used by the distributed scanner to collect and store information about Modbus devices.

4.1   Passive Scanning

Passive scanning uses a packet parser to examine the contents of Modbus messages. Messages are analyzed to determine the identity of the master unit and field devices involved in transactions, and message PDUs are parsed to discover the state of field devices. Note that traffic generated by the active scanning process (described in Section 4.2) is ignored to prevent the scanning process from being designated as a master unit in the database. All the information gathered is stored in the database tables described in the previous section.

Eventually, passive scanning discovers all the active devices in a Modbus network. The database is updated only when a network packet contains new information. Nevertheless, information retrieval and database updates consume significant network bandwidth, possibly impacting control system availability. This problem is alleviated by queuing database updates that involve data transfers exceeding 1 KB per second.

4.2   Active Scanning

Active scanning determines the functionality and state of devices in a Modbus network. In addition, it discovers inactive and disabled devices.

The active scanning algorithm exploits the Modbus protocol to safely determine if function codes are implemented by field devices. In the case of a function code that implements a read operation, the active scanning process sends a request message with the function code; a valid response from the addressed device implies that the function code is implemented by the device. For a function code corresponding to a write operation, a special malformed packet is sent so that a response is received without altering device memory.

Table 3. Sample *Active Scan State* data.

Device IP Address	Unit ID	Next Phase	Next Number	Next Scan	Time Between
192.168.30.1	1	Function Code	10	2007-03-28 16:40:00	00:05:00
192.168.30.2	3	Coils Maximum	0, 32767	2007-03-28 11:40:00	00:09:00

A slave device always checks the function code before acting on a Modbus message [6]. It returns an exception code of 1 if the function code is not implemented; an exception code of 2 (resp. 3) is returned when the function code is implemented, but a malformed request with an illegal data address (resp. illegal data value) was received by the device. The active scanning process interprets the exception response and updates the corresponding device record in the database. The function codes implemented by a Modbus device are determined by systematically querying the device for every function code in the range [0, 127].

Upon obtaining information about the functionality of a device, the active scanning process determines the range and size of each memory table in the device. Read-only requests are used for this purpose and a search is conducted using the starting and ending addresses to determine the valid addresses in each memory table. Note that although the Modbus documentation specifies tables with 65,536 addresses, some devices may not implement such large tables.

Scanning actions are scheduled so as not to interfere with normal operations. In fact, scanning may be scheduled over several days in the case of a large Modbus network.

An active scan of a device involves fourteen phases. The first phase tests whether or not the device implements function codes from 0 to 127. The next twelve phases determine the minimum, maximum and offset values for each of the four types of device memory. The final phase tests diagnostic sub-functions implemented under function code 8.

Table 3 presents two sample entries from the *Active Scan State* table. The first entry indicates that the function codes of Device 1 at the IP address 192.168.30.1 are being examined; and function code 10 is the next one to be tested. The second entry indicates that the maximum value of the coil memory table of Device 3 at IP address 192.168.30.2 is being identified. The *Next Number* field of the table stores the minimum and maximum values of the memory addresses used in the search. The *Next Scan* value indicates when the next scan operation will be performed, and the *Time Between* value specifies the interval between successive scan operations.

Our experiments have shown that a complete scan of a device involves an average of 300 request messages. To reduce bandwidth, consecutive messages are sent after a relatively long time interval (e.g., four minutes apart in our laboratory testbed). The time interval should be increased for networks with large numbers of field devices.

5.   Experimental Results

A major design goal is to ensure that the distributed scanner has minimal impact on normal Modbus network operations. This section evaluates the impact of the scanner on a laboratory testbed and a virtual environment intended to model a small-scale industrial environment. Scanner performance is evaluated with respect to three metrics: scalability, distributability and link utilization.

5.1   Experimental Setup

The distributed Modbus network scanner was evaluated using a laboratory-scale SCADA testbed as well as a larger virtual environment. The SCADA testbed incorporated two Allen-Bradley PLCs with Logix 5555 processors [1]; both devices used Prosoft MVI56-MNET Modbus TCP/IP interface modules for communication [9]. The testbed also incorporated two Direct Logic 205 PLCs with DL260 processors using D2-DCM Ethernet communication modules [2, 3].

The distributed scanner components used with the SCADA testbed were executed on two computers running Windows XP Service Pack 2. The master scanner and database were hosted on an Intel Xeon 3 GHz machine with 2 GB RAM. The remote sensor was hosted on an Intel Pentium III 1 GHz machine with 496 MB RAM.

A virtual experimental facility was created to evaluate the scalability of the distributed scanner in industrial environments. Figure 3 illustrates the virtual SCADA environment. Virtual PLCs were created using Jamod Java libraries [12]. The master and slave devices were located on separate machines; otherwise, traffic between the master and slaves is transmitted at the operating system level and is not visible to a scanner. Each group of slaves was placed on a separate VMWare guest [11] to ensure that they would only see their network adapter. Each guest, which was assigned 512 MB RAM, hosted up to 50 slave devices. The VMWare guests used Windows XP Service Pack 2.

The distributed scanner for the virtual environment incorporated three computers (Table 4). One computer created a virtual router using IMUNES, a popular network simulator based on Unix FreeBSD [13]. The other two computers, which ran Windows XP Service Pack 2, were configured to communicate through the virtual router.

The traffic volumes generated during passive and active scanning of the physical and virtual environments are summarized in Table 5. Passive scanning produces traffic volumes that are within a few hundred bytes for the two environments. The active scanning results are also similar. The minor differences seen for the two environments may be attributed to lost packets and other network transmission errors. Therefore, it appears that the virtual envi-

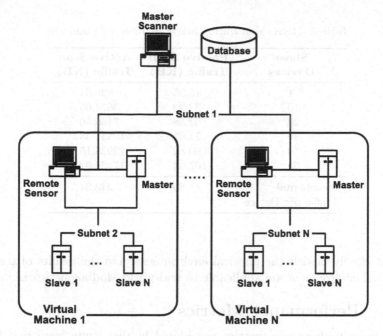

Figure 3. Virtual environment.

Table 4. Virtual environment components.

Host	Role	Hardware
Computer 1	Master Scanner and Database	Intel Xeon 3 GHz, 2 GB RAM
Computer 2	3 VMWare guests with Remote Sensor, Master and Slaves	Intel Xeon 3 GHz, 2 GB RAM
Computer 3	IMUNES virtual router	Pentium III 800 MHz, 768 MB RAM

Table 5. Scanning results for the physical and virtual environments.

	Subnets	Passive Scan KB Sent	Active Scan KB Sent
Physical	1	15.720	528.191
	2	31.911	1056.350
Virtual	1	15.952	528.511
	2	31.788	1057.051

Table 6.   Bytes sent during active and passive scanning.

Slave Devices	Passive Scan Traffic (KB)	Active Scan Traffic (KB)
1	15.95	528.51
10	33.23	3674.05
20	52.38	7166.56
30	71.63	10531.38
40	90.82	13928.15
50	107.64	17324.92
Incremental Traffic per Device	1.89	342.31

ronment closely models the physical environment, and the results of tests on the virtual environment are applicable to real-world Modbus networks.

5.2   Performance Metrics

The three performance metrics considered in this study were scalability, distributability and link utilization. The scanner is deemed to be scalable if the volume of scanning traffic increases linearly with the number of devices in a subnet. The scanner is distributable if the traffic increases linearly as the number of subnets grows given that each subnet has the same number of devices. Link utilization is measured as the fraction of the available bandwidth used by the scanner, i.e., bytes per second divided by link speed.

Scalability   The scalability of the distributed scanner was evaluated using the virtual environment. Traffic volumes generated during passive and active scanning were measured for subnets with numbers of devices ranging from 1 to 50.

Table 6 presents the results obtained for passive and active scanning. In both cases, the traffic volume grows linearly with the number of devices, which shows that the scanner is scalable. In the case of passive scanning, each additional device causes an average of 1.89 KB of incremental traffic to be sent from the remote sensor to the master scanner. For active scanning, each device adds an average of 342.31 KB of traffic.

Distributability   The scanner satisfies the distributability metric when the volume of traffic it generates grows linearly with the number of subnets. In the tests, the number of subnets ranged from 1 to 3 and the number of devices per subnet were 1, 5 and 10.

The results in Tables 7 and 8 show that the traffic volume generated during passive and active scanning is proportional to the number of subnets. Note that the relationship holds regardless of the number of devices per subnet.

Table 7. Traffic generated during passive scanning.

1 Subnet		2 Subnets		3 Subnets	
Slaves	KB Sent	Slaves	KB Sent	Slaves	KB Sent
1	15.952	2	31.788	3	46.992
5	23.817	10	47.320	15	69.645
10	33.360	20	66.140	30	100.930

Table 8. Traffic generated during active scanning.

1 Subnet		2 Subnets		3 Subnets	
Slaves	KB Sent	Slaves	KB Sent	Slaves	KB Sent
1	528.511	2	1057.051	3	1584.456
5	1926.827	10	3855.527	15	5778.640
10	3674.047	20	7347.702	30	11022.781

Link Utilization Link utilization measures the impact of scanner transmissions on network bandwidth. In the case of passive scanning, traffic is generated by three types of events: (i) when the remote sensor establishes a connection to the master scanner, (ii) when a new device is detected in the network, and (iii) when the function codes implemented in previously detected devices are being determined.

Table 9. Link utilization during passive scanning.

Link Speed	Connection	New Device	Update FCs
52 Kbps	25.38%	1.63%	2.54%
128 Kbps	10.31%	0.66%	1.03%
384 Kbps	3.44%	0.22%	0.34%
768 Kbps	1.72%	0.11%	0.17%
1.5 Mbps	0.88%	0.06%	0.09%
10 Mbps	0.13%	0.01%	0.01%

The results in Table 9 show that passive scanning uses only a small fraction of the available bandwidth after the initial connection phase. Since the initial connection occurs only during start up, the operator of the distributed scanner can plan for this situation.

To forestall link flooding, especially during the initial scanning of a network, the distributed scanner imposes a limit on the number of packets sent per second. Figure 4 shows a graphic of the number of packets transmitted during

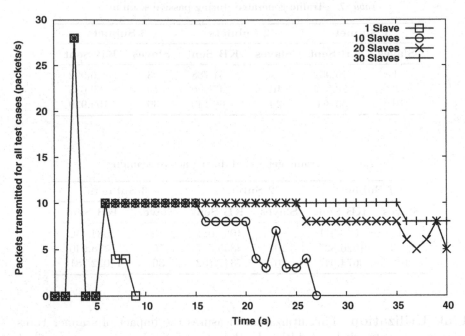

Figure 4.   Device discovery with limited transmissions.

passive scanning of a subnet with the number of slaves ranging from 1 to 30. As expected, there is an initial spike as new devices are detected. However, the limits imposed on the packet rate soon take effect, helping prevent excessive link utilization.

Table 10.   Link utilization during one active scanning step.

Link Speed	% Link Used
52 Kbps	3.32%
128 Kbps	1.35%
384 Kbps	0.45%
768 Kbps	0.22%
1.5 Mbps	0.12%
10 Mbps	0.02%

Unlike passive scanning, the active scanning process executes its scan steps following a schedule that prevents excessive link utilization. A typical scanning schedule spreads the active scan over a twenty-four hour period. Measurements show that a single scan step produces 1,725 bytes of traffic directed at the master scanner. Table 10 shows link utilization during active scanning with an unreasonably high rate of one scan step per second. In fact, active scanning consumes only 3.32% of the bandwidth even for a slow (52 Kbps) link.

6. Conclusions

Despite the scale, cost and significance of the oil and gas pipeline infrastructure, asset owners and operators do not currently have the means to remotely verify the integrity of the thousands of field devices that are vital to pipeline operations. Our distributed scanner addresses this need by remotely conducting stateful analyses of Modbus devices, verifying their configurations and assessing their integrity. Tests on a laboratory system and a virtual environment that models a small-scale industrial facility indicate that the distributed scanner is scalable, distributable and operates satisfactorily in low bandwidth environments. Equally important is the fact that the scanner is designed to have minimal impact on normal pipeline control operations. In particular, the scanner accommodates the delicate TCP/IP stacks of field devices and scanning activities can be scheduled based on network size and bandwidth.

Our future work will focus on testing the distributed scanner in simulated moderate-scale and large-scale pipeline control environments. A demonstration project involving an operating pipeline is also planned. We hope this work will spur the development of sophisticated situational awareness systems that provide control center operators with a comprehensive view of network topology along with detailed information about the configuration, status and integrity of field devices, communications links and control center software.

Acknowledgements

This work was partially supported by the Institute for Information Infrastructure Protection (I3P) at Dartmouth College, Hanover, New Hampshire, under Award 2003-TK-TX-0003 and Award 2006-CS-001-000001 from the U.S. Department of Homeland Security.

References

[1] Allen-Bradley, Logix5000 Controllers Common Procedures Programming Manual, Milwaukee, Wisconsin, 2004.

[2] Automation Direct, D2-DCM Data Communications Module User Manual (web2.automationdirect.com/static/manuals/d2dcm/d2dcm.pdf), 2003.

[3] Automation Direct, DL205 User Manual (Volumes 1 and 2) (www.auto mationdirect.com), 2003.

[4] J. Gonzalez, Security Strategies for Process Control Networks, Ph.D. Dissertation, Department of Computer Science, University of Tulsa, Tulsa, Oklahoma, 2006.

[5] J. Gonzalez and M. Papa, Passive scanning in Modbus networks, in *Critical Infrastructure Protection*, E. Goetz and S. Shenoi (Eds.), Springer, Boston, Massachusetts, pp. 175–187, 2007.

[6] Modbus IDA, Modbus Application Protocol Specification v1.1a, North Grafton, Massachusetts (www.modbus.org/specs.php), 2004.

[7] Modbus IDA, Modbus Messaging on TCP/IP Implementation Guide v1.0a, North Grafton, Massachusetts (www.modbus.org/specs.php), 2004.

[8] Modbus.org, Modbus over Serial Line Specification and Implementation Guide v1.0, North Grafton, Massachusetts (www.modbus.org/specs.php), 2002.

[9] ProSoft Technology, MVI56-MNET ControlLogix Platform Modbus TCP/IP Interface Module User Manual (www.prosoft-technology.com/content /download/2801/26796/file/mvi56_mnet_user_manual1.pdf), 2007.

[10] R. Shayto, Industry-Scale Distributed Scanners for Modbus Networks, Ph.D. Dissertation, Department of Computer Science, University of Tulsa, Tulsa, Oklahoma, 2007.

[11] VMWare, VMWare Server Virtual Machine Guide (www.vmware.com/pdf /server_vm_manual.pdf), 2007.

[12] D. Wimberger, Jamod – Java Modbus Implementation (jamod.sourceforge .net), 2004.

[13] M. Zec, Implementing a clonable network stack in the FreeBSD Kernel, *Proceedings of the 2003 USENIX Annual Technical Conference*, pp. 137–150, 2003.

Chapter 10

DESIGNING SECURITY-HARDENED MICROKERNELS FOR FIELD DEVICES

Jeffrey Hieb and James Graham

Abstract Distributed control systems (DCSs) play an essential role in the operation of critical infrastructures. Perimeter field devices are important DCS components that measure physical process parameters and perform control actions. Modern field devices are vulnerable to cyber attacks due to their increased adoption of commodity technologies and that fact that control networks are no longer isolated. This paper describes an approach for creating security-hardened field devices using operating system microkernels that isolate vital field device operations from untrusted network-accessible applications. The approach, which is influenced by the MILS and Nizza architectures, is implemented in a prototype field device. Whereas, previous microkernel-based implementations have been plagued by poor inter-process communication (IPC) performance, the prototype exhibits an average IPC overhead for protected device calls of 64.59 μs. The overall performance of field devices is influenced by several factors; nevertheless, the observed IPC overhead is low enough to encourage the continued development of the prototype.

Keywords: Distributed control systems, field devices, microkernels, security

1. Introduction

Field devices employed in distributed control systems (DCSs) connect sensors and actuators to control networks, providing remote measuring and control capabilities. Early DCSs were isolated proprietary systems with limited exposure to cyber threats. However, modern DCSs often engage commercial computing platforms and network technologies, which significantly increase their vulnerability to cyber attacks. While major disasters have thus far been averted, incidents such as the 2003 Slammer worm penetration of the Davis-Besse nuclear power plant network in Oak Harbor (Ohio) and the 2006 hacker

Please use the following format when citing this chapter:

Hieb, J. and Graham, J., 2008, in IFIP International Federation for Information Processing, Volume 290; *Critical Infrastructure Protection II*, eds. Papa, M., Shenoi, S., (Boston: Springer), pp. 129–140.

attack on a water treatment facility in Harrisburg (Pennsylvania) underscore the significance of the cyber threat.

Field devices are attractive targets for cyber attacks on control systems. Since these devices are used for measurement and control of physical systems, preventing these attacks is essential to securing DCSs and, by extension, the critical infrastructures assets they operate. Unlike early field devices, which were highly specialized systems, modern field devices use commercially-available hardware and software and can be attacked quite easily.

The need to secure field devices and their operating systems has been discussed by several researchers (see, e.g., [8, 10]). Guffy and Graham [2] have applied multiple independent layers of security (MILS) to creating security-hardened remote terminal units (RTUs). Hieb and Graham [6] have investigated techniques for creating security-hardened RTUs with reduced commercial kernels or microkernels. Hieb, Patel and Graham [7] have discussed security enhancements for DCSs involving protocol enhancements and a minimal kernel RTU (a reduced version of LyxnOS, a commercial RTOS).

This paper describes an approach for creating security-hardened field devices by applying elements of the MILS and Nizza microkernel-based security architectures. The approach protects field device operations and data by isolating them from less trustworthy application software that may be network accessible. Field device performance is an important issue because DCSs are much less tolerant to delays and jitter than traditional IT systems. To enhance performance, the approach leverages the inter-process communication (IPC) primitive provided by the microkernel. Preliminary results indicate that the observed IPC overhead is low enough to warrant further development of the security-hardened microkernel.

2.   Microkernel-Based Security Architectures

Multiple independent levels of security (MILS) [1] and Nizza [5] are two microkernel-based security architectures. The MILS architecture, which was developed for high assurance and high performance computing, is based on Rushby's separation kernel [9]; it enforces strict security and separation policies on data and processes within a single processor [14]. The Nizza architecture is based on the L4 microkernel and protects security critical code. The MILS and Nizza architectures are presented in Figures 1 and 2, respectively.

MILS and Nizza employ isolated partitions, each with its own protection domain, that allow software and data of different security levels or sensitivity to be decoupled from potentially less secure software. Secure compartmentalization of components and IPC allow the trusted computing base (TCB) to remain small, comprising only the kernel and security-critical code; application software resides outside the TCB. In the MILS architecture, this enables high assurance application layer reference monitors to be inserted between application software components [1, 4]. In Nizza, security-critical code is removed from commercial applications and placed in a protected isolated compartment,

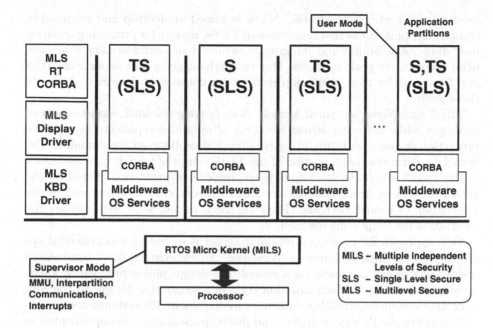

Figure 1. MILS architecture.

keeping the TCB small. Singaravelu and colleagues [13] describe an application of Nizza to the secure signing of email.

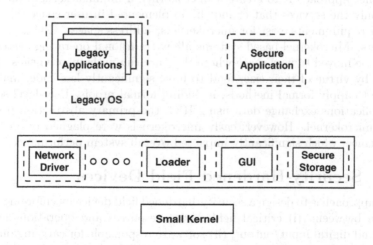

Figure 2. Nizza architecture.

MILS and Nizza primarily focus on protecting the confidentiality of data. MILS is designed for government and military systems that have multilevel security (MLS) requirements, where independent systems have historically been used for different security levels. Nizza is aimed at desktop and commodity computing applications that require small TCBs, mainly for protecting sensitive user data. Availability and integrity – rather than confidentiality – are the principal security goals in DCSs. Our research suggests that aspects of MILS and Nizza can be used to develop security-hardened field devices that satisfy these goals.

MILS and Nizza use small kernels that provide minimal services to user processes while enforcing strong isolation of system components in separate protection domains and supporting communication between the domains. The kernel constitutes a major portion of the TCB; thus, the reliability or assurance of the overall system largely depends on the level of protection offered by the kernel. Providing strong assurance requires rigorous system testing and/or the application of formal methods. These methods do not scale well and are the motivation for using a microkernel.

One approach for creating a minimal kernel is to reduce a commercial operating system such as Linux or Windows. Unfortunately, most commercial operating systems are based on a monolithic design philosophy, which yields large kernels with poor fault isolation [14]. In a monolithic design, all the core operating system functionality – memory management, file systems, access control, network stacks, device drivers and interrupt handling – is implemented in the kernel. Thus, all the software that implements this functionality is executed in privilege mode by the processor where it is not subject to any security or protection enforcement. Although it is possible to reduce kernel size, it is difficult to cut down a monolithic kernel to a size that permits formal methods to be applied.

Another approach is to create a microkernel, a minimal kernel that implements only the services that cannot be implemented in user space [9]. Three minimal requirements exist for microkernels: address spaces, IPC and unique identifiers. Microkernel-based systems allow traditional operating system services to be moved to user space where they are run without privileges. Microkernels, by virtue of their size, tend to have significantly less code, making it possible to apply formal methods, including formal proofs. User-level services and applications exchange data using IPC, the primary abstraction provided by the microkernel. However, early microkernels were plagued by poor IPC performance, which significantly impacted overall system performance.

3.   Security-Hardened Field Devices

Our approach is to design a security-hardened field device by enforcing strong isolation between: (i) critical field device resources and operations such as analog and digital input/output, (ii) software responsible for carrying out local control algorithms, and (iii) network-connected field device applications. The application code that implements network connectivity for field devices includes network drivers and protocol stacks; any exploitation of this code must not affect other components. This would enable critical field device code to continue to execute even when network components are attacked, resulting in graceful

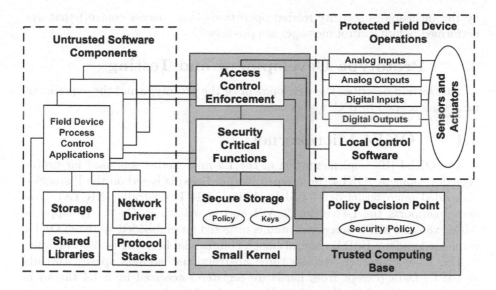

Figure 3. Security-hardened field device with a reduced kernel.

degradation as opposed to complete failure. Our approach also isolates security-critical data and code (e.g., cryptographic keys and cryptographic operations) in a separate compartment where they are protected from unauthorized access by a compromised network component. Field device integrity can be further enhanced by using a device-wide security policy enforcement component placed between the critical code and network accessible application code.

The partitioning is provided by a microkernel that supplies primitives for creating and enforcing the isolated compartments. Note that it is necessary to extract and isolate security-related code from control system software. For example, in a field device that supports security-enhanced DNP3 [7], the code that performs authentication and message integrity checking for DNP3 messages must be removed from the main body of code and placed in its own protected compartment. The isolation of security-related code has the added benefit of reducing the complexity of control applications, especially when security-related code has to be added or upgraded.

The architecture supports the enforcement of a security policy. The policy may include high-level specifications (e.g., RTU role-based access control [7]) or low-level device-specific requirements. Figure 3 presents a security-hardened field device with a reduced kernel architecture.

It is important to ensure that the security architecture does not impact field device performance, especially because industrial control systems have a very low tolerance for delay and jitter. IPC overhead (i.e., the time taken for IPC operations) can significantly affect field device performance because IPC is used extensively to implement communications between field device application code and protected operations. Device performance is also negatively impacted by the inclusion of security-related operations (e.g., access control) that are performed before control messages are processed.

## 4.		Prototype Development and Testing

This section describes the development of the prototype and the experimental results related to IPC performance.

### 4.1		OKL4 Microkernel

The OKL4 [12] implementation of the L4 microkernel was used for prototype development. OKL4 (from Open Kernel Labs) is based on the Pistachio-embedded microkernel developed by National ICT Australia (NICTA). The kernel supports the L4 version 2 API and is written in C++. It supports ARM, x86 and MIPS processors, and is targeted for embedded systems. OKL4 is released under a BSD license, although commercial licensing is also available.

The L4 microkernel provides three abstractions: address spaces, threads and IPC. Data (except from hardware registers) accessed by a L4 thread is contained in the thread's address space. An L4 address space is a partial mapping from virtual memory to physical memory. L4 threads are the basic unit of execution in L4; they share data by mapping parts of their address spaces to other address spaces. Each thread has a unique identifier (UID) and a register set that includes an instruction pointer and a stack pointer. Threads communicate with each other using IPC primitives provided by the L4 kernel; L4 IPC is synchronous and unbuffered. L4 supports the following basic IPC primitives:

- `receive()`: Wait for a message from a specific thread

- `reply_wait()`: Send a reply message to a client thread and wait for the next request

- `send()`: Send a message to a thread

- `wait()`: Wait for a message from a thread

An L4 system is composed of address spaces populated by threads that execute code in their address spaces. Each thread, identified by a thread UID, operates on data stored in its address space. The L4 kernel ensures that threads do not execute instructions in other address spaces or access data residing in other address spaces.

### 4.2		Hardware Platform

Gumstix [3] was selected as the hardware development platform. It provides a range of embeddable computers powered by ARM XScale processors and has been used in a number of commercial devices, indicating the platform may provide a path for possible commercialization. The Connex 400 was chosen for

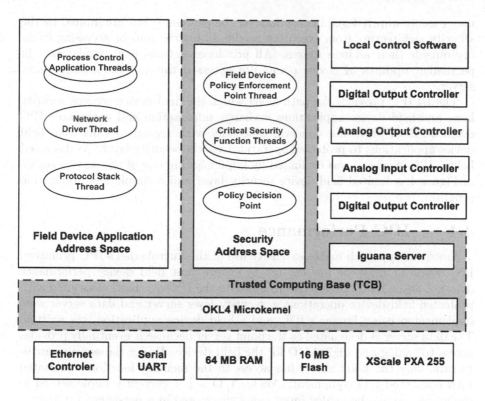

Figure 4. OKL4-based security-hardened field device.

the development. It has an XScale PXA 255 (32-bit) processor running at 400 MHz with 64 MB RAM and 16 MB of flash memory. In addition to the Gumstix motherboard, the development platform includes the Netstix and Console ST daughter boards. Netstix provides an Ethernet controller that can be used as a network interface for the field device. The console ST board provides two UART serial interfaces, one of which serves as a console interface.

4.3 System Development

The approach outlined in Section 3 was applied to the development of a prototype security-hardened field device using the OKL4 microkernel and the XScale PXA 255 processor. Figure 4 provides a high-level view of the development platform implementation. Protected field device components are implemented as "servers" as in Iguana [11], a transparent, lightweight interface to the L4 kernel included with OKL4. Each server is assigned its own address space where it is protected from other system components by the L4 kernel. The security functions and policy enforcement component are both part of a single security layer address space. This address space provides an interface (via IPC) to user applications and is located in the TCB. User applications may execute unprivileged instructions on the processor, but are limited by the security architecture from executing privileged instructions or accessing memory outside their address spaces. All privileged actions (e.g., reads) and, in particular, updates of device points are accessed through the security layer server.

The L4 IPC provides the path along which the field device servers, security layer and field device applications exchange information and cooperate. IPC overhead is of particular concern, especially with regard to calls from field device applications to protected operations via the security layer. As discussed below, IPC overhead was evaluated by implementing one of the servers shown in Figure 4, a limited field device security layer and a simple test application program.

4.4   IPC Performance

Since our approach makes extensive use of the microkernel's IPC primitive, IPC overhead must be low enough to ensure that field device performance does not affect DCS operations. To evaluate the IPC overhead associated with protected field device operations, a security layer server and data server were implemented using Iguana's IDL, and a field device application was written. The data server is designated as the point server because it eventually provides access to analog and digital I/O for the field device. Under the security architecture, only the point server has access to the memory locations associated with connected I/O equipment. Analog I/O is not currently implemented in the prototype, so the analog input value was stored in a persistent variable.

The primary goal was to determine only the IPC overhead of a call. The security layer server has access to all the field device servers, enabling it to enforce access control for these resources. It also creates address spaces for field device applications and maps them to needed resources. Thus, the security layer maintains control of the resources available to field device applications. Field device application threads are started by the security layer, which waits for an IPC request from a field device application.

Figure 5 shows an example case where the policy enforcement point thread receives a request to read an analog input. If the request is allowed, then the operation is performed and the result passed back to the user level thread that made the call. This involves several IPC operations as shown in Figure 5. Initially, the field device policy enforcement point thread and the field device point service call IPC_Wait (1) and (2) (IPC_Wait is a blocking IPC that waits for an incoming IPC message). IPC activity is initiated by the application thread IPC_Send to the policy enforcement point thread (3). When the send succeeds, the field device application thread calls IPC_Receive to wait for a response IPC (4). Next, the policy enforcement point security layer issues an IPC_Send to the appropriate field device server thread (5). The policy enforcement point thread then calls IPC_Receive to wait for a response from the server (6). The server responds with an IPC_Send to the policy enforcement point thread (7). Finally, the policy enforcement point thread calls IPC_Send

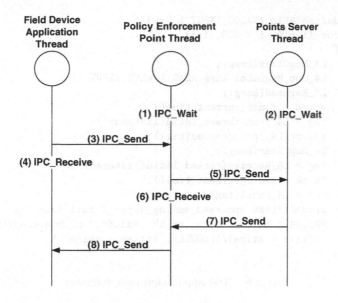

Figure 5. IPC operations involved in policy enforcement.

to return the response to the field device application thread that initiated the IPC sequence (8).

A code fragment from the test application is shown in Figure 6. The test loop iterates 300 times. Each loop instance records the start and finish times of a loop instance using the timer_current_time() call provided by Iguana. Iguana's time tick is one microsecond and the timer_current_time() returns the current tick count. Subtracting the final time from the start time gives the number of microseconds elapsed between (3) and (7). To ensure that protected operation calls are indeed reaching the point server and are being correctly returned, different values were written to and read from the point server. The observed results of the reads and writes were used to confirm that the field device application thread was retrieving values from the point server. No policy was enforced to ensure that only the IPC overhead was measured; the elapsed time between (3) and (8) represents the total IPC overhead of a protected call.

The elapsed time reported by the code fragment in Figure 6 also includes the overhead of the timer_current_time() call. A separate test program without the L4_IPC calls was used, leaving just the two calls to timer_current_time(). This program obtained a measure of the timer overhead, which was determined to be 59.63 μs. The time was rounded down to 59 μs when calculating the actual IPC overhead so that the rounding error is added to the IPC overhead.

The test program was run a total of four times on the development platform. The first value reported for each run was more than 1,000 μs, but the remaining sample times were closely grouped around 123 μs. The higher elapsed time for the first measurement of each run is very likely because the kernel performs a

```
define READ_ANALOG_INPUT_1 0x01
for (i = 0; i < 300; i++)
{
  L4_MsgClear(&msg);
  L4_Set_MsgLabel(&msg,READ_ANALOG_INPUT_1);
  L4_MsgLoad(&msg);
  stime = timer_current_time();
  tag = L4_Send(thread_l4tid(listener));
  assert(L4_IpcSucceeded(tag));
  L4_MsgClear(&msg);
  tag = L4_Receive(thread_l4tid(listener));
  ftime = timer_current_time();
  val = L4_Label(tag);
  printf("test app read_analog_input_1 call took  \%"
  PRIu64 " milliseconds, or \%" PRIu64 " microseconds\n",
  ((ftime - stime)/1000ULL), (ftime - stime) );
}
```

Figure 6. Test application code fragment.

one-time initialization for thread IPCs. Consequently, the first recorded time was dropped from the performance calculations.

Table 1. IPC overhead for protected calls.

Description	Value
Average reported elapsed time	123.19 μs
Standard deviation	0.784908
95% confidence interval	0.002
Timer overhead	59 μs
Actual average IPC overhead for protected operation call	64.19 μs

A total of 500 samples were selected from the remaining times. The results are shown in Table 1. The mean value is 123.19 μs with a standard deviation of 0.785 and a 95% confidence interval of 0.002. This value includes the 59 μs of timer overhead. After subtracting the timer overhead, the actual IPC overhead for the entire sequence shown in Figure 6 is 64.19 μs. Since L4 IPC calls are synchronous and there are a total of four sends in the sequence, the observed IPC overhead is distributed across four IPC send-receive pairs. Assuming that the overhead is evenly distributed, a single IPC from one L4 thread to another takes an average of 16.05 μs. These times are significantly better than the 100 μs reported for first-generation microkernels and are low enough to encourage further prototype development.

5. Conclusions

Embedded operating systems used in field devices provide little, if any, security functionality. This exposes industrial control systems and the critical infrastructure assets they operate to a variety of cyber attacks. Creating security-hardened field devices with microkernels that isolate vital monitoring and control functions from untrusted applications is an attractive solution. This strategy also produces a small TCB, which reduces vulnerabilities and facilitates the application of formal methods. Unlike most microkernel-based implementations for field devices that have been plagued by poor IPC performance, the prototype constructed using the OKL4 microkernel running on a 400 MHz XScale PXA 255 microprocessor exhibits low IPC overhead (64.59 μs) for protected device calls. While the system is not yet complete and other performance issues remain to be considered, the low IPC overhead is encouraging enough to warrant the continued development of the prototype.

References

[1] J. Alves-Foss, C. Taylor and P. Oman, A multi-layered approach to security in high assurance systems, *Proceedings of the Thirty-Seventh Annual Hawaii International Conference on System Sciences*, pp. 302–311, 2004.

[2] B. Guffy and J. Graham, Evaluation of MILS and Reduced Kernel Security Concepts for SCADA Remote Terminal Units, Technical Report TR-ISRL-06-02, Intelligent Systems Research Laboratory, Department of Computer Engineering and Computer Science, University of Louisville, Louisville, Kentucky, 2006.

[3] Gumstix, Products, Portola Valley, California (www.gumstix.com/prod ucts.html).

[4] N. Hanebutte, P. Oman, M. Loosbrock, A. Holland, W. Harrison and J. Alves-Foss, Software mediators for transparent channel control in unbounded environments, *Proceedings of the Sixth Annual IEEE SMC Information Assurance Workshop*, pp. 201–206, 2005.

[5] H. Hartig, M. Hohmuth, N. Feske, C. Helmuth, A. Lackorzynski, F. Mehnert and M. Peter, The Nizza secure-system architecture, *Proceedings of the International Conference on Collaborative Computing: Networking, Applications and Worksharing*, 2005.

[6] J. Hieb and J. Graham, Security-enhanced remote terminal units for SCADA networks, *Proceedings of Nineteenth ISCA International Conference on Computer Applications in Industry and Engineering*, pp. 271–276, 2006.

[7] J. Hieb, S. Patel and J. Graham, Security enhancements for distributed control systems, in *Critical Infrastructure Protection*, E. Goetz and S. Shenoi (Eds.), Springer, Boston, Massachusetts, pp. 133–146, 2007.

[8] V. Igure, S. Laughter and R. Williams, Security issues in SCADA networks, *Computers and Security*, vol. 25(7), pp. 498–506, 2006.

[9] J. Liedtke, On micro-kernel construction, *ACM SIGOPS Operating Systems Review*, vol. 29(5), pp. 237–250, 1995.

[10] A. Miller, Trends in process control systems security, *IEEE Security and Privacy*, vol. 3(5), pp. 57–60, 2005.

[11] National ICT Australia, Project Iguana, Eveleigh, Australia (ertos.nicta.com.au/software/kenge/iguana-project/latest).

[12] Open Kernel Labs, Products, Chicago, Illinois (www.ok-labs.com).

[13] L. Singaravelu, C. Pu, H. Hartig and C. Helmuth, Reducing TCB complexity for security-sensitive applications: Three case studies, *ACM SIGOPS Systems Review*, vol. 40(4), pp. 161–174, 2006.

[14] A. Tanenbaum, J. Herder and H. Bos, Can we make operating systems reliable and secure? *IEEE Computer*, vol. 39(5), pp. 44–51, 2006.

Chapter 11

COMBATING MEMORY CORRUPTION ATTACKS ON SCADA DEVICES

Carlo Bellettini and Julian Rrushi

Abstract   Memory corruption attacks on SCADA devices can cause significant disruptions to control systems and the industrial processes they operate. However, despite the presence of numerous memory corruption vulnerabilities, few, if any, techniques have been proposed for addressing the vulnerabilities or for combating memory corruption attacks. This paper describes a technique for defending against memory corruption attacks by enforcing logical boundaries between potentially hostile data and safe data in protected processes. The technique encrypts all input data using random keys; the encrypted data is stored in main memory and is decrypted according to the principle of least privilege just before it is processed by the CPU. The defensive technique affects the precision with which attackers can corrupt control data and pure data, protecting against code injection and arc injection attacks, and alleviating problems posed by the incomparability of mitigation techniques. An experimental evaluation involving the popular Modbus protocol demonstrates the feasibility and efficiency of the defensive technique.

Keywords: SCADA systems, memory corruption attacks, Modbus protocol

1.   Introduction

This paper describes the design and implementation of a run-time system for defending against memory corruption attacks on SCADA devices. SCADA systems are widely used to operate critical infrastructure assets such as the electric power grid, oil and gas facilities, and water treatment plants. Recent vulnerability analyses of SCADA protocol implementations have identified several memory corruption vulnerabilities such as buffer overflows and faulty mappings between protocol elements (handles and protocol data unit addresses) and main memory addresses [8, 27]. These include [19, 40] for Inter Control Center Protocol (ICCP) [20, 42] for OLE for Process Control (OPC) [21], respectively.

Please use the following format when citing this chapter:

Bellettini, C. and Rrushi, J., 2008, in IFIP International Federation for Information Processing, Volume 290; *Critical Infrastructure Protection II*, eds. Papa, M., Shenoi, S., (Boston: Springer), pp. 141–156.

Very few defensive techniques have been devised specifically for SCADA systems. Consequently, most of the techniques discussed in this paper are drawn from efforts related to traditional computer systems. All these techniques, which the exception of pointer taintedness detection [10, 11], focus on protecting control data (e.g., saved instruction pointers, saved frame pointers and pointers in various control tables) from corruption. The techniques do not protect against attacks that corrupt non-control data, also called "pure data," which includes user identification data, configuration data and decision-making data [12]. Furthermore, the techniques only protect against pre-defined attack techniques. This problem, which is referred to as the "incomparability of defensive techniques" [34], is stated as follows: for any two categories of techniques A and B there are attacks prevented by A that are not prevented by B, and there are attacks prevented by B that are not prevented by A. The approach described in this paper overcomes the limitations of current defensive techniques in terms of attack vector coverage. Also, it protects against control data attacks as well as pure data attacks.

We have evaluated our defensive technique using a Modbus protocol [26] implementation running under Linux. In particular, we employed FreeMOD-BUS [44] running on a Debian machine (OS kernel 2.6.15) with 1024 MB main memory and an IA-32 processor with a clock speed 1.6 GHz. The Modbus client and server ran on the same physical machine and communicated via a null-modem cable between /dev/ttyS1 and /dev/ttyS0. The experimental results indicate that the defensive technique is both feasible and efficient for real-time operation in industrial control environments.

2.   Related Work

Simmons, *et al.* [38] have proposed code mutation as a technique for detecting buffer overflow exploits in SCADA systems before the exploits are executed. The technique involves altering SCADA executable code without changing the logic of the original algorithms. Code mutation is one of the first approaches proposed for protecting SCADA systems from memory corruption attacks. The other techniques discussed below were originally developed for traditional computer systems.

Instruction set randomization [6, 23] counters attacks that hijack the execution flow of a targeted program in order to execute injected shellcode. This defensive technique prevents the injected shellcode from being executed by encrypting program instructions with a random key; the encrypted code is loaded into memory and is decrypted just before it is processed by the CPU.

Kc, *et al.* [23] randomize ELF [40] executables by extending the objcopy utility to create a binary by XORing the original instructions with a 32-bit key. This key is then embedded in the header of the executable. When a new process is generated from a randomized binary, the operating system extracts the key from the header and stores it in the process control block. After the process is scheduled for execution, the key is loaded into a special register of the CPU via a privileged instruction; the key is then XORed with the instructions before they are processed by the CPU. This approach protects against attacks on remote services, but not from local attacks. Also, it has a considerable performance cost and does not handle dynamic libraries. In fact, because a key is associated with a single process, it is difficult to use dynamic libraries whose code is shared by different processes. A solution is to copy the shared library code to a memory area where it could be XORed with the key of the corresponding process; this enables each process to create and use a private copy of the shared code. However, the memory consumption is high and the strategy conflicts with the rationale for having shared libraries.

Barrantes, *et al.* [6] have developed the RISE tool that generates a pseudo-random key whose length is equal to the total number of bytes of the program instructions. The instructions are XORed with the key when they are loaded into the emulator and are decrypted right before being executed. When a process needs to execute shared library code, the operating system makes a private copy of the code, encrypts it and stores the encrypted code in the virtual memory assigned to the process. Thus, the use of shared libraries consumes a large amount of main memory. RISE is based on `valgrind` [29] and adds a latency of just 5% to a program running under `valgrind`. Instruction set randomization cannot prevent control data attacks or pure data attacks that operate in a `return-into-libc` manner because these attacks do not use injected shell-code [28].

The instruction set randomization technique can be subverted. Sovarel, *et al.* [39] have demonstrated the efficiency of incremental key guessing where an attacker can distinguish between incorrect and correct key byte guesses. The incremental key guessing exploit injects either a return instruction (which is one byte long for the IA-32 processor) or a jump instruction (two bytes long) encrypted with one or two guessed bytes, respectively. If an attacker employs a return instruction in a stack overflow exploit [1], the stack is overflowed so that the saved frame pointer is preserved. The saved instruction pointer is then modified to point to the encrypted return instruction that is preliminarily injected and the original saved instruction pointer is stored next to it. If the guess of the encryption byte is correct, the CPU executes the injected return instruction and the vulnerable function returns normally; if the guess is incorrect, the targeted process crashes.

The subversion technique requires knowledge of the saved frame pointer and the saved instruction pointer. An attacker may also inject a short jump with a -2 offset. If the attacker's guess of the two encryption bytes is correct, the jump instruction is executed and proceeds to jump back to itself, causing an infinite loop; an incorrect guess causes the targeted process to crash. After successfully guessing the first byte or the first two bytes, the attacker changes the position of the byte(s) to be guessed and proceeds as in the previous step. Because a failed key guess causes the targeted process to crash, incremental subversion is possible only for programs that are encrypted with the same key every time they execute. Incremental subversion is also applicable to programs whose forked children are encrypted with the same key, in which case the technique is directed at a child process.

PointGuard [15] XORs pointers with a 32-bit key when they are stored in main memory, and XORs them again with the same key right before they are loaded into CPU registers. The encryption key is generated randomly at load time and is kept secret. An attacker cannot corrupt a pointer with a value that is useful (from the attack point of view) as the encryption key is not known. This is because the corrupted pointer is decrypted before being loaded into a CPU register; thus, it will not accomplish the attacker's task [15]. However, PointGuard does not counter injected shellcode. Also, uncorrupted bytes in a partially-corrupted pointer are decrypted correctly. This means that an attacker can corrupt the least significant byte of a pointer in a process running on a Little Endian architecture and then employ a brute force technique to land in a memory location where shellcode or a program instruction is stored. The subversion may be carried out on any architecture by exploiting a format bug [18, 30, 37] to corrupt any one byte of a target pointer [2].

StackGuard [16] places a load-time-generated random value or a string terminating value (called a "canary") on the stack next to the saved instruction pointer. The integrity of the canary is checked upon function return. If the original value of the canary has been modified, a stack overflow has occurred, the incident is reported in a log file and program execution is aborted [16].

StackShield [43] creates a separate stack to hold a copy of each saved instruction pointer. It saves a copy of the saved instruction pointer at function call and copies the saved value back to the saved instruction pointer location at function return; this ensures that the function correctly returns to its original caller. However, Bulba and Kil3r [9] have shown that StackShield can be bypassed by corrupting the saved frame pointer using a frame pointer overwrite attack [24]. Also, StackGuard can be bypassed by attack techniques that do not need to pass through a canary in order to corrupt the saved instruction pointer of a vulnerable function. Examples include heap overflows, longjmp overflows, format strings and data/function pointer corruption.

The StackGuard limitation can be addressed by XORing a saved instruction pointer with a random canary at function call and at function return. The attack fails if the saved instruction pointer is corrupted without also modifying the corresponding canary. When a function completes its execution, XORing the canary with the corrupted instruction pointer will not yield a pointer to the memory location defined by the attacker.

FormatGuard [14] is a countermeasure against format string attacks. It compares the number of actual parameters passed to a format function against the number of formal parameters. If the number of actual parameters is less than the number of formal parameters, FormatGuard reports the fact as an incident in a log file and aborts program execution. Robins [35] has proposed libformat, a library that aborts program execution if it calls a format function with a format string that is writable and contains a %n format directive.

Baratloo, *et al.* [5] utilize the `libsafe` library to intercepts calls to functions that are known to cause buffer overflows and replace each function with one that implements the same functionality, but with buffer overflows restricted to the current stack frame. Note that `libsafe` does not protect against heap overflows or attacks that corrupt data/function pointers. With regard to format string vulnerabilities, `libsafe` rejects dangerous format directives such as `%n` that attempt to corrupt saved instruction pointers. Baratloo, *et al.* [4] have created the `libverify` library that offers the same kind of protection as StackShield. The main difference is in the way the copy of a saved instruction pointer is compared with the saved pointer on the stack at function return.

Krennmair [25] has developed ContraPolice for protecting against heap overflows [3, 13, 17, 22]. ContraPolice places a random canary before and after the memory region to be protected. Integrity checks are performed on the canary before exiting from a function that copies data to the protected memory region. Program execution is aborted when the canary indicates corruption.

The PaX kernel patch [33] for Linux employs non-executable pages for IA-32 to make the stack and heap non-executable [33]. Page privilege flags are used to mark pages as non-executable; a page fault is generated when a process accesses such a page. PaX then checks if a data access occurred or the CPU tried to execute an instruction (in which case the program execution is aborted). PaX performs well against shellcode injection, but not against attacks structured in a `return-into-libc` manner.

The defensive techniques discussed in this section focus on a few attacks, often on a single attack. None of the techniques can protect against all attacks that exploit memory corruption vulnerabilities, which raises the issue of incomparability of mitigation techniques. To the best of our knowledge, the only approach capable of protecting a process from control data and pure data attacks is pointer taintedness detection [10, 11]. A pointer is considered to be tainted when its value is obtained via user input or is derived from user input. If a pointer is tainted during the execution of a process, an attack is underway and a response should be triggered. Pointer taintedness detection is a effective technique, but it requires substantial changes to the underlying hardware to implement its memory model.

3.   Countering Memory Corruption Attacks

The computer security community has traditionally relied on patching memory corruption vulnerabilities to combat control data and pure data attacks. However, software patches only address known vulnerabilities; the patched systems would still be exposed to attacks that exploit vulnerabilities that exist, but that have not been identified or disclosed. Also, patching SCADA systems often degrades their real-time performance characteristics.

Intrusion detection and response systems are often used for attack prevention. The problem is that an intrusion detection system generally performs its analysis and raises alarms after an intrusion has been attempted. Some modern intrusion detection systems (e.g., Snort [36]) perform real-time intrusion prevention tasks. Similarly, a fast proactive defense mechanism could be used to block the exploitation of memory vulnerabilities.

Building attack requirement trees for known attacks that target memory corruption vulnerabilities can assist in developing defensive mechanisms. An attack requirement tree is a structured means for specifying conditions that must hold for an attack to be feasible [7]. The root node of the tree is the attack itself, while every other node is a requirement (or sub-requirement) for the attack. Internal nodes are either AND nodes or OR nodes. An AND node is true when all its child nodes are true; an OR node is true if if any one of its child nodes is true.

We use an attack requirement tree corresponding to a specific attack as a pattern for characterizing the family of memory corruption attacks. The example attack we consider smashes a buffer on a stack to corrupt the saved instruction pointer and return execution to injected shellcode. The attack requirement tree highlights two issues:

- The main instrument employed to satisfy one or more critical nodes in an attack requirement tree is the input data fed to a targeted process. In our example, the corrupting value of the saved instruction pointer and the shellcode injected into the address space of a targeted process constitute the input data (supplied by the attacker).

- The nodes are true because the attacker has full control of the input data in the address space of the targeted process. In our example, an attacker defines the content of shellcode and the shellcode is stored in memory in exactly the way the attacker defined it. Furthermore, an attacker can define the value that overwrites the saved instruction pointer. Thus, during a memory corruption attack, a saved instruction pointer is overwritten by the value defined by the attacker.

Obviously, it is not possible to eliminate the attack instrument. However, it is feasible to eliminate the control that an attacker has on the content of the input data stored in main memory. The idea is to prevent the attacker from being able to define the bytes stored in memory. As shown in Figure 1, the attacker develops shellcode that spawns a shell (Figure 1(a)) and feeds it along with other attack data to a targeted process. Figure 1(b) shows the shellcode stored in the main memory of a Little Endian Intel machine in the manner defined by the attacker. Under these conditions, an attacker could hijack program execution to the injected shellcode and cause its execution. If users, including malicious users, specify the content of input data while it is within the process that defines the content stored in main memory, an attacker cannot control the content of input data stored in main memory.

A process should store input data in main memory so that transformed data is converted to its original form before it is used. Figure 1(c) presents the shell-spawning shellcode encrypted in a stream cipher mode using the key 0xd452e957 and stored in main memory as ciphertext. The input data stored in main memory is different from the input data defined by an attacker at

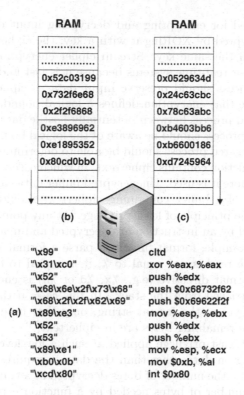

RAM

....
....
0x52c03199
0x732f6e68
0x2f2f6868
0xe3896962
0xe1895352
0x80cd0bb0
....
....

RAM

....
....
0x0529634d
0x24c63cbc
0x78c63abc
0xb4603bb6
0xb6600186
0xd7245964
....
....

(b)   (c)

(a)

```
"\x99"              cltd
"\x31\xc0"          xor %eax, %eax
"\x52"              push %edx
"\x68\x6e\x2f\x73\x68"   push $0x68732f62
"\x68\x2f\x2f\x62\x69"   push $0x69622f2f
"\x89\xe3"          mov %esp, %ebx
"\x52"              push %edx
"\x53"              push %ebx
"\x89\xe1"          mov %esp, %ecx
"\xb0\x0b"          mov $0xb, %al
"\xcd\x80"          int $0x80
```

Figure 1. Potentially hostile data sanitized by stream cipher encryption.

the moment the attack data is provided as input to a targeted process. If the attacker hijacks control to the transformed shellcode, it is highly likely that the CPU will execute it, but the machine instructions in the transformed shellcode would not be recognized.

This situation also holds for a saved instruction pointer. An attacker is able to define (in the input data) the address of injected shellcode as the value that overwrites an instruction pointer saved on the stack. However, if a targeted process transforms the input data before storing it in memory, then the saved instruction pointer is overwritten with the transformed value, not with the address of the injected shellcode that the attacker intended. Consequently, while it is likely that execution will be hijacked, control will not pass to the injected shellcode. This technique applies to all attack techniques that exploit memory vulnerabilities by corrupting control data or pure data.

4.   Proposed Approach

The principal idea behind enforcing logical boundaries on potentially hostile data is to encrypt input data before it enters the address space of a protected process. All the data read from sockets, environment variables, files and standard input devices are encrypted and then stored in main memory. The stream cipher mode is used for encrypting and decrypting input data. Specifically, input data is encrypted by XORing it with a key; the ciphertext is decrypted by XORing it with the same key. Stream cipher encryption using the XOR operation is ideal for real-time systems because it is fast and efficient.

A protected process should preserve input data as ciphertext throughout its execution. Note that encryption defines a logical boundary in the address space of a protected process between potentially hostile data and control/pure data. A protected process should be aware of the logical boundaries of data. In particular, the protected process should be able to determine if a buffer needed by a machine instruction contains ciphertext, in which case, the buffer data has to be decrypted before it is used. Unencrypted buffer data can be used directly.

The decryption of a buffer containing ciphertext should be performed in compliance with the principle of least privilege. At any point in time, only the data items required by an instruction are decrypted and made available to the instruction. For example, format functions parse a format string one byte at a time. If the byte read is not equal to %, it is copied to output; otherwise, it means that a format directive (e.g., %x, %d or %n) is encountered and the related value is retrieved from the stack. In this case, if the format function needs to parse a byte of the format string, only that byte is decrypted and made available; the remaining bytes are in ciphertext.

The principle of least privilege applied at such a low level prevents a function from operating on data other than the data it requires. To alleviate the performance penalty, the number of bytes decrypted at a time could be slightly greater than the number of bytes needed by a function – but such an action should be performed only if it is deemed safe. The plaintext version of data should not be preserved after an operation completes; otherwise, plaintext attack data (e.g., shellcode) could be exploited in an attack. When a protected process has to copy or move input data to another memory location, the data is stored as ciphertext as well. Data created by concatenating strings, where at least one string is stored as ciphertext, should also be preserved as ciphertext.

Each process generates a random sequence of bytes that is used as a key for encrypting/decrypting input data. This key is generated before the main function is executed. Child processes also randomly generate their own keys immediately after being forked but before their program instructions are executed. Thus, parent and child processes generate and use their own keys.

A child process that needs to access ciphertext data stored and handled by its parent process uses the key of the parent process. To counter brute force attacks, the lifetime of a key should extend over the entire period of process execution. A brute force attack against a non-forking process or against a parent process would require the key to be guessed correctly at the first attempt. If this is not done, the protected process crashes and a new key is generated the next time the process is created. The same situation holds for child processes: if the key of the targeted child process is not guessed during the first try, the process crashes and a new child process with a new key is forked when the attacker attempts to reconnect to the parent process. A brute force attack fails because the new child process generates and uses a new random key.

A key is stored within the address space of the process that created it and is available to the process throughout its execution. Care should be taken to guarantee the integrity of the key when it is stored and loaded from memory.

By encrypting process input, intervention occurs at two vital points of an attack. The first point is when attack data is stored in buffers to execute various types of buffer overflow attacks that corrupt control data or pure data. The second point is when attack data is stored in main memory.

Without the encryption key, an attacker cannot place the correct data required to execute a buffer overflow attack. In addition, the attacker cannot inject valid shellcode because it would have to be in ciphertext (like the original shellcode). In the case of a format string attack, due to the application of the least privilege principle for decryption, when a format function processes a directive (e.g., %n), the bytes to be stored and their starting memory location are not available. Thus, the attacker loses the ability define a value and the address where the value is to be stored.

The second point of intervention is when attack data is stored in memory. This is when an attacker, who has corrupted control data or pure data, could cause execution to return to shellcode. It is also at this point that an attacker could inject data into the stack by passing it as an argument to a function. This is referred to as arc injection (a `return-into-libc` type of attack). Preserving potentially malicious data as ciphertext in main memory thus eliminates the ability of an attacker to use shellcode or to perform arc injection.

Note that an intervention at the first point prevents an attacker from transferring control to the desired memory location. Therefore, an intervention at the second point can be considered to be redundant. Nevertheless, we include it in the specification of our protection strategy as a second line of defense.

5. Experimental Results

Our experimental evaluation of the protection technique employed a Modbus control system. Modbus is an application-layer protocol that enables SCADA devices to communicate according to a master-slave model using various types of buses and networks. Modbus was chosen for the implementation because it is popular, simple and representative of industrial control protocols. We instrumented the code of FreeMODBUS, a publicly available Modbus implementation, to evaluate the feasibility and efficiency of the protection technique. Several vulnerabilities were introduced into FreeMODBUS in order to execute memory corruption attacks.

The implementation of the defensive technique involved kernel domain intervention and user domain intervention. Kernel domain intervention requires system calls to be extended so that all input data to protected processes is encrypted. The second intervention takes place in the user domain, where additional instructions are introduced to Modbus programs to enable them to access and use the encrypted information.

5.1   Kernel Domain Intervention

Logical boundaries on potentially hostile data are enforced by having the operating system encrypt all input data delivered to protected processes. This functionality is best implemented as a kernel domain activity that ensures that input data is encrypted as soon as it is generated. Our approach involved extending system calls responsible for reading data (e.g., read(), pread(), readv(), recv(), recvfrom() and recvmsg()).

The extension incorporates an additional parameter (encryption key) for each system call, which is used to encrypt the input data passed to a protected process. Thus, when a Modbus process needs a service from the operating system, it fills CPU registers with system call parameters, one of which is encryption key. Next, the Modbus process generates an interrupt and control is transferred to the procedure at the system call kernel location, which checks the system call number, uses it to index the system call table, and issues the system call. Each extended system call retrieves input data and encrypts it with the key received from the calling process in the user domain.

5.2   User Domain Intervention

A protected Modbus process in the user domain always receives its input data as ciphertext; therefore, it should be provided with the appropriate mechanisms to use and protect input data. These tasks may be performed at compile time using an *ad hoc* GCC extension module, or by manually instrumenting Modbus program source code before compiling it, or by employing a binary rewriting tool to insert additional instructions in a Modbus binary. Our FreeMODBUS experiments implemented the first two methods.

Modbus data items include discrete inputs (1-bit read-only data from the I/O system), coils (1-bit data alterable by Modbus processes), input registers (16-bit read-only data provided by the I/O system), and holding registers (16-bit data alterable by Modbus processes). These items are stored in the main memory of Modbus devices and addressed using values from 0 to 65,535.

A Modbus implementation generally maintains a pre-mapping table that maps a data item address used by the Modbus protocol to the actual location in memory where the data item is stored. In general, Modbus instructions that work on potentially hostile data include those that consult the pre-mapping table and those that read from or write to the memory area holding Modbus data items. Thus, it is relatively easy to identify points in a Modbus program where instrumentation instructions should be inserted. Note that this is much more difficult to accomplish in traditional computer systems.

The task of spotting potentially malicious data is essentially a taintedness tracking problem. This makes our approach specific to implementations of control protocols such as Modbus. The main GCC executable named gcc is a driver program that calls a preprocessor and compiler named cc1, an assembler named as, and a linker named collect2. GCC transforms the preprocessed source code into an abstract syntax tree representation, then converts it into a register transfer language (RTL) representation, before it generates assembly code for the target platform [31]. A GCC extension module instruments Modbus program code by adding additional assembly language instructions during assembly code generation. The CPU registers are visible at this stage; therefore, it is easier to repair the assembly instructions that store (on the stack) the contents of the CPU register that holds the encryption key in order to make that register available for some other use. Therefore, the additional assembly instructions that the GCC extension module inserts into the final Modbus assembly file implement the protection technique without affecting the computations of a protected Modbus program.

Assembly instructions are inserted at several points in a program. For example, the GCC extension module inserts in the .init section assembly instructions that call an interface to the kernel's random number generator that provides the 32-bit key. These instructions read four bytes from the file /dev/urandom. The .init section is appropriate for this task because it usually holds instructions for process initialization [40]. GCC also inserts assembly instructions in .init that issue the mmap() system call to allocate mapped memory from the Linux kernel.

Other instructions are inserted to store keys at the correct memory locations and to invoke mprotect() to designate these memory locations as read-only. Instructions that generate and store a key are also inserted in the process that forks child processes; these instructions are positioned after the child process is forked but before its original instructions are executed.

During our experiments we considered all Modbus data items (including input registers and discrete inputs) as potentially hostile; consequently, they were stored in memory as ciphertext. Just before Modbus instructions processed data items, their encrypted versions were copied to a mapped memory region, where they were decrypted in place. We refer to this portion of memory as the "temporary storage area." Note that the GCC extension module inserts instructions in .init that issue a call to mmap() to allocate the mapped memory used as the temporary storage area, and then issue a call to mprotect() to designate the memory as non-executable.

The GCC extension module thus generates additional assembly language instructions for every function that operates on potentially hostile data. These additional instructions are interleaved with the assembly instructions that implement the original functions. The additional instructions copy the ciphertext data to the temporary storage area and decrypt portions of the ciphertext as and when function instructions need them. Some of the original assembly instructions are modified in order to obtain data from the temporary storage area rather than from the original locations. The GCC extension module also inserts assembly instructions in the .fini section. These instructions, which are executed at process termination, issue a call to munmap() to remove previous memory mappings.

Another technique for implementing defensive capabilities in a Modbus program is to instrument its source code. In FreeMODBUS, C instructions that operate on potentially hostile data are identified and extra C code for decrypting ciphertext is introduced. Likewise, additional C code is included for generating keys and implementing the temporary storage area.

5.3   Performance Overhead

When analyzing the performance costs involved in enforcing logical boundaries on potentially hostile data, we noticed that most of the overhead is due to constant invocations of the mmap() and mprotect() system calls. However, these calls can be eliminated if special care is taken when storing keys. Using mmap() and mprotect() calls to designate the temporary storage area as non-executable is reasonable only if they do not affect the real-time performance of the Modbus device being protected.

One question that arises relates to the feasibility of encrypting input data at the kernel level. Since our technique already compiles a program and makes it pass the encryption key to a system call, the program could directly encrypt data returned from the system call. In other words, there is no need for the kernel to perform the initial encryption of input data.

Our motivation for performing input data encryption at the kernel level is to reduce the memory consumption incurred by the protection strategy. System calls as implemented in most operating systems read input data and store them in internal buffers. Therefore, an encryption extension of a system call would encrypt input data in place so that it does not consume additional memory. If a process were to encrypt input data in the user domain, then it certainly would not place it directly in the destination buffer. This is exactly what our technique tries to avoid. Consequently, a protected process would have to allocate an additional buffer, place the input data there, encrypt it and copy the encrypted data to the original destination. If the process receiving input data from a system call were to encrypt the data itself, it would consume additional memory while introducing the overhead of executing extra instructions.

The computational overhead depends on the number of data items in Modbus device memory, the number of data items incorporated in Modbus request frames in typical transactions, and the number of instructions that operate on input data. The instruction counter is a CPU performance equation variable [32] that is incremented by our protection technique. In fact, our technique requires additional instructions to be inserted in Modbus code. The number of instructions that perform basic boundary enforcement operations such as generating, storing and deleting keys or creating and releasing the temporary storage area is constant for all protected processes. The number of instructions that transfer data to the temporary storage area and decrypt them there depends on how often a Modbus protected process operates on ciphertext.

The number of clock cycles per instruction (CPI) and the clock cycle time depend on the CPU architecture. Enforcing logical boundaries on potentially hostile data in a Modbus process has no affect on the pipeline CPI, but it causes an overhead in the memory system CPI and contributes to the miss rate because it uses additional memory. The performance overhead introduced by enforcing logical boundaries on potentially malicious data during the execution of Modbus processes varies from 0.8% for transactions with typical frames that request a few data items to 2% for transactions with full 253-byte protocol data units. Furthermore, our protection technique does not rely on complementary defensive techniques such as address space randomization or StackGuard. Consequently our technique avoids the performance penalties introduced by operational security mechanisms.

6. Conclusions

Control data and pure data attacks can be countered by preserving input data as ciphertext in main memory and by instrumenting SCADA device code to decrypt potentially malicious data before processing according to the principle of least privilege. Our experiments demonstrate that the kernel-level stream encryption of input data using random keys preserves the logical boundary between potentially malicious data and clean data in the address space of processes. This enforcement of logical boundaries causes attackers to lose the precision with which they can corrupt control data and pure data. It also eliminates the execution of injected shellcode and the use of injected pure data while preserving the functionality of the protected processes. To the best of our knowledge, the protection technique is the only one that is capable of combating pure data attacks on C/C++ implementations of SCADA protocols such as Modbus without requiring hardware modification. We hope that this work will stimulate efforts focused on defending against unknown and zero-day attacks that rely on memory corruption.

References

[1] Aleph One, Smashing the stack for fun and profit, *Phrack*, vol. 7(49), 1996.

[2] S. Alexander, Defeating compiler-level buffer overflow protection, *;login: The USENIX Magazine*, vol. 30(3), pp. 59–71, 2005.

[3] Anonymous, Once upon a `free()`, *Phrack*, vol. 10(57), 2001.

[4] A. Baratloo, N. Singh and T. Tsai, Transparent run-time defense against stack smashing attacks, *Proceedings of the USENIX Annual Technical Conference*, 2000.

[5] A. Baratloo, T. Tsai and N. Singh, `libsafe`: Protecting critical elements of stacks, White Paper, Avaya, Basking Ridge, New Jersey (pubs.research .avayalabs.com/pdfs/ALR-2001-019-whpaper.pdf), 1999.

[6] E. Barrantes, D. Ackley, T. Palmer, D. Stefanovic and D. Zovi, Randomized instruction set emulation to disrupt binary code injection attacks, *Proceedings of the Tenth ACM Conference on Computer and Communications Security*, pp. 281–289, 2003.

[7] C. Bellettini and J. Rrushi, SCADA protocol obfuscation: A proactive defense line in SCADA systems, presented at the *SCADA Security Scientific Symposium*, 2007.

[8] C. Bellettini and J. Rrushi, Vulnerability analysis of SCADA protocol binaries through detection of memory access taintedness, *Proceedings of the IEEE SMC Information Assurance and Security Workshop*, pp. 341–348, 2007.

[9] Bulba and Kil3r, Bypassing StackGuard and StackShield, *Phrack*, vol. 10(56), 2000.

[10] S. Chen, K. Pattabiraman, Z. Kalbarczyk and R. Iyer, Formal reasoning of various categories of widely exploited security vulnerabilities by pointer taintedness semantics, in *Security and Protection in Information Processing Systems*, Y. Deswarte, F. Cuppens, S. Jajodia and L. Wang (Eds.), Kluwer, Boston, Massachusetts, pp. 83-100, 2004.

[11] S. Chen, J. Xu, N. Nakka, Z. Kalbarczyk and R. Iyer, Defeating memory corruption attacks via pointer taintedness detection, *Proceedings of the International Conference on Dependable Systems and Networks*, pp. 378–387, 2005.

[12] S. Chen, J. Xu, E. Sezer, P. Gauriar and R. Iyer, Non-control data attacks are realistic threats, *Proceedings of the Fourteenth USENIX Security Symposium*, pp. 177–192, 2005.

[13] M. Conover and w00w00 Security Team, w00w00 on heap overflows (www.w00w00.org/files/articles/heaptut.txt), 1999.

[14] C. Cowan, M. Barringer, S. Beattie, G. Kroah-Hartman, M. Frantzen and J. Lokier, FormatGuard: Automatic protection from `printf` format string vulnerabilities, *Proceedings of the Tenth USENIX Security Symposium*, pp. 191–200, 2001.

[15] C. Cowan, S. Beattie, J. Johansen and P. Wagle, PointGuard: Protecting pointers from buffer overflow vulnerabilities, *Proceedings of the Twelfth USENIX Security Symposium*, pp. 91–104, 2003.

[16] C. Cowan, C. Pu, D. Maier, H. Hinton, P. Bakke, S. Beattie, A. Grier, P. Wagle and Q. Zhang, StackGuard: Automatic adaptive detection and prevention of buffer overflow attacks, *Proceedings of the Seventh USENIX Security Symposium*, pp. 63–78, 1998.

[17] I. Dobrovitski, Exploit for CVS `double free()` for Linux pserver, Neohapsis Archives (www.security-express.com/archives/fulldisclosure/2003-q1/0545.html), 2003.

[18] Gera and Riq, Advances in format string exploitation, *Phrack*, vol. 10(59), 2002.

[19] iDefense Labs, LiveData Protocol Server heap overflow vulnerability, Sterling, Virginia (labs.idefense.com/intelligence/vulnerabilities/display.php?id=523), 2007.

[20] International Electrotechnical Commission, Telecontrol Equipment and Systems – Part 6-503: Telecontrol Protocols Compatible with ISO Standards and ITU-T Recommendations – TASE.2 Services and Protocol, IEC Publication 60870-6-503, Geneva, Switzerland, 2002.

[21] F. Iwanitz and J. Lange, *OPC – Fundamentals, Implementation and Application*, Huthig, Heidelberg, Germany, 2006.

[22] M. Kaempf, Vudo `malloc` tricks, *Phrack*, vol. 11(57), 2001.

[23] G. Kc, A. Keromytis and V. Prevelakis, Countering code injection attacks with instruction set randomization, *Proceedings of the Tenth ACM Conference on Computer and Communications Security*, pp. 272–280, 2003.

[24] Klog, Frame pointer overwriting, *Phrack*, vol. 9(55), 1999.

[25] A. Krennmair, ContraPolice: A `libc` extension for protecting applications from heap smashing attacks (synflood.at/papers/cp.pdf), 2003.

[26] Modbus IDA, MODBUS Application Protocol Specification v1.1a, North Grafton, Massachusetts (www.modbus.org/specs.php), 2004.

[27] L. Mora, OPC exposed: Part I, presented at the *SCADA Security Scientific Symposium*, 2007.

[28] Nergal, Advanced `return-into-lib(c)` exploits: PaX case study, *Phrack*, vol. 10(58), 2001.

[29] N. Nethercote and J. Seward, `valgrind`: A program supervision framework, *Electronic Notes in Theoretical Computer Science*, vol. 89(2), pp. 44–66, 2003.

[30] NOP Ninjas, Format string technique (julianor.tripod.com/bc/NN-form ats.txt), 2001.

[31] D. Novillo, From source to binary: The inner workings of GCC, *Red Hat Magazine* (www.redhat.com/magazine/002dec04/features/gcc), December 2004.

[32] D. Patterson and J. Hennessy, *Computer Organization and Design*, Morgan Kaufmann, San Francisco, California, 2007.

[33] PaX-Team, Documentation for the PaX Project (pax.grsecurity.net/docs), 2008.

[34] J. Pincus and B. Baker, Mitigations for low-level coding vulnerabilities: Incomparability and limitations, Microsoft Corporation, Redmond, Washington, 2004.

[35] T. Robbins, `libformat`, 2001.

[36] M. Roesch and C. Green, Snort Users Manual 2.3.3, Sourcefire (www.snort .org/docs/snort_manual), 2006.

[37] scut and team teso, Exploiting format string vulnerabilities (julianor.trip od.com/bc/formatstring-1.2.pdf), 2001.

[38] S. Simmons, D. Edwards and N. Wilde, Securing control systems with multilayer static mutation, presented at the *Process Control Systems Forum Annual Meeting* (www.pcsforum.org/events/2007/atlanta/documents /west.pdf), 2007.

[39] A. Sovarel, D. Evans and N. Paul, Where's the FEEB? The effectiveness of instruction set randomization, *Proceedings of the Fourteenth USENIX Security Symposium*, pp. 145–160, 2005.

[40] TIS Committee, Tool Interface Standard (TIS) Executable and Linking Format (ELF) Specification (www.x86.org/ftp/manuals/tools/elf.pdf), 1995.

[41] US-CERT, LiveData ICCP Server heap buffer overflow vulnerability, Vulnerability Note VU#190617, Washington, DC (www.kb.cert.org/vuls /id/190617), 2006.

[42] US-CERT, Takebishi Electric DeviceXPlorer OPC Server fails to properly validate OPC server handles, Vulnerability note VU#926551, Washington, DC (www.kb.cert.org/vuls/id/926551), 2007.

[43] Vendicator, StackShield: A stack smashing technique protection tool for Linux (www.angelfire.com/sk/stackshield), 2000.

[44] C. Walter, FreeMODBUS: A Modbus ASCII/RTU and TCP implementation (v1.3), FreeMODBUS, Vienna, Austria (freemodbus.berlios.de), 2007.

Chapter 12

MITIGATING ACCIDENTS IN OIL AND GAS PRODUCTION FACILITIES

Stig Johnsen

Abstract   Integrated operations are increasingly used in oil and gas production facilities to improve yields, reduce costs and maximize profits. They leverage information and communications technology (ICT) to facilitate collaboration between experts at widely dispersed locations. This paper discusses the safety and security consequences of implementing integrated operations for oil and gas production. It examines the increased accident risk arising from the tight coupling of complex ICT and SCADA systems, and proposes technological, organizational and human factors based strategies for mitigating the risk.

Keywords: Oil and gas production, integrated operations, accident mitigation

1.   Introduction

This paper discusses the safety and security consequences of using integrated operations for oil and gas production. Integrated operations leverage modern information and communications technology (ICT) in planning, organizing and performing tasks. The goal is increased value creation through collaboration across disciplines, corporations and geography [1].

The implementation of integrated operations is a large-scale change process involving technology, human resources and organizational factors. It is leading to organizational changes and new work processes both onshore and offshore. Significant segments of operations are being moved to a geographically distributed network where the actors are from a variety of organizations, reside in different locations and are interconnected by ICT systems. A key technological challenge is to integrate ICT and SCADA systems so that real-time data can be shared by the various actors and organizations.

This paper presents the results of a theoretical investigation and interviews with key personnel from the Norwegian oil and gas industry. In particular, it focuses on the increased risk of "normal accidents" due to the complexity

Please use the following format when citing this chapter:

Johnsen, S., 2008, in IFIP International Federation for Information Processing, Volume 290; *Critical Infrastructure Protection II*, eds. Papa, M., Shenoi, S., (Boston: Springer), pp. 157–170.

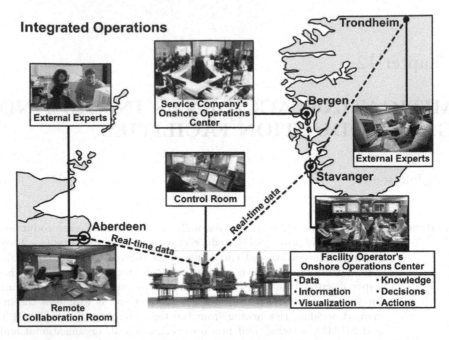

Figure 1.   Interconnectivity and actors involved in integrated operations.

and tight coupling of ICT and SCADA systems. It also examines the theory of normal accidents [10] and related work in resilience engineering and high reliability organizations.

Our hypothesis is that the safety and security of integrated operations can be improved by focusing on resilience and performing mitigating actions that reduce the probability of normal accidents. We also argue that it is important to analyze, report and share incidents based on perspectives involving organizational, human and technical factors.

2.   Integrated Operations

Integrated operations are attractive because they reduce costs, increase income and improve the yield from oil and gas fields. Several operations and maintenance tasks are being outsourced and this trend is likely to increase. Integrated operations provide for better utilization of expertise, facilitating interactions between professionals at widely dispersed sites. The increased connectivity, geographical distances, outsourcing and use of suppliers lead to a network of actors, which by accident, misunderstanding or intention can cause unforeseen incidents or accidents that could result in significant economic loss, environmental damage and casualties.

Figure 1 shows the interconnectivity and principal actors involved in integrated operations. The trend has been to move from teams located near the operational environment to large-scale remote operations. In remote operations,

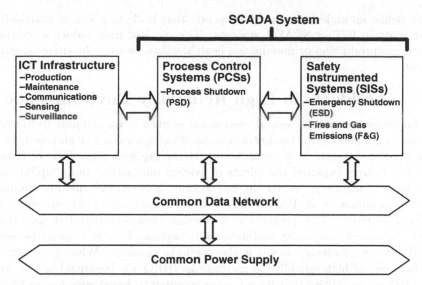

Figure 2. Systems used in integrated operations.

most team members may not be located at the site of operations, eliminating personal contact with other workers and the awareness of operating conditions (e.g., sound of mechanical equipment and smell of leaking gas) and environmental conditions (e.g., storm or calm). This situation poses great challenges because technical expertise and situational awareness must be shared to conduct production operations and to avoid incidents and accidents. Thus, it can be very difficult to maintain the safety and security of integrated operations.

The technologies used to manage production are changing from proprietary stand-alone systems to standardized IT systems and networks, which are often connected to the Internet. The standardization and increased interconnectivity of production systems, SCADA systems and ICT infrastructures increases the likelihood of undesirable incidents. Indeed, there has been an increase in the number of incidents related to SCADA systems, but the incidents are seldom reported. The incidents range from reduced production at oil and gas platforms to significant health, safety, security and environmental (HSSE) events. A production stoppage of just one day at a Norwegian Continental Shelf facility can result in a loss of two to three million dollars.

Figure 2 presents the major technical systems used in integrated operations. They include the ICT infrastructure, process control systems (PCSs) and safety instrumented systems (SISs). The ICT infrastructure consists of networks and supporting systems used for production (e.g., SAP), maintenance, communications (telephones and videoconferencing systems) and sensing and surveillance (radar and CCTV). PCSs are used for production; they include sensors and process shutdown (PSD) systems. SISs are used for emergency shutdown (ESD) and to deal with fires and gas (F&G) emissions. PCSs and SISs are collectively called "safety and automation systems" or SCADA systems.

We define an undesirable incident as one that leads to a loss of availability or integrity in ICT or SCADA systems. The incident may reduce or disrupt oil and gas production or may have a health, safety, security or environmental impact.

3.   Accidents in High Reliability Environments

This section examines several theoretical studies in an attempt to identify the challenges and the mitigating actions used to improve safety and security in integrated operations. In *Normal Accidents: Living with High Risk Technologies* [10], Perrow explored the effects of system interaction and coupling and their impact on safety. When the interactions between systems are complex and the couplings tight, Perrow argued that an accident could represent the "normal" outcome. This perspective is relevant because integrated operations lead to increased complexity and increased coupling. Perrow's theory is based on "What can go wrong," but it is also useful to consider "What goes right."

The study of high reliability organizations (HROs) is beneficial in this context. HROs are entities that have (or are required to have) very few incidents and accidents. The three original HRO entities in the United States were the air traffic control system, nuclear power stations and U.S. Navy nuclear aircraft carriers. U.S. Navy nuclear aircraft carrier operations are based on the assumption that errors have catastrophic consequences. In general, the carriers have managed their tasks well despite the technical complexity and the pressure to perform [12].

HROs may be defined (somewhat imprecisely) as "hazardous systems that produce near accident-free performance" [9]. It is difficult to use the available data to support the claim of near accident-free performance in HROs. Nevertheless, it is recommended that the oil and gas industry strive for near accident-free performance in integrated operations.

Resilience is also an important concept in the context of integrated operations. Resilience is "the intrinsic ability of a system to adjust its functioning prior to or following changes and disturbances, so that it can sustain operations even after a major mishap or in the presence of continuous stress" [4].

Perrow defines two dimensions of normal accidents, "interaction" and "coupling." Interactions between systems range from linear (expected or familiar sequences) to complex (unexpected or unfamiliar sequences). Complex systems are characterized by proximity, common mode connections, interconnected subsystems, limited substitution, feedback loops, multiple and interacting controls, indirect information and limited understanding. A goal for integrated operations should be to design systems whose interactions are closer to linear than complex.

Coupling between systems ranges from loose to tight. Loosely coupled systems have flexible performance standards and can handle failures, delays and changes without destabilization. Tightly coupled systems have no buffering; consequently, what happens in one system directly impacts the other. These systems cannot accommodate delays in processing. They are characterized by invariant sequences and little to no slack with respect to supplies, equipment and personnel. A goal in integrated operations should be to design systems that have tight coupling as opposed to loose coupling (e.g., by incorporating buffers and redundancies). Also, it is important to ensure that loosely coupled systems do not drift to tightly coupled systems due to breakdowns in buffering or loss of redundancy.

Empirical investigations of HROs have identified several key characteristics [9, 12]. HROs generally operate in environments with the potential for conflicting goals; however, when there is an absolute safety commitment from the top, conflicting goals are prioritized to ensure safety. HRO operations are distributed, but there is a focus on shared beliefs and values among the distributed teams; good communication among team members is critical. Public attention focused on HROs ensures that the key actors are always alert. Also, there is a strong focus on proactive learning about accidents and dormant faults. HROs generally have relatively abundant resources to deal with change; however, the organizations should be flexible and should handle unplanned activities in a safe manner. The organizations operate under the assumption that no individual is perfect; organizational redundancy is maintained in key areas. Although a high degree of system complexity and tight coupling exist, there is extensive system insight and errors are not tolerated.

Ideals such as commitment to safety should be communicated from top management when integrated operations are implemented. The distributed environment requires the establishment of common shared values and beliefs among actors. The two issues are also an important part of a safety and security culture [11]. Communication must be tailored to all the groups within and outside the organization.

Extensive system insight is a mitigating factor [10] as limited understanding often contributes to incidents in complex systems. Proactive learning is an excellent way to gain system insight and maintain readiness. Every undesirable incident should, therefore, be reported and analyzed to foster learning by the various actors. To avoid incidents and accidents, it is important to be ever alert and to avoid complacency. Errors should not be tolerated in tightly coupled systems; this helps ensure a preoccupation with failures [15].

Reason [11] describes four components of a safety culture: a just culture, a reporting culture, a learning culture and a flexible culture. Together, these four components create an informed environment where managers and operators have the most current knowledge about human, technical, organizational and environmental factors that determine the safety of the system as a whole. A just culture fosters an atmosphere of trust where personnel are encouraged to provide essential safety-related information, and a clear line exists between acceptable and unacceptable performance. A reporting culture encourages personnel to report their errors and near misses. A learning culture creates an environment where there is the willingness and competence to draw the right conclusions, and the will to implement major reforms when needed. A flexible culture ensures that control passes to experts during a crisis and reverts to the traditional bureaucratic hierarchy when the emergency has passed.

Drawing on studies of HROs, Johnsen, *et al.* [7] have developed the CheckIT tool that attempts to measure and improve the safety and security culture through group-based discussions and actions. The idea is to improve the culture from one of denial to a rule-based culture to the ideal proactive reporting culture. Cultural improvements can be achieved in many ways; two key elements are management commitment and group discussions that nurture shared beliefs and values.

Weick [15] has identified five characteristics of HROs: (i) preoccupation with failures, (ii) reluctance to simplify, (iii) sensitivity to operations, (iv) commitment to resilience, and (v) deference to expertise.

- **Preoccupation with Failures:** Long periods of accident-free operations often breed complacency, but it is during these periods that one should be preoccupied with potential failures. HROs scrutinize incidents and search for possible errors because they may provide signals of precursors to larger failures. Turner [14] notes that a major disaster is often preceded by several serious incidents that are ignored due to complacency. Research in the area of safety also makes the same claim (see, e.g., [11]). An important aspect is a reporting culture where personnel report errors, near misses and unsafe acts. This culture is important in integrated operations because of the dependence on technical systems. Unfortunately, there is very limited reporting of ICT and SCADA incidents by the oil and gas industry [5]; this may increase the risk to integrated operations.

- **Reluctance to Simplify:** Simplification increases the likelihood of surprises because key details are overlooked or ignored. It is important to obtain accurate information and create a mental model that is complete and nuanced. In HROs, redundancy in personnel and systems are treated as vital for collecting and interpreting information that is necessary to avert disasters. In a complex environment such as integrated operations, it is important to establish a redundant set of communications systems.

- **Sensitivity to Operations:** In HROs, the entire workforce strives to maintain situational awareness, to understand what can go wrong and how to recover when things go wrong. HRO personnel attempt to maintain a perspective of the entire situation, not just the segments for which they are responsible. In integrated operations, situational awareness must be shared among all the relevant actors in the virtual organization and should be leveraged when incidents occur.

- **Commitment to Resilience:** HROs anticipate errors and are not disabled by them because they can quickly mobilize themselves to deal with errors. This should be a goal for integrated operations that is generally achieved by extensive training using realistic scenarios.

- **Deference to Expertise:** In critical situations, decision-making tasks often migrate to personnel with the most expertise, even if they are low in the organizational hierarchy. Learning activities must be supported throughout the organization. During an incident, decision-making power should be transferred to personnel who are the most knowledgeable.

Decisions and their premises must be evaluated and explored in a learning environment where the guiding variables are questioned and adjusted [2]. Second-order learning [2] should be explored when implementing integrated operations. This is because experience must be built continuously when new technology is implemented and the guiding variables influencing the organization should be continuously monitored and adjusted.

Resilience [4] requires that an organization be constantly watchful and ready to respond. Also, the organization should continuously update its knowledge, competence and resources by learning from successes as well as failures. Several issues should be considered in order to design for resilience.

- **Looking Ahead:** This involves anticipation (knowing what to expect) as well as looking for threats and having a constant sense of unease.

- **Looking Out:** This involves constant attention to detail, looking at performance indicators, having the time to think and perform actions.

- **Responding:** This involves effective response, maintaining plans, procedures, resources, readiness and flexibility.

- **Learning:** This involves knowing what has happened, having reporting schemes and accident models, and focusing on communication and feedback.

The studies we have examined provide a foundation for discussing the safety and security of integrated operations. The principles discerned from our study are listed below. Note that the principles overlap in many respects and, thus, appear to validate each other.

- Commitment to safety and security must come from the top; safety and security are goals.

- Focus on communication; establishment of shared beliefs; reluctance to simplify.

- Focus on proactive learning; preoccupation with failures; creation of a reporting culture.

- Commitment to resilience; importance of being alert and responding appropriately; flexible organizations.

- Extensive system insight; sensitivity to operations; focus on interactions ranging from simple to complex.

- No complacency related to coupling; avoidance of drift from loose coupling to tight coupling; implementation of necessary buffers and barriers; non tolerance of errors.

It is difficult to prove that these principles lead to error-free operations. Nevertheless, it is clear that in practically every incident or accident, one or more of the principles mentioned were violated.

4.   Accidents and Integrated Operations

The consequences of an accident in the oil and gas industry can be very serious. The 1988 fire at the Piper Alpha production platform on the North Sea, which was caused by an oil and gas leak, resulted in the loss of 169 lives.

Production processes involved in integrated operations are complex and tightly coupled. Offshore oil and gas production, in particular, is highly complex. The complexity is increased by the presence of interconnected systems with unintended feedback loops and multiple, interacting controls.

Oil and gas production processes are also tightly coupled. They are based on invariant sequences, delays are unacceptable, and there is often only one method to achieve the goal. However, it is possible to shutdown the production process using at least two independent systems, the process shutdown (PSD) system that completely shuts down production, and the emergency shutdown (ESD) system.

Three main subsystems are used to manage production, the ICT infrastructure, PCSs and SISs. Our interviews with operators and suppliers have revealed that ICT systems, PCSs and SISs often use common networks and power supplies. PCSs and SISs also share the same operator interfaces on workstations (HMIs). Moreover, when PCSs and SISs are delivered by the same supplier, the systems have many common elements and are very tightly integrated.

PCSs and SISs are interconnected with ICT systems in order to obtain real-time production data and to perform control actions. It is often the case that failures in ICT components disrupt PCSs. In one incident on a North Sea platform, a malfunctioning computer system flooded a network with error packets, which caused the PCS to crash [5]. In fact, according to data from CERN [6], unanticipated ICT traffic could cause as much as 30% of SCADA network components to malfunction. The interconnections between ICT systems, PCSs and SISs are seldom tested or certified. A dangerous situation can arise if an SIS is rendered non-operational due to erroneous ICT traffic. This may cause the ESD to be locked, leading to a serious accident.

The scenario we used to explore what could happen in a production system is based on a real incident where a supplier connected a laptop infected with a virus to a production network. We applied the STEP methodology [3] to describe this scenario:

- **Actors:** The actors involved in the incident are identified. These actors are drawn under each other on the left-hand side of the STEP diagram (Figure 3).

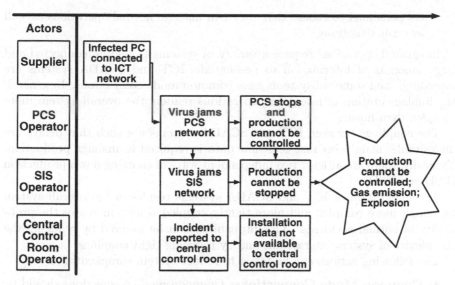

Figure 3. STEP diagram for a SCADA scenario.

- **Events:** The events that influenced the incident and how it was handled are identified. The "who," "what" and "how" of events are described. The events are placed in the correct locations of the time-actor sheet.

- **Causal Links:** The relationships between events and their causes are identified. Causal links are expressed in the diagram by drawing arrows between the events.

The STEP diagram is analyzed to identify the weak points. Next, barrier analysis is performed to identify the (existing and missing) barriers that hinder the root causes and threats, as well as the (existing and missing) barriers that reduce negative consequences and impacts.

Analysis of the STEP diagram in Figure 3 identifies several weak points and actions and barriers associated with the weak points:

- **Virus Scanning:** All computers must be scanned for viruses and other malware before being connected to the network. A staging facility must be used to scan the computers. Personnel should take steps to ensure that viruses and other malware are not introduced into computers and networks.

- **Patch Management:** All computer systems, software and network components should have the latest patches.

- **SIS-PCS Connectivity:** A firewall should be positioned between an SIS and PCS.

- **SCADA System Expertise:** Detailed documentation and training about SCADA systems and their operation should be provided to technical personnel to ensure that they can manage normal operations as well as crisis situations.

Integrated operations require a variety of systems to be interconnected and large amounts of information to be shared. ICT and SCADA systems are integrated, and some subsystems have common mode connections. In general, the implementation of integrated operations renders the overall system more complex than linear.

The couplings between ICT and SCADA systems are such that delays are undesirable, mainly because real-time data is required to manage production. Typically, there are at least two independent ways of shutting down production (PSD and ESD).

The integration of ICT and SCADA systems results in the overall system becoming more complex and more tightly coupled, which increases the probability of normal accidents. This probability can be lowered by reducing the complexity of system interactions and by reducing tight coupling.

The following actions can be taken to reduce system complexity:

- **Common Mode Connections:** Common mode connections should be reduced by separating networks, system components and power supplies. The separation of PCSs and SISs should be mandatory, but this is seldom enforced and the status of common faults is rarely explored.

- **Interconnected Systems:** Systems have to be interconnected in order to share information, but the interconnections should be simplified to the extent possible. For example, "one-way" connections could be established for data exchange. Also, data exported from SCADA systems to ICT components should be designated as read-only to enhance security. Furthermore, changes to SCADA data should be implemented using redundant systems with human intervention and/or supervision.

- **System Understanding:** It is important to establish a good understanding of the systems used in integrated operations. ICT and SCADA systems should undergo comprehensive testing and evaluation under normal and abnormal scenarios, including virus infections and denial-of-service attacks. Information collected about systems and incidents should be disseminated to improve understanding and awareness.

The following actions can be taken to reduce tight coupling between systems:

- **Processing Delays:** The need for real-time data should be critically evaluated. Processing delays should be introduced, if possible.

- **Equipment and Personnel:** The introduction of slack with regard to equipment and personnel should be explored. Additional resources may be needed to provide slack.

- **Redundancy:** Redundancies may be incorporated (e.g., independent shutdown systems) to reduce tight coupling. It is important that the redundant systems are tested regularly.

5.   Interview Results and Mitigating Actions

We interviewed personnel from several large oil and gas companies in Norway to identify the key issues relating undesirable incidents in ICT and SCADA systems used in production. Several incidents involving virus and worm infections occurred annually. However, these incidents mainly affected ICT systems. In installations implementing integrated operations, there was at most one incident each year that impacted offshore SCADA networks.

In practically every installation, ICT and SCADA professionals belong to different parts of the overall organization; they have different educational backgrounds and apply different standards and methods. For example, ICT personnel adopt standards such as ISO/IEC 27002 (Information Technology – Code of Practice for Information Security Management (formerly ISO/IEC 17799)). On the other hand, SCADA personnel comply with the IEC 61508 (Functional Safety of Electrical/Electronic/Programmable Electronic Safety-Related Systems) and ISA SP99 (Manufacturing and Control Systems Security) standards.

Our interviews with industry experts have identified several key safety and security issues along with mitigating actions:

- **Incident Reporting:** Incidents are seldom reported or analyzed. There does not appear to be an open reporting culture; information about undesirable accidents is not shared with and between organizations. Clearly, incidents should be analyzed thoroughly and disseminated using a standardized reporting scheme that documents all the major issues. Key actors such as the control room operators should be alerted to incidents as they happen. Proactive scenario analyses, as illustrated by the STEP diagram in Figure 3, should be explored. These analyses should be used to raise incident awareness and develop mitigation strategies.

- **Technical, Organizational and Human Factors Issues:** Unwanted incidents are regarded as technical issues; organizational and human factors issues are rarely considered. ICT and SCADA professionals adopt different standards and practices. Clear responsibility, unambiguous work procedures and common situational awareness are important when incidents develop into dangerous situations. Common situational awareness must be maintained under normal operations as well as during incidents. It is important to focus on organizational and human factors issues such as common goals, beliefs and values. Incidents should be analyzed and reported using a standardized scheme that documents technical, organizational and human factors issues.

- **Probability of Normal Accidents:** Implementing integrated operations increases the probability of normal accidents. ICT and SCADA have different architectures, and SCADA systems are vulnerable to unanticipated ICT traffic. The integration of ICT and SCADA systems results in shared networks, power supplies and operator interfaces for ICT, PCS and SIS systems, leading to common cause failures. Integrated systems are rarely tested and certified for independence and resilience. It is important to perform thorough testing and certification of all systems, and to ensure that all normal accident scenarios are reported and analyzed.

Based on our analysis of the theory and interactions with industry experts, we have identified several barriers that should be explored during accident analysis. The following questions should be considered as a starting point when identifying the barriers in an organization:

- **Organizational Barriers:** Is there a management commitment to safety and security from the top of the organization? Has an open reporting culture been established among operators and suppliers? Has a risk assessment been performed for process control, safety and ICT systems and networks? Has a practice been established for remote access that ensures human supervision from the central control room? Has an incident handling team been established and has a short, precise incident handling plan been established? Is there clear responsibility for ICT/SCADA network operations? Are there procedures in place for reporting security and safety incidents? Has a scenario analysis been performed between the operator and suppliers? Have all incidents been documented and analyzed by teams with the relevant actors?

- **Technical Barriers:** Have proactive indicators been established to indicate the level of attacks? Have the interconnections between ICT and SCADA systems been tested and certified, and has the SCADA network been tested and certified for ICT traffic? Have firewalls been implemented based on a best practice scheme and are firewall logs analyzed systematically? Do the process control, safety and ICT systems have adequate, updated and active protection against malware?

- **Human Factors Barriers:** Have all the involved actors been informed about relevant incidents and have there been open discussions about incidents and vulnerabilities in the various systems? Has an analysis of safety culture (knowledge, awareness and actions) been performed among the relevant actors? Have suppliers and other operators been educated about information security requirements, do they know how incidents should be handled and do they know about acceptable ICT system use and operations?

6.   Conclusions

The implementation of integrated operations in oil and gas production facilities in the Norwegian Continental Shelf has contributed to increased complexity and tight coupling between ICT and SCADA systems. Our research has identified three areas of concern: the increased probability of normal accidents due to the integration of ICT and SCADA systems, the inadequate reporting and analysis of ICT and SCADA incidents, and the designation of undesirable incidents as technical issues that are rarely analyzed in the context of organizational and human factors issues.

Normal accidents can be mitigated by building resilient systems and creating high reliability organizations. This can be accomplished by developing defensive strategies and performing barrier analyses that consider human factors, organizational factors and technical solutions. Incident reporting is also critical; strong efforts should be undertaken to document, analyze and share information about incidents among the various actors.

References

[1] K. Andersen, IO in StatoilHydro – Drilling and well, presented at the *Forum for Human Factors in Control* (www.criop.sintef.no/Participant s%20and%20projects/0–HFC%20-%20M%C3%B8tereferat%20april%2008 .pdf), 2008.

[2] C. Argyris and D. Schon, *Organizational Learning: A Theory of Action Perspective*, Addison-Wesley, Reading, Massachusetts, 1978.

[3] K. Hendrick and L. Benner, *Investigating Accidents with STEP*, Marcel Dekker, New York, 1986.

[4] E. Hollnagel, D. Woods and N. Leveson, *Resilience Engineering*, Ashgate, Aldershot, United Kingdom, 2006.

[5] M. Jaatun, S. Johnsen, M. Line, O. Longva, I. Tondel, E. Albrechtsen and I. Waero, Incident Response Management in the Oil and Gas Industry, SINTEF Report A4086, SINTEF, Trondheim, Norway (www.sintef.no/up load/10977/20071212_IRMA_Rapport.pdf), 2007.

[6] S. Johnsen, R. Ask and R. Roisli, Reducing risk in oil and gas production operations, in *Critical Infrastructure Protection*, E. Goetz and S. Shenoi (Eds.), Springer, Boston, Massachusetts, pp. 83–95, 2007.

[7] S. Johnsen, C. Hansen, M. Line, Y. Nordby, E. Rich and Y. Qian, CheckIT – A program to measure and improve information security and safety culture, *International Journal of Performability Engineering*, vol. 3(1), pp. 174–186, 2007.

[8] S. Johnsen, M. Lundteigen, E. Albrechtsen and T. Grotan, Trusler og muligheter knyttet til eDrift, SINTEF Report A04433, SINTEF, Trondheim, Norway (www.sintef.no/upload/Teknologi_og_samfunn/Sikkerhet %20og%20p%C3%A5litelighet/Rapporter/STF38%20A04433.pdf), 2005.

[9] T. LaPorte and P. Consolini, Working in practice but not in theory: Theoretical challenges of "high-reliability organizations," *Journal of Public Administration Research and Theory*, vol. 1(1), pp. 19–48, 1991.

[10] C. Perrow, *Normal Accidents: Living with High Risk Technologies*, Princeton University Press, Princeton, New Jersey, 1999.

[11] J. Reason, *Managing the Risks of Organizational Accidents*, Ashgate, Aldershot, United Kingdom, 1997.

[12] K. Roberts, New challenges in organizational research: High reliability organizations, *Organization and Environment*, vol. 3(2), pp. 111–125, 1989.

[13] K. Stouffer, J. Falco and K. Scarfone, Guide to Industrial Control Systems (ICS) Security, NIST Special Publication 800-82, National Institute of Standards and Technology, Gaithersburg, Maryland, 2007.

[14] B. Turner and N. Pidgeon, *Man-Made Disasters*, Butterworth-Heinemann, Oxford, United Kingdom, 1997.

[15] K. Weick and K. Sutcliffe, *Managing the Unexpected: Assuring High Performance in an Age of Complexity*, Jossey-Bass, San Francisco, California, 2001.

IV

SECURITY STRATEGIES

Chapter 13

AUTOMATED ASSESSMENT OF COMPLIANCE WITH SECURITY BEST PRACTICES

Zahid Anwar and Roy Campbell

Abstract   Several standards and best practices have been proposed for critical infrastructure protection. However, the scale and complexity of critical infrastructure assets renders manual compliance checking difficult, if not impossible. This paper focuses on the automated assessment of security compliance of electrical power grid assets. A security model based on predicate calculus is used to express infrastructure elements (e.g., devices, services, protocols, access control implementations) as "facts" and security standards and best practices as "rules" that specify constraints on the facts. A tool chain is applied to automatically generate the security model from specifications and to check compliance with standards and best practices. The tool chain also supports the visualization of network topology and security assessment results to reveal possible points of attack.

Keywords: Security best practices, compliance assessment, first order logic

1.   Introduction

The Industrial Security Incident Database (ISID) [4] reveals an alarming number of attacks on cyber infrastructures, more than half of them originating from external sites. The electrical power grid is especially vulnerable to attack. An experimental cyber attack on an electrical power plant generator made headlines in September 2007 [14]. While the details of the attack have not been released, it is clear that researchers were able to hack into the SCADA network and change its configuration to cause significant damage to the generator.

To address security problems, the Federal Energy Regulatory Commission (FERC) has approved eight cyber security and critical infrastructure protection standards proposed by NERC [9, 20]. However, there is considerable flexibility

Please use the following format when citing this chapter:

Anwar, Z. and Campbell, R., 2008, in IFIP International Federation for Information Processing, Volume 290; *Critical Infrastructure Protection II*, eds. Papa, M., Shenoi, S., (Boston: Springer), pp. 173–187.

with regard to their implementation. For example, CIP-005 Requirement 4 (R4) states:

> "*The responsible entity shall perform a cyber vulnerability assessment of the electronic access points to the electronic security perimeter(s) at least annually.*"

Obviously, there are several ways of securing the electronic perimeter. Two of the most popular techniques are firewall deployment and access control.

Similarly, CIP-009 Requirement 2 (R2) discusses the security implications of operating procedures and disaster recovery procedures, their relative orderings, timeframes and requirements. While the NERC standards do not discuss implementation, several entities have published guidelines for implementing security best practices for SCADA systems [3, 7, 11, 15, 17]. Most of these guidelines are informal English descriptions of SCADA infrastructure configurations, firewall rules, allowable services and security protocols. Our strategy is to formalize these best practices and to use them in automated conformance checking of SCADA network configurations.

We use predicate logic to model SCADA and enterprise networks along with their security properties. The model creates a comprehensive network dependency graph containing information about physical connections (e.g., links) and logical connections (e.g., service dependencies). This information is automatically obtained from SCADA specification languages such as the Common Information Model (CIM) [8]. Best practices modeled as rules defined in terms of facts are used to determine whether or not the dependency graph satisfies the security constraints.

2.   Related Work

A survey of SCADA security implementations reveals a lack of authentication mechanisms, limited patch protection and uncontrolled Internet connections [13]. This situation exposes SCADA systems to a variety of exploits, including simple SQL injection attacks. However, even when the vulnerabilities of individual components are known, no adequate tools are available for reasoning about the overall security of a system.

The SINTEF CORAS Project [19] has developed a risk analysis methodology that models threats as unwanted system features. The system and its associated threats are modeled using Unified Modeling Language (UML) diagrams that support security risk assessments. An XML schema is available for communicating risk and vulnerability assessment data in a standardized format.

Masera and Nai Fovino [12] have proposed a service-oriented architecture for conducting security assessments. A service-oriented description of a system (where components and subsystems are interconnected by "service chains") is used to identify attacks and reason about the propagation of faults and failures. Our model is not limited to checking for particular attacks; instead, it allows for conformance checking against security standards and best practices that defend against a variety of attacks simultaneously.

Chandia and colleagues [5] have proposed a standards-based security services suite that provides security functionality at different levels of the network infrastructure. Their approach involves message monitoring, protocol-based solutions, tunneling services, middleware components and cryptographic key management, along with a network forensic system for analyzing attacks. Our approach is different in that it involves the static analysis of security conformance of implementations instead of implementing security solutions.

While the use of attack graph models to identify vulnerabilities in large-scale networks is fairly mature, little work has focused on the automated generation of these models, especially for cyber infrastructures. Also, few researchers have investigated the use of dependency graphs for vulnerability assessment and automated checking against security standards and best practices.

3.   Security Model

Our security model captures the static aspects of SCADA systems, including network topology, devices, services, connectivity and security properties. A SCADA system is expressed as a dependency graph G and a set of rules expressing security standards and best practices.

3.1   Dependency Graph

A dependency graph G is defined as a tuple $(D, E, S, V, S_T, D_T, S_p)$ where D is the set of devices, $E \subseteq D \times D$ is the set of edges between two physically connected devices, S is the set of services, V is the set of vulnerabilities, S_T is the set of service types, D_T is the set of device types and S_p is the set of security protocols.

The following functions provide attribute mappings to the various devices and dependencies:

- *devof* : $S \rightarrow D$ maps a service to the device that hosts it.
- *hostedsvs* : $D \rightarrow \mathbb{P}\{S\}$ s.t. *devof*$(S) = D$ maps a device to the services it hosts.
- *defsvs* : $D \rightarrow S$ maps a device to its default service.
- *depdtsvs* : $S \rightarrow \mathbb{P}\{S\}$ maps a service to the set of services on which it depends.
- *trusteddevs* : $D \rightarrow \mathbb{P}\{D\}$ maps a device to a set of trusted devices.
- *secprots* : $S \rightarrow \mathbb{P}\{S_p\}$ maps a service to a set of security protocols it uses.
- *typeofsvs* : $S \rightarrow stype$ where $stype \in S_T$ maps a service to its type.
- *typeofdvs* : $D \rightarrow dtype$ where $dtype \in D_T$ maps a device to its type.
- *knownvuls* : $stype \rightarrow \mathbb{P}\{V\}$ maps a service to its set of known vulnerabilities.
- *priv* : $S \rightarrow privlvl$ where $privlvl \in \{none \leq user \leq root\}$ maps a service to its privilege level.
- *exploitability* : $V \rightarrow likelihood$ where $likelihood \in \mathbb{R}$ $(0 \leq n \leq 1)$ maps a vulnerability to the likelihood it will be exploited.

The dependency graph G is modeled as facts in first order predicate logic.

3.2   Security Standards and Best Practices

Security standards and best practices are expressed as rules whose terms are constraints on G.

Intranet Services.   Services between a process control network (PCN), an enterprise network (EN) and the Internet should be allowed strictly on a need basis. IAONA's template for protocol access in industrial environments states that incoming DNS, HTTP, FTP, telnet and SMTP traffic to a PCN should be discouraged unless absolutely required [10].

We express this best practice as:

- $\forall d_1, \forall d_2 \in D \ [typeof(d_1, EN) \wedge typeof(d_2, PCN) \wedge$
  $\forall s_1, \forall s_2 \in S \ [devof(s_1, d_1) \wedge devof(s_2, d_2) \wedge depends(s_1, s_2)$
  $\Rightarrow s_2 \notin \{dns, http, ftp, telnet, smtp\}]]$

with the auxiliary functions:

- $typeof : \forall d \in D, \forall x \in D_T (typeofdvs(d) = x) \Rightarrow typeof(d, x)$
- $devof : \forall s \in S, \forall d \in D(devof(s) == d) \Rightarrow devof(s, d)$
- $depends : \forall d_1, \forall d_2 \in D, \exists s_1, \exists s_2 \in S[devof(s_1, d_1) \wedge$
  $devof(s_2, d_2) \wedge depdtsvs(s_1, s_2) \Rightarrow depends(d_1, d_2)].$

The rule checks if a service dependency exists from an EN device to a PCN device, where both devices are in a substation. If a dependency exists, then it should not be of the type DNS, HTTP, FTP, telnet or SMTP.

Access Control Implementation.   The American Gas Association's document on cryptographic protection of SCADA communications [1] states that in a proper access control implementation, a service should provide an authentication scheme and also use communication protocols that guarantee confidentiality and integrity.

We express this best practice as:

- $\forall d_{alice}, \forall d_i, \forall d_j, \forall d_{bob} \in D \ [depends(d_{alice}, d_{bob}) \wedge$
  $d_i \in path(d_{alice}, d_{bob}) \wedge d_j \in path(d_{alice}, d_{bob}) \wedge (d_i, d_j) \in E$
  $\Rightarrow (secprots(defsvs(d_i)) \cap secprots(defsvs(d_j))) \neq \emptyset \wedge$
  $(keys(d_{alice}) \cap keys(d_{bob})) \neq \emptyset]$

with the auxiliary functions:

- $path : path(d_1, d_k) = d_1, d_2, ...d_{k-1}, d_k$ s.t. $\forall_{1 \leq i < k-1}(d_i, d_{i+1} \in E)$
- $keys : D \rightarrow \mathbb{P}\{K\}$

where *path* is a mapping from a pair of devices to the set of paths between them and *keys* is a mapping from a device to the set of pre-shared keys it has with other devices.

Table 1. Firewall architectures.

Type (Rating)	Description
Dual-Homed Server (1)	This design installs two network interface cards on devices requiring access to both networks, which violates the principle of no direct Internet access from the PCN. This configuration was severely affected by the Slammer worm in January 2003.
Dual-Homed Host Firewall (2)	The host-based firewall on a dual-homed machine prevents traffic from traversing the PCN-EN boundary. However, it offers low granularity with multiple shared servers when remote PCN management is required.
Packet Filtering Router (2)	This design uses a Layer 3 switch with basic filters to block unwanted traffic. It offers limited protection because it is not stateful and assumes that the EN is highly secure.
Two-Port Dedicated Firewall (3)	This aggressively configured stateful firewall provides considerable security. The shared device is positioned in the PCN or EN and the firewall is configured with the appropriate rules.
Two-Zone Firewall-Based DMZ (4)	This design positions shared devices in their own DMZs, which eliminates direct communication between the plant floor and the EN. Multiple DMZs ensure that only desired traffic is forwarded between zones. However, compromised entities in the DMZs may be used as staging points for attacks against PCN devices.
Firewall and VLAN Design (4.5)	This design partitions PCNs into subnets so that devices that require little or no communication are placed in separate networks and only communicate via Layer 3 switches.

The best practice predicate checks if a service s_i implements access control, confidentiality and integrity correctly. It does this by checking if all its dependent services have a common shared-key mechanism. The helper function *path* checks if the default service on each pair of devices along the path from the queried service to the dependent services share common security properties. Function *keys* checks if all the dependent services use a pre-shared key.

Firewall Deployment. NISCC's document on SCADA firewall deployment [3] states that traffic from an enterprise LAN must be separated from an industrial control LAN by a firewall. Table 1 presents five firewall architectures and their security ratings. We express the firewall best practices as:

- $\forall d_e, \forall d_p, \forall d_s \in D$ [$typeof(d_e, EN) \wedge typeof(d_p, PCN) \wedge$
  $depends(d_e, d_s) \wedge depends(d_p, d_s) \wedge (d_s \in path(d_e, d_p)) \wedge$
  $\exists s_f \in S[devof(s_f, d_s) \wedge typeof(s_f, firewall) \Rightarrow dualhomedfirewalled]]$
- $\forall d_e, \forall d_p, \forall d_s \in D$ [$typeof(d_e, EN) \wedge typeof(d_p, PCN) \wedge$
  $depends(d_e, d_s) \wedge depends(d_p, d_s) \wedge$
  $\exists d_{f1}, \exists d_{f2}, \exists d_{f3} \in D$ [$(d_{f1} \in path(d_e, d_s)) \wedge (d_{f2} \in path(d_p, d_s)) \wedge$
  $(d_{f3} \in path(d_e, d_p)) \wedge typeof(d_{f1}, firewall) \wedge typeof(d_{f2}, firewall) \wedge$
  $typeof(d_{f3}, firewall) \Rightarrow dmz$

with the auxiliary predicate:

- $typeof : \forall s \in S, \forall x \in S_T(typeofsvs(s) = x) \Rightarrow typeof(s, x).$

This predicate identifies the shared network devices (e.g., historians, aggregators and access points). Servers accessed by dependent services running on devices in the PCN and EN are characterized as shared. The proper placement of these devices with respect to firewalls determines the architecture to be used. The first predicate states that if all the paths between the two dependent PCN and EN devices pass through the shared device and the shared device is running a personal firewall service, then a dual-homed host firewall with a security rating of 2 should be used. The second predicate checks if all possible paths between PCN and ECN devices d_p and d_e, d_p and the shared device d_s, and d_e and d_s pass through firewalls, in which case, the shared device should be placed in a isolated DMZ with a security rating of 4. Predicates for the other four firewall architectures are specified along the same lines.

4.   Tool Chain Architecture and Implementation

This section discusses the architecture and implementation of the security assessment tool chain (Figure 1).

4.1   Parsing Specification Files

The dependency graph of the SCADA network is generated from annotated specifications written in CIM [8] with the help of a parser tool and stored in a Prolog database. CIM is an object-oriented cyber infrastructure modeling language developed by EPRI for representing objects encountered in electric utilities. The objects are represented as classes that have attributes and relationships (with other classes). The CIM RDF schema, which is documented as IEC Standard 61970-501, is self-describing because it is based on XML.

CIM RDF classes are mapped to entities in our security model. Figure 2 shows the XML description and the Prolog version of an actuator for a disconnect switch (DS3). The XML attributes provide detailed information about switch functions and the SCADA elements that control it.

The parser begins by identifying the principal entities such as devices, connections and services, and populates their attributes based on the properties and relationships of CIM objects. Some attributes (e.g., inter-service

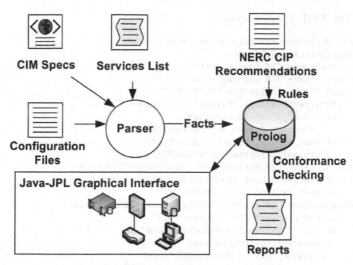

Figure 1. Security assessment tool chain.

data dependencies and security protocols used by services) are not covered by CIM. These attributes are incorporated by parsing the firewall configuration logs, manually annotating the CIM XML or looking-up a services-to-security-properties table when a services entity is encountered. Services running on a device may be determined by running nmap port scans; communicating services are identified by parsing firewall logs.

Discovering service dependencies from firewall logs is not a new technique. Several open source tools are available for traffic analysis and network dependency visualization based on firewall logs (e.g., psad [16] and afterglow [18]).

4.2   Predicate Calculus Implementation

The predicate calculus security model is implemented as a form of Horn Clause Logic using SWI-Prolog (version 5.6). The devices, services, connectivity and dependencies identified by the parser are asserted as Prolog facts. Table 2 lists the Prolog facts that describe the interconnections and service dependencies of a sensor, which reports readings to a historian and an administrator's computer through a firewall. The connected predicate shows a bidirectional link between two devices.

4.3   Rules Implementation

The rules and helper functions were implemented to check for conformance with best practices. Prolog rules are essentially goals that check for other subgoals to hold true; subgoals are other rules or primitive facts.

Table 3 summarizes the Prolog implementation of an American Gas Association access control best practice. We explain the Prolog listing from the bottom up. The ck_ConformanceTo_CIP002-08 rule (Line 32) takes three arguments:

CIM XML Specification

```
<!-- Describes our Substation Architecture -->
<SubstationArchitecture>
 <class name="CIM_LogicalSwitch"
  Superclass="CIM_LogicalDevice">
  <cim:CIM_LogicalSwitch ID="ActDS3"
   cim:type="DisconnectSwitch" cim:State="Closed"
   cim:PowerSystemResourceName=
     "Disconnect Switch No 3 Actuator"
   cim:Manufacturer="General Electric"
   cim:Controllerforresource="#DS3">
  <class name="CIM_SerialLink" Superclass="CIM_Link">
   <cim:CIM_SerialLink ID="SlinkActDS3" cim:source="PLC2"
    cim:dest="ActDS3"/> </class>
  <class name="CIM_Firmware" Superclass="CIM_Service">
   <cim:CIM_Firmware ID="F.wareActDS3"
    cim:ver="1.0" cim:type="ModbusSlave"
    cim:PowerSystemResourceName=
      "Actuator Service for ActDS3"
    cim:secprops="TLS" cim:dependsupon="PLC2Master"
    cim:port="502"/> </class>
  </cim:CIM_LogicalSwitch>
 </class>
 .
 .
</SubstationArchitecture>
```

Prolog Primitive Facts

```
device( ActDS3,      //ID
 DisconnectSwitch,   //Type
 Closed,             //State
 FwareActDS3         //Services
).

connected( PLC2,     //Start Node
 ActDS                //End Node
).

service( FwareActDS3,//Service ID
 1.0,                //Version Number
 ModbusSlave,        //Service Type
 [PLC2Master],       //Dependent Upon
 [TLS],              //Security Protocols
 502                 //Connecting Port
).
```

Figure 2. CIM XML and Prolog specifications of a substation.

two communicating devices and a *Path* variable. It then calls a helper rule *path* (Line 1), which finds a path (list of nodes) from A to B. This is accomplished using a recursive travel rule: a path from A to B is obtained if A and B are connected (Line 5) and a path from A to B is obtained provided that A is connected to a node C different from B that is not on the previously visited

Table 2. SCADA device models described as Prolog facts.

```
1   % device (ID , TYPE, GROUP, SERVICES_LIST , COORDX, COORDY)
2   device(adminpc, pc , en ,[ ssh1 , sqlclient1 ],10,20).
3   device(historian , pc , en ,[ rlogind1 , postgresqld ],10,30).
4   device(sensor , pc , pcn ,[ rlogin2 , sqlclient2 ],30,10).
5   device(serviceproxy , router , firewall ,[ firewalld ],10,10).
6
7   % service (ID , TYPE, VER, PRIV_LEVEL , PROTOCOL, ACL)
8   service(sqlclient1 , database_client ,2003, user , odbc , _).
9   service(sqlclient2 , database_client ,2000, user , odbc , _).
10  service( postgresqld , database_server ,1998, root , odbc , [ ←↩
        sqlclient1 , sqlclient2 ]).
11
12  % bydirectionlink (SRC , DEST)
13  connected (adminpc , serviceproxy ).
14  connected (historian , serviceproxy ).
15  connected (sensor , serviceproxy ).
```

Table 3. Access control implementation.

```
1   path(A, B, Path ) :−
2           travel(A, B, [A], Q) ,
3           reverse(Q, Path ).
4
5   travel(A, B, P, [B|P]) :−
6           connected (A, B).
7
8   travel(A, B, Visited , Path ) :−
9           connected (A, C),
10          C \== B,
11          \+member(C, Visited ),
12          travel(C, B, [C| Visited ] , Path ).
13
14  is_access_control (DevA , DevB) :−
15          keys (DevA , AuthMechA ),
16          keys (DevB , AuthMechB ),
17          match ( AuthMechA , AuthMechB ).
18
19  is_end2end_conf_integ ( SecPropsList , [ Head ]) :−
20          defsvs (Head , dservice ) ,
21          secprots ( dservice , SPList ),
22          SecPropsList = SPList .
23
24  is_end2end_conf_integ ( SecPropsList , [ Head| Tail ]) :−
25          defsvs (Head , dservice ) ,
26          secprots ( dservice , SPList1 ),
27          is_end2end_conf_integ ( SPList2 , Tail ),
28          intersection ( SPList1 , SPList2 , CommonSPList ),
29          nth0 (0 , CommonSPList , _) ,
30          SecPropsList=SPList1 .
31
32  ck_ConformanceTo_CIP002 −08(DevA , DevB , Path ) :−
33          path (DevA , DevB , Path ),
34          is_access_control (DevA , DevB ),
35          is_end2end_conf_integ (Path ).
```

part of the path, and a path is found from C to B (Line 8). Avoiding repeated nodes ensures that the program halts. Once the path is known, checking access control (Line 14) is a matter of comparing if both the communicating nodes use

Table 4.   Java-JPL code for querying and importing path information.

```
1    Variable X = new Variable("X");
2    Variable Y = new Variable("Y");
3    Variable P = new Variable("P");
4    Term arg[] = { X,Y,P };
5    Query q = new Query("path" , arg);
6
7    while (q.hasMoreElements()) {
8        Term bound_to_x = (Term) ((Hashtable) q.nextElement()).get(↵
             "P");
9        String[] strarray = jpl.Util.atomListToStringArray(↵
             bound_to_x);
10       for (int i=0; i<strarray.length; i++) {
11           System.out.println(strarray[i]);
12       }
13   }
```

a pre-shared key or PKI authentication. Checking confidentiality and integrity (Lines 19 and 24) amounts to checking if every pair of consecutive nodes on a path share an encryption channel (e.g., IPSec or TLS).

4.4   Graphical User Interface

A Java-based GUI front-end to Prolog facilitates user interaction with the system. The implementation leverages JPL, a set of Java classes and C functions, which provides a Java-Prolog interface by embedding a Prolog engine in Java VM. Annotating each device in a CIM specification with (x, y) coordinates enables SCADA network data to be imported and viewed in a Java grid panel. This approach allows for more user interaction than other network visualization tools (e.g., Graphviz [2] and CAIDA [6]). For example, a user can hover over a device icon to see a detailed listing of its security attributes or click on devices of interest and formulate a query. Table 4 presents JPL code that imports information about all possible paths between two devices in the form of Prolog lists for display (Table 3 describes the predicate implementation).

Three JPL variables (Lines 1–3) are created to hold the two devices and the list of possible paths between them. A query is then formulated and sent to the Prolog engine, which populates these values. The JPL library provides several utility functions such as atomListToStringArray to perform conversions between Java and Prolog types.

5.   Evaluation

Our implementation involves approximately 1,620 lines of Prolog code (not including network and workflow encodings) and 3,500 lines of Java code. The twelve best practices rules took roughly 30 hours to encode in Prolog. The implementation was tested with several substation network-level scenarios (involving less than 100 machines). Each scenario executed in a few seconds on

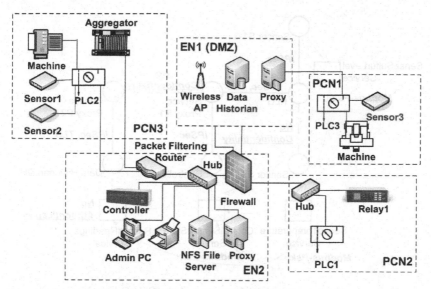

Figure 3. SCADA architecture with two ENs and three PCNs.

an Intel Core2Duo 2.0 GHz machine running Ubuntu Linux 7.10. This section presents the results of access control and firewall deployment evaluations for one of these scenarios.

Figure 3 presents a typical SCADA architecture containing two subnets (EN1 and EN2) with several enterprise machines and devices, and three subnets (PCN1, PCN2 and PCN3) with process control devices. EN1 has two important devices, the Wireless AP (access point) and Data Historian. The data relationships are as follows. The Data Historian is a shared device that logs events in several SCADA devices. It is accessed by local and remote users for supervisory purposes. The Data Historian connects directly to devices in PCN1 via a proxy server; this configuration enables the vendor to maintain the machine remotely via the Internet. The Data Historian also logs events from Relay1 in PCN2 and is accessed by the Admin PC and NFS File Server in EN3. Sensor1 and Sensor2 in PCN3 are managed by the Controller in EN3 and their events are logged by the Data Historian. Services provided by the Controller are accessed by the Admin PC.

5.1 Test 1: Access Control Implementation

Figure 4 shows the dependency graph of the two sensors in PCN3 that report their readings to two enterprise devices (Controller and Data Historian) through several proxy servers and PLCs, not all of which support IPSec or TLS stacks for confidentiality.

Table 5 summarizes the results of running a "correct implementation of access control" query for confidentiality and integrity (C/I), authentication (Auth) and CIP conformance (Conf) on the sensors.

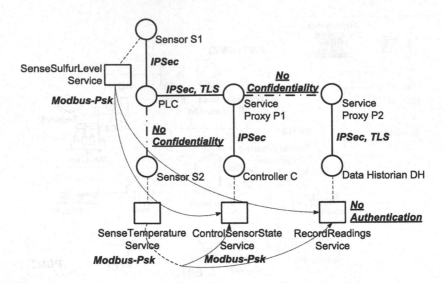

Figure 4.   Access control conformance of the SCADA architecture.

Table 5.   Access control implementation results.

Source	Sink	Path	C/I	Auth	Conf
S1	C	S1 → PLC → P1 → C	Yes	Yes	Yes
S1	DH	S1 → PLC → P1 → P2 → DH4	No	No	No
S2	C	S2 → PLC → P1 → C	No	Yes	No
S2	DH	S2 → PLC → P1 → P2 → DH	No	No	No

The invocation ck_ConformanceTo_CIP002(sensors,sinks,Paths) reveals that the data association channel between the sensors and controller enforces integrity because of an end-to-end pre-shared key. However the channel between sensor S2 and the controller does not have confidentiality because the hop between S2 and the PLC does not support a confidentiality protocol. A similar problem occurs along the paths between the sensors and the data historian where the hop between the two proxies is not confidential. The only channel that passes the test successfully is between S1 and the controller because the sensor supports IPSec as an encryption protocol.

5.2   Test 2: Firewall Deployment

Firewall deployment was evaluated by starting with the original configuration, identifying the offending link, incorporating the appropriate firewall, and repeating the conformance checking of the new configuration. Table 6 presents the results. The original configuration has a security rating of 2 due to the direct historian-PCN1 link that was incorporated for vendor convenience. This

Table 6. Firewall deployment results.

Num	Substation Architecture	Rating	Offending Link
1	Original configuration (Figure 3)	2	DH-PCN1
2	Same as 1 with DH-PCN1 link removed	2	S2-PacketFilteringRouter-C
3	Same as 2 with router replaced with a stateful firewall	3	C-AdminPC
4	Same as 3 with C moved to the DH subnet	4	None

link poses a serious threat to the substation as it potentially allows direct Internet access to the plant floor. Note that the security rating of the entire substation is dependent on the security rating of the weakest link. Removing this link (by incorporating a new firewall or relocating PCN devices) and repeating the analysis produces a security rating of 2. This is due to the presence of a packet filtering router that separates devices in PCN3 from the controller in EN3. Upon replacing the router with a stateful firewall, the new configuration has a security rating of 3 with all the shared devices positioned behind the proper firewalls. Finally, moving the shared controller to same subnet as the historian produces a DMZ configuration (security rating 4) with all the shared devices located in a separate subnet.

6. Conclusions

The predicate-calculus-based security model described in this paper expresses infrastructure elements as facts and security standards and best practices as rules that specify constraints on the facts. The implemented tool chain automatically generates a security model from SCADA infrastructure specifications and checks it for compliance with security standards and best practices. The tool chain provides a rich front-end to the predicate logic engine, which enables security administrators to compose their own queries during security assessments. It also supports the visualization of network topology and security assessment results to reveal possible points of attack.

Although the approach has been tested on infrastructures with less than 100 nodes, it is scalable to large infrastructures because best practices are typically specified at the substation level. Moreover, checking system conformance against best practices is a static process that is typically performed offline.

The model allows the implementation of checks against other standards and best practices with minimal changes; however, the generation of the security model from CIM specifications could be improved. Our future work will focus on integrating security tools such as Nessus that automatically provide details of services running on devices along with device dependencies and vulnerabilities. Also, the security model will be extended to include SCADA infrastructures that are complementary to the power grid (e.g., water supply and telecommunications systems).

References

[1] American Gas Association, Cryptographic Protection of SCADA Communications; Part 1: Background, Policies and Test Plan, AGA Report No. 12 (Part 1), Draft 5, Washington, DC (www.gtiservices.org/security /AGA12Draft5r3.pdf), 2005.

[2] AT&T Research, Graphviz – Graph Visualization Software, Florham Park, New Jersey (www.graphviz.org).

[3] British Columbia Institute of Technology, Good Practice Guide on Firewall Deployment for SCADA and Process Control Networks, National Infrastructure Security Co-ordination Centre, London, United Kingdom, 2005.

[4] British Columbia Institute of Technology, Industrial Security Incident Database, Burnaby, Canada.

[5] R. Chandia, J. Gonzalez, T. Kilpatrick, M. Papa and S. Shenoi, Security strategies for SCADA networks, in *Critical Infrastructure Protection*, E. Goetz and S. Shenoi (Eds.), Springer, Boston, Massachusetts, pp. 117–131, 2007.

[6] Cooperative Association for Internet Data Analysis, The CAIDA web site, La Jolla, California (www.caida.org).

[7] R. Dacey, Critical Infrastructure Protection: Challenges in Securing Control Systems, Report GAO-04-140T, United States General Accounting Office, Washington, DC (www.gao.gov/new.items/d04140t.pdf), 2004.

[8] Distributed Management Task Force, Common Information Model (CIM) Infrastructure Specification, Document DSP0004 Version 2.3 Final, Portland, Oregon (www.dmtf.org/standards/published_documents /DSP0004V2.3_final.pdf), 2005.

[9] Federal Energy Regulatory Commission, Mandatory Reliability Standards for Critical Infrastructure Protection, Docket No. RM06-22-000; Order No. 706, Washington, DC (ferc.gov/whats-new/comm-meet/2008/011708/E-2 .pdf), 2008.

[10] Industrial Automation Open Networking Association, The IAONA Handbook for Network Security, Version 1.3, Magdeburg, Germany (www.iaona.org/pictures/files/1122888138–IAONA_HNS_1_3-reduced_050 725.pdf), 2005.

[11] Instrumentation Systems and Automation Society, Security Technologies for Manufacturing and Control Systems (ANSI/ISA-TR99.00.01-2004), Research Triangle Park, North Carolina, 2004.

[12] M. Masera and I. Nai Fovino, A service-oriented approach for assessing infrastructure security, in *Critical Infrastructure Protection*, E. Goetz and S. Shenoi (Eds.), Springer, Boston, Massachusetts, pp. 367–379, 2007.

[13] D. Maynor and R. Graham, SCADA security and terrorism: We're not crying wolf! presented at the *Black Hat Federal Conference*, 2006.

[14] J. Meserve, Sources: Staged cyber attack reveals vulnerability in power grid, Cable News Network, Atlanta, Georgia (www.cnn.com/2007/US /09 /26/power.at.risk), September 26, 2007.

[15] National Institute of Standards and Technology, Standards for Security Categorization of Federal Information and Information Systems, FIPS Publication 199, Gaithersburg, Maryland, 2004.

[16] M. Rash, psad: Intrusion detection for iptables (www.cipherdyne.com /psad).

[17] R. Ross, A. Johnson, S. Katzke, P. Toth, G. Stoneburner and G. Rogers, Guide for Assessing the Security Controls in Federal Information Systems, NIST Special Publication 800-53A, National Institute of Standards and Technology, Gaithersburg, Maryland, 2008.

[18] SourceForge.net, AfterGlow (afterglow.sourceforge.net).

[19] Y. Stamatiou, E. Skipenes, E. Henriksen, N. Stathiakis, A. Sikianakis, E. Charalambous, N. Antonakis, K. Stolen, F. den Braber, M. Sodal Lund, K. Papadaki and G. Valvis, The CORAS approach for model-based risk management applied to a telemedicine service, *Proceedings of the European Medical Informatics Conference*, pp. 206–211, 2003.

[20] K. Ziegler, NERC cyber security standards to become mandatory in United States, *Electric Energy Industry News*, January 21, 2008.

Chapter 14

COLLABORATIVE ACCESS CONTROL FOR CRITICAL INFRASTRUCTURES

Amine Baina, Anas Abou El Kalam, Yves Deswarte and Mohamed Kaaniche

Abstract   A critical infrastructure (CI) can fail with various degrees of severity due to physical and logical vulnerabilities. Since many interdependencies exist between CIs, failures can have dramatic consequences on the entire infrastructure. This paper focuses on threats that affect information and communication systems that constitute the critical information infrastructure (CII). A new collaborative access control framework called PolyOrBAC is proposed to address security problems that are specific to CIIs. The framework offers each organization participating in a CII the ability to collaborate with other organizations while maintaining control of its resources and internal security policy. The approach is demonstrated on a practical scenario involving the electrical power grid.

Keywords: Access control, policies, models, collaboration, interoperability

1.   Introduction

Critical infrastructures (CIs) are logical/physical facilities that are essential to public welfare; their disruption or failure could have a dramatic impact on the economy and social well-being of a nation. The most significant CIs are those dedicated to electricity generation, transport and distribution (electrical power grid), telecommunications, supply services (energy, food, fuel, water and gas), transportation systems (roads, railways and airports) and financial services (banks, stock exchanges and insurance companies).

Due to interdependencies existing between the various infrastructures, cascading and escalating failures are possible [15, 21]. A cascading failure occurs when a failure in one infrastructure causes the failure of one or more components in a second infrastructure. An escalating failure occurs when a failure in one infrastructure exacerbates an independent failure in a second infrastructure; this second failure has increased severity and/or requires significant

Please use the following format when citing this chapter:

Baina, A., El Kalam, A.A., Deswarte, Y. and Kaaniche, M., 2008, in IFIP International Federation for Information Processing, Volume 290; *Critical Infrastructure Protection II*, eds. Papa, M., Shenoi, S., (Boston: Springer), pp. 189–201.

recovery or restoration time. A prime example is the North American blackout of August 14, 2003 [4]. A small failure in monitoring software prevented an electrical line incident from being confined; the failures propagated across the electrical power grid resulting in losses exceeding six billion dollars. In general, failures may occur as a result of accidental faults or malicious actions such as intrusions, denial-of-service attacks and worm propagation.

The North American blackout was caused by a failure in a computer system. Information technology and communications systems are used so widely in the various critical infrastructures that they have come to be known as the critical information infrastructure (CII). CIIs involve vulnerable information and communication technologies (ICT) that are easily compromised by attackers. Consequently, securing CII assets is an important component of any critical infrastructure protection effort.

In Europe, America and elsewhere, regional, national and multinational energy companies may be in competition, but they have to cooperate to produce, transport and distribute electric power. CIIs play a major role in these efforts – they are open, distributed systems that support collaboration between the various entities involved in operating critical infrastructures. CIIs are required to be flexible and extensible; it is equally important that they implement sophisticated access control strategies given the diverse entities that share the information and communication assets.

This paper focuses on security problems related to access control, collaboration and interoperability in CIIs. In particular, it shows how PolyOrBAC [2], a security framework based on the OrBAC access control model [1, 18] and web services technology, can be adapted to cope with CII security needs.

2.   CRUTIAL Architecture

This section describes a generic CII architecture (CRUTIAL [10]), which models interconnected infrastructures such as those encountered in the electrical power grid, provides an excellent framework for applying PolyOrBAC to protect CIIs from accidents and as well as from malicious acts.

The CRUTIAL architecture is presented in Figure 1. It can be viewed as a WAN comprising multiple LANs interconnected by CRUTIAL information switches (CISs). A LAN incorporates various logical and physical systems; it has its own applications and access control policy, and provides services to other entities. Each LAN belongs to an organization involving different actors and stakeholders (e.g., power generation companies, power plants, substations, energy authorities, external maintenance service providers, and transmission and distribution system operators). Multiple LANs are connected by a single CIS if they are part of the same organization and located in the same area. In this case, each LAN is dedicated to a component (e.g., substation) in order to manage a different access control policy for each component.

All the CII organizations in the CRUTIAL architecture are interconnected by CISs. Therefore, to provide controlled cooperation, each CIS must contain mechanisms that enforce the local security policy of each collaborating

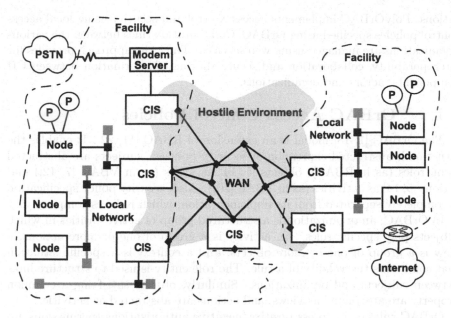

Figure 1. Generic CII architecture.

organization. Also, collaboration mechanisms should be implemented using web services. These policies and mechanisms must allow authorized access to resources and prevent all unauthorized access.

3. PolyOrBAC Framework

XACML is a popular language for specifying policies and managing access control in distributed and decentralized systems [16]. However XACML's flexibility and expressiveness comes at the cost of complexity and verbosity. It is hard to work directly with the language and policy files. Tools are being developed, but until they are widely available, it will be difficult for average users to work with XACML-based systems.

We use the OrBAC access control model as an alternative to XACML to implement access control for each CII component and to facilitate collaboration between components. Two approaches are possible. One approach is to impose a global, centralized security policy for all the organizations. This approach is not appropriate for a CII because of its dynamic character – organizations should be able to join or leave the CII without disturbing the rest of the architecture. Also, organizations are mutually suspicious. Each organization has specific rules and security policies and would prefer to maintain its autonomy. An organization would likely refuse to open its information systems to competitors or change its security policy.

The second approach is to use PolyOrBAC [2] to manage collaboration between CII organizations while maintaining the autonomy of individual organizations. PolyOrBAC implements access control and security using local access control policies specified using OrBAC. Collaboration rules between the various organizations are managed using web services. Thus, the approach provides for interoperability, collaboration and secure sharing of information between CII components, actors and organizations.

3.1   OrBAC Access Control Policies

The OrBAC [1, 18] model is an extension of RBAC [11, 22]. It enables the structured, abstracted expression of security policies: subjects are abstracted using roles (as in RBAC), objects [5, 14] as views (as in VBAC [7, 12]) and actions [5, 14] as activities (as in TBAC [20]). Also, security policy specification is completely separated from its implementation, which reduces complexity.

In OrBAC, an organization is a structured group of active entities in which subjects play specific roles. An activity is a group of one or more actions, a view is a group of one or more objects, and a context is a specific situation that conditions the validity of a rule. The role entity is used to structure links between subjects and organizations. Similarly, objects satisfying a common property are abstracted as views, and actions are abstracted as activities.

OrBAC rules can express positive/negative authorizations (permissions/interdictions) and obligations. Security rules have the following form: Permission (org ; r ; v ; a ; c), Prohibition (org ; r ; v ; a ; c) or Obligation (org ; r ; v ; a ; c). The rules imply that in context c, organization org grants role r permission (or prohibition or obligation) to perform activity a on view v.

OrBAC considers two different levels for the security policy: the abstract level and the concrete level. At the abstract level, the security administrator defines security rules using abstract entities (roles, activities, views) without worrying about how each organization implements these entities. At the concrete level, when a user requests an access, an authorization is granted (or not) according to the relevant rules, organization, role, instantiated view/activity and parameters. The derivation of permissions (i.e., instantiation of security rules) is formally expressed as:

$\forall org \in Organizations, \forall s \in Subjects, \forall activ \in Activities,$
$\forall o \in Objects, \forall r \in Roles, \forall a \in Actions, \forall v \in View, \forall c \in Contexts :$
Permission ($org, r, v, activ, c$) $\wedge$ Empower (org, s, r) $\wedge$
Consider ($org, a, activ$) $\wedge$ Use (org, o, v) $\wedge$
Hold (org, s, a, o, c) $\Rightarrow$ is-permitted(s, a, o).

The security rule specifies that if in organization org, role r can perform activity *activ* on view v when context c is True; and in organization org, r is assigned to subject s; and in organization org, action a is a part of activity *activ*; and in organization org, object o is part of view v; and context c is True for (org, s, a, o); then subject s may perform action a on object o.

3.2   OrBAC Limitations

OrBAC can be used to specify complex security policies that are encountered in real-world information technology systems. Also, it facilitates security policy management and updates.

However, in the CII context, it is necessary to specify security requirements and rules for each CII organization or subsystem, manage the collaboration between organizations, and enforce (within each CIS) the different security policies. OrBAC can handle the first requirement, but not the second. In particular, it is not possible to specify rules pertaining to multiple independent organizations in a collaborative system using a single OrBAC policy. Also, permissions cannot be associated with users belonging to other partner organizations or sub-organizations. Consequently, while OrBAC can express the security policy of an organization, it is inadequate for modeling collaboration and interoperability between multiple organizations.

3.3   Web Services

Web services technology offers powerful mechanisms for implementing collaboration. Software applications written in different programming languages and running on diverse platforms can use web services to exchange data over computer networks in a manner similar to inter-process communication on a single computer. Web services use well-known open standards and protocols such as XML [6], SOAP [19], WSDL [17] and UDDI [8], which are readily used with current web interfaces. Since web services are based on the HTTP protocol, they can cross firewalls without changing established security requirements. Moreover, the execution of a web service does not require substantial resources (memory, power and CPU time) and a small quantity of code is sufficient for implementation. Finally, web services can be easily coupled with OrBAC.

3.4   PolyOrBAC Framework

PolyOrBAC uses OrBAC to specify local access control policies (for each organization) and collaboration rules involving multiple organizations. Web services are used to enforce collaboration. A CII component (organization or subsystem) may have its own security objectives and can cooperate with the other components. Each organization has its own resources, services and applications with its own objectives, operations, security rules and policy. Figure 2 shows a scenario where Alice from Organization A wishes to invoke web service Service1 offered by Organization B.

During the initial publication step, each organization determines which resources and/or services it will provide to external partners. Web services are developed on the organization's application servers; they are defined in the organization's OrBAC security policy and are referenced in the organization's CIS to be accessible to external users.

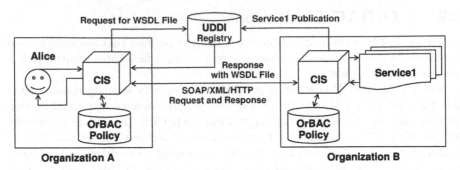

Figure 2. PolyOrBAC framework.

During the discovery step, when Alice wishes to use Service1, Organization A contacts the UDDI web service registry to search for Service1 (which is published beforehand by the offering organization (Organization B)). Then, Organization A receives the WSDL file with the description of Service1 and the URL of the site (in Organization B) that hosts Service1.

During the negotiation step, Organizations A and B mutually authenticate each other, they negotiate and come to an agreement, establish a contract and jointly define security rules governing access to Service1. These rules and contracts are registered in the OrBAC format in each CIS database that contains the security policy.

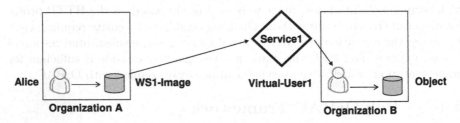

Figure 3. Virtual user and web service image.

During the invocation step, when Alice wishes to use Service1, she is first authenticated by Organization A. Organization A might wish to avoid using the UDDI registry every time it invokes Service1. Also, it might want to have a local representation of Service1 to manage the access control policy locally. To accomplish this, Organization A creates a local WS1-Image accessed by authorized users in A (Figure 3). Organization B may wish to have a local representation of (the remote) Organization A that requests Service1 to virtualize the distant access from Organization A and to manage it like a local access in Organization B. To accomplish this, Organization B creates a local Virtual-User1 with an OrBAC role that enables it to perform the activity corresponding to Service1. Each organization thus controls access to its own resources and services. It is responsible for authenticating its own users when they use services hosted by other organizations.

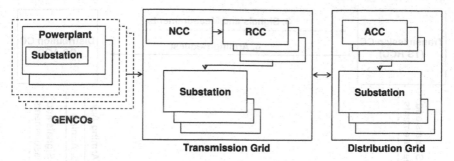

Figure 4. Generic electrical power grid architecture.

The request involves an access (controlled by A's OrBAC policy) to the local object WS1-Image representing Service1 as well as a remote access (controlled by B's OrBAC policy) to B's actions corresponding to Service1. The CISs belonging to Organizations A and B check that all exchanges between A and B are compatible with the agreed contract, and maintain logs of all exchanges to serve as evidence in case of dispute. If the invocation of Service1 is authorized, A sends a SOAP/XML request to the URL of Service1, B executes the request, and sends the result of Service1 to A, which transmits it to Alice.

4. Case Study

This section descibes a case study involving the application of PolyOrBAC to an electrical power grid CII.

4.1 Electrical Power Grid Scenario

Figure 4 presents a generic electrical power grid architecture. One or more electricity generation companies (GENCOs) – each operating several power plants — are connected to transmission grids. Each transmission grid, which is managed by transmission system operators (TSOs), comprises transmission substations monitored by one national and several regional control centers, and is connected to one or more distribution grids. Each distribution grid, which is managed by distribution system operators (DSOs), is composed of distribution substations monitored by area control centers; the grid provides electricity to subscribers (industries and residences) over distribution lines [13].

PolyOrBAC is useful when infrastructure components are required to execute remote actions and access resources from other partner organizations. We employ a real-world scenario to illustrate the application of PolyOrBAC to the electrical power grid CII. The scenario considers the possible cascading effects caused by attacks on the communication channels between TSO/DSO control centers and their substations during emergency conditions (e.g., line overloads). We assume that during emergency conditions a TSO is authorized by a DSO to activate defensive actions that include load shedding. The scenario involves four classes of organizations: transmission regional control centers (TS

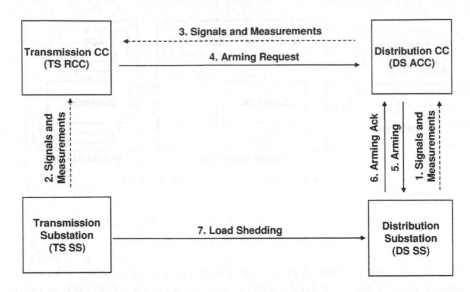

Figure 5.   Exchanged commands and signals.

RCCs) managed by TSOs, transmission substations (TS SSs), distribution area control centers (DS ACCs) managed by DSOs, and distribution substations (DS SSs). Figure 5 presents the commands and signals exchanged between these organizations in normal and emergency situations.

During normal operations, the DS SSs send several signals and measurements (power, voltage, frequency) to the TS RCC via their DS ACCs (1 and 3). On the other hand, the TS SSs send signals and measurements (power, voltage, frequency) to their TS RCC (2). The TS RCC monitors the electrical power system and identifies emergency conditions that could be remedied with opportune load shedding applied to specific areas of the grid. To actuate a defensive action, the TS RCC chooses a subset of HV (high voltage) or MV (medium voltage) DS SSs from the list of participating DS SSs in the emergency plan; these DS SSs are subsequently armed by the TS RCC.

In the arming step, the TS RCC sends the requests to preventively arm the selected DS SSs to the concerned DS ACCs (4) to prepare for load shedding. The DS ACCs send the arming order to DS SSs that arm the appropriate monitoring control and defense terminal unit (MCDTU) (5); the armed DS SSs then send acknowledgements to the DS ACC (6). When an emergency situation is detected, the TS SS sends a load shedding command to all the DS SSs participating in the emergency plan, at which point only the previously armed DS SSs perform load shedding over their MCDTUs (7).

4.2   Scenario Interpretation

This section details the web service invocations that are involved in the scenario based on the PolyOrBAC security policy.

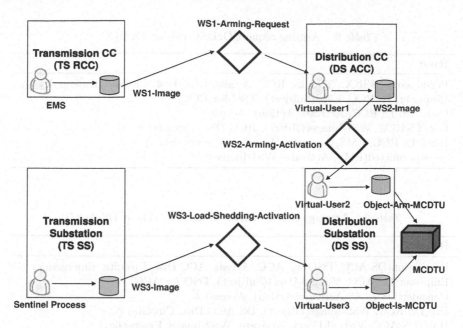

Figure 6. PolyOrBAC applied to the electrical power grid scenario.

Table 1. Instantiated web services.

Service	Provider	Client
WS1-Arming-Request	DS ACC	EMS in the TS RCC
WS2-Arming-Activation	DS SS	Virtual user in the DS ACC
WS3-Load-Shedding-Activation	DS SS	Sentinel process in the TS SS

Figure 6 summarizes the web services, virtual users representing remote organizations that can request web services, ws-images (local images of remote web services that can be invoked), and resources involved in the scenario. The scenario involves four organizations (TS RCC, DS ACC, TS SS and DS SS) and three web services (Table 1).

We assume that the electrical management system (EMS) in the TS RCC orders the DS ACC to arm its DS SS MCDTUs. When the EMS activates WS1-Image, the execution of WS1-Arming-Request is automatically activated. The access of WS1-Image by the EMS is checked against the TS RCC policy and is granted according to the OrBAC rule (Table 2) that manages access control for the Arming Request web service at the level of the organization that invokes the service (i.e., TS RCC).

On the DS ACC side, WS1-Arming-Request tells Virtual-User1 in DS ACC to access object WS2-Image. This access (WS2-Image by Virtual-User1) is checked against the DS ACC policy and is granted according to the OrBAC rule

Table 2.   Arming request OrBAC rule at TS RCC.

Rule
Permission(TS RCC, TSO for RCC, Access, RCC Dist. Circuits, Emergency) ∧ Empower(TS RCC, EMS(Subject), TSO for RCC) ∧ Consider(TS RCC, Activate(Action), Access) ∧ Use(TS RCC, WS1-Image(Object), RCC Dist. Circuits) ∧ Hold(TS RCC, EMS, Activate, WS1-Image, Emergency) ∧ ⇒ is-permitted(EMS, Activate, WS1-Image)

Table 3.   Arming request/activation OrBAC rule at DS ACC.

Rule
Permission(DS ACC, DSO for ACC, Access, ACC Dist. Circuits, Emergency) ∧ Empower(DS ACC, Virtual-User1(Subject), DSO for ACC) ∧ Consider(DS ACC, Activate(Action), Access) ∧ Use(DS ACC, WS2-Image(Object), DS ACC Dist. Circuits) ∧ Hold(DS ACC, Virtual-User1, Activate, WS2-Image, Emergency) ∧ ⇒ is-permitted(Virtual-User1, Activate, WS2-Image)

(Table 3) that manages access control for the Arming Request and Activation web services at the level of the organization that provides the service (i.e., DS ACC).

Table 4.   Arming activation OrBAC rule at DS SS.

Rule
Permission(DS SS, DSO for SS, Access, DS SS Dist. Circuits, Emergency) ∧ Empower(DS SS, Virtual-User2(Subject), DSO for SS) ∧ Consider(DS SS, Activate(Action), Access) ∧ Use(DS SS, Object-Arm-MCDTU(Object), DS SS Dist. Circuits) ∧ Hold(DS SS, Virtual-User2, Activate, Object-Arm-MCDTU, Emergency) ∧ ⇒ is-permitted(Virtual-User2, Activate, Object-Arm-MCDTU)

When Virtual-User1 activates object WS-Image2, WS2-Arming-Activation is automatically activated, then Virtual-User2 activates Object-Arm-MCDTU in DS SS, and the physical arming command is executed over the MCDTU. This access (Virtual-User2 to Object-Arm-MCDTU) is checked against the DS SS policy and is granted according to the OrBAC rule (Table 4), which manages access control for the Arming Activation web service in DS SS. WS3-Load-Shedding-Activation is negotiated and activated in the same way.

5. Conclusions

The PolyOrBAC security framework provides excellent support for the access control and collaboration requirements in CIIs. Web services are leveraged to provide decentralized management of access control policies and to enable organizations to mutually negotiate contracts for collaboration. Organizations retain their own resources, services, applications, operating systems, functioning rules, goals and security policy rules. However, each organization is responsible for authenticating its users when they use other organizations' services. The framework also facilitates the management and integration of new organizations in a CII and ensures user privacy and non-disclosure of data and services. Moreover, the framework can handle hardware and software heterogeneities; network segments and physical/logical equipment belonging to the collaborating CII organizations can be integrated seamlessly [9].

The framework is currently being implemented in a Java environment using IBM Eclipse IDE and SWI-Prolog. Our future research will focus on meeting availability requirements using obligation rules and integrity requirements by monitoring information flows of different degrees of criticality [24]. Our research will also attempt to incorporate results from trust negotiation [23] and trust-based access control [3] in the PolyOrBAC framework.

Acknowledgements

This research was partially supported by CRUTIAL, a European FP6-IST Project and by PolSec, a LAAS Project. The authors also wish to thank Fabrizio Garrone and Giovanna Dondossola for their contributions to the case study described in this paper.

References

[1] A. Abou El Kalam, S. Benferhat, A, Miege, R. El Baida, F. Cuppens, C. Saurel, P. Balbiani, Y. Deswarte and G. Trouessin, Organization based access control, *Proceedings of the Fourth IEEE International Workshop on Policies for Distributed Systems and Networks*, pp. 120–134, 2003.

[2] A. Abou El Kalam, Y. Deswarte, A. Baina and M. Kaaniche, Access control for collaborative systems: A web services based approach, *Proceedings of the IEEE International Conference on Web Services*, pp. 1064–1071, 2007.

[3] W. Adams and N. Davis, Toward a decentralized trust-based access control system for dynamic collaboration, *Proceedings of the Sixth Annual IEEE SMC Information Assurance Workshop*, pp. 317–324, 2005.

[4] M. Amin, North America's electricity infrastructure: Are we ready for more perfect storms? *IEEE Security and Privacy*, vol. 1(5), pp. 19–25, 2003.

[5] D. Bell and L. LaPadula, Secure Computer Systems: Unified Exposition and MULTICS Interpretation, Technical Report ESD-TR-75-306, MTR-2997 Rev. 1, MITRE Corporation, Bedford, Massachusetts, 1976.

[6] T. Bray, J. Paoli, C. Sperberg-McQueen, E. Maler, F. Yergeau and J. Cowan (Eds.), Extensible Markup Language (XML) 1.1, Recommendation, World Wide Web Consortium, Cambridge, Massachusetts (www .w3.org/TR/2004/REC-xml11-20040204), 2004.

[7] G. Brose, A view-based access control model for CORBA, in *Secure Internet Programming: Security Issues for Mobile and Distributed Objects (LNCS 1603)*, J. Vitek and C. Jensen, Springer-Verlag, London, United Kingdom, pp. 237–252, 2001.

[8] L. Clement, A. Hately, C. von Riegen and T. Rogers (Eds.), UDDI Version 3.0.2, Organization for the Advancement of Structured Information Standards, Billerica, Massachusetts (uddi.org/pubs/uddi_v3.htm), 2005.

[9] F. Cuppens, N. Cuppens-Boulahia, T. Sans and A. Miege, A formal approach to specify and deploy a network security policy, in *Formal Aspects in Security and Trust*, T. Dimitrakos and F. Martinelli (Eds.), Springer, Berlin-Heidelberg, Germany, pp. 203–218, 2004.

[10] G. Dondossola, G. Deconinck, F. Di Giandomenico, S. Donatelli, M. Kaaniche and P. Verissimo, Critical utility infrastructural resilience, *Proceedings of the Workshop on Security and Networking in Critical Real-Time and Embedded Systems*, 2006.

[11] D. Ferraiolo, R. Sandhu, S. Gavrila, D. Kuhn and R. Chandramouli, Proposed NIST standard for role-based access control, *ACM Transactions on Information and System Security*, vol. 4(3), pp. 224–274, 2001.

[12] T. Fink, M. Koch and C. Oancea, Specification and enforcement of access control in heterogeneous distributed applications, *Proceedings of the International Conference on Web Services*, pp. 88–100, 2003.

[13] F. Garrone, C. Brasca, D. Cerotti, D. Codetta Raiteri, A. Daidone, G. Deconinck, S. Donatelli, G. Dondossola, F. Grandoni, M. Kaaniche and T. Rigole, Analysis of New Control Applications, Deliverable D2, The CRUTIAL Project, CESI Ricerca, Milan, Italy (crutial.cesiricerca.it/content /files/Documents/Deliverables%20P1/WP1-D2-final.pdf), 2007.

[14] M. Harrison, W. Ruzzo and J. Ullman, Protection in operating systems, *Communications of the ACM*, vol. 19(8), pp. 461–471, 1976.

[15] J. Laprie, K. Kanoun and M. Kaaniche, Modeling interdependencies between the electricity and information infrastructures, *Proceedings of the Twenty-Sixth International Conference on Computer Safety, Reliability and Security*, pp. 54–67, 2007.

[16] M. Lorch, S. Proctor, R. Lepro, D. Kafura and S. Shah, First experiences using XACML for access control in distributed systems, *Proceedings of the ACM Workshop on XML Security*, pp. 25–37, 2003.

[17] N. Kavantzas, D. Burdett, G. Ritzinger, T. Fletcher, Y. Lafon, and C. Barreto (Eds.), Web Services Choreography Description Language Version 1.0, Candidate Recommendation, World Wide Web Consortium, Cambridge, Massachusetts (www.w3.org/TR/2005/CR-ws-cdl-10-20051109), 2006.

[18] A. Miege, Definition of a Formal Framework for Specifying Security Policies: The OrBAC Model and Extensions, Ph.D. Thesis, Department of Computer Science, Ecole Nationale Superieure des Telecommunications (TELECOM ParisTech), Paris, France, 2005.

[19] N. Mitra (Ed.), SOAP Version 1.2, Recommendation, World Wide Web Consortium, Cambridge, Massachusetts (www.w3.org/TR/2003/REC-soap12-part0-20030624), 2003.

[20] S. Oh and S. Park, Task-role-based access control model, *Information Systems*, vol. 28(6), pp 533–562, 2003.

[21] S. Rinaldi, J. Peerenboom and T. Kelly, Identifying, understanding and analyzing critical infrastructure interdependencies, *IEEE Control Systems*, vol. 21(6), pp. 11–25, 2001.

[22] R. Sandhu, E. Coyne, H. Feinstein and C. Youman, Role-based access control models, *IEEE Computer*, vol. 29(2), pp. 38–47, 1996.

[23] K. Seamons, T. Chan, E. Child, M. Halcrow, A. Hess, J. Holt, J. Jacobson, R. Jarvis, A. Patty, B. Smith, T. Sundelin and L. Yu, TrustBuilder: Negotiating trust in dynamic coalitions, *Proceedings of the DARPA Information Survivability Conference and Exposition*, vol. 2, pp. 49–51, 2003.

[24] E. Totel, J. Blanquart, Y. Deswarte and D. Powell, Supporting multiple levels of criticality, *Proceedings of the Twenty-Eighth Annual Symposium on Fault Tolerant Computing*, pp. 70–79, 1998.

V

INFRASTRUCTURE INTERDEPENDENCIES

Chapter 15

MODELING DEPENDENCIES IN CRITICAL INFRASTRUCTURES

Albert Nieuwenhuijs, Eric Luiijf and Marieke Klaver

Abstract   This paper describes a model for expressing critical infrastructure dependencies. The model addresses the limitations of existing approaches with respect to clarity of definition, support for quality and the influence of operating states of critical infrastructures and environmental factors.

Keywords: Critical infrastructures, dependencies, modeling, system analysis

1.   Introduction

A critical infrastructure (CI) comprises those assets and parts thereof that are essential to maintaining vital societal functions, including the supply chain, health, safety, security and the economy [5]. CI dependencies are important for understanding the cascading effects in the various CI sectors that can have serious societal impact.

However, the models and methodologies available for dependency analysis are very limited. Recent studies of the Dutch national infrastructure [7, 11, 12] have demonstrated the need for a clear, methodical understanding of dependencies. Moreover, real-world dependencies and event data from CI incident databases (e.g., [16]) contain complexities that are not captured by existing dependency models; these complexities are, therefore, often ignored. When important aspects of CI dependencies are not modeled adequately, risk assessments conducted using these dependencies are suspect at best.

This paper describes a model for expressing CI dependencies that is based on a system analysis approach. The model addresses the limitations of existing approaches with respect to clarity of definition, support for quality and the influence of operating states of CIs and environmental factors.

Please use the following format when citing this chapter:

Nieuwenhuijs, A., Luiijf, E. and Klaver, M., 2008, in IFIP International Federation for Information Processing, Volume 290; *Critical Infrastructure Protection II*, eds. Papa, M., Shenoi, S., (Boston: Springer), pp. 205–213.

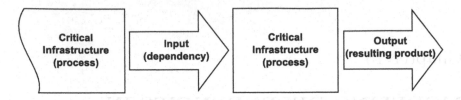

Figure 1. Modeling dependencies.

2.   Background

A dependency is a relationship between two products or services in which one product or service is required for generating the other product or service. A product is a tangible or intangible entity created as a result of direct human, machine or system activity. A service is an intangible product. An interdependency is the mutual dependency of products or services [8].

Numerous models have been developed to capture the essential properties of dependencies [4, 9, 10, 14, 15]. Dependencies are classified on the basis of various features, including sector, product (e.g., cyber or physical), coupling (tight or loose), buffered or non-buffered, and policy.

Our experience performing dependency analyses has shown that current methodologies (e.g., [9, 10, 14, 15]) do not provide enough support for modeling the complexities that arise in real-world scenarios. The primary problem is the absence of a clear definition of dependencies. In particular, common cause scenarios are often mistaken for dependencies. In our view, dependencies always deal with the relationships between two infrastructures. Therefore, a vulnerability or threat shared by two infrastructures should neither be included as a type of dependency nor as an aspect of a dependency. Whereas dependencies are the subject of dependency analysis, common cause threats and scenarios are components of risk analysis.

A second problem is the lack of support for modeling essential real-world factors. These include: (i) quality factors other than on/off availability that influence the output of CI products and services, (ii) process states in which the outputs of CI products and services may be produced, and (iii) environmental factors that influence the dependent inputs and processes that output CI products and services.

Our systems approach for modeling CI dependencies was developed to address these shortcomings.

3.   Modeling Dependencies

The systems approach views a CI as a process. A CI has one or more dependencies as required input(s) to the process. The approach is equivalent to process modeling, and, in this context, dependencies are modeled as response functions (Figure 1).

In the following, we define the "quality" and "response" elements that describe dependencies, along with the "state of operation" and the "environmental" factors that influence dependencies.

3.1   Quality

Most approaches for modeling dependencies implicitly assume the complete availability or complete non-availability of a CI product or service. However, our experience working on CI incidents around the world [16] and examining CI incidents described in literature (e.g., [13]) has shown that the dependency of a CI product or service is characterized by more than just on/off availability. CI products and services that are input to a CI process also need to adhere to certain levels of quality. These levels of quality may involve various indicators, often specific to a product or service. Key indicators of quality include:

- Quantity/volume (of food, water or power)

- Speed (of transport or information services)

- Reliability (of information)

- Temperature (of heating or cooling water)

- Pressure (of gas or drinking water supply)

- Frequency and voltage (of electrical power)

- Biological and chemical purity (of food, drinking water, surface water or chemicals)

Note that when we refer to input(s) or output(s), all the quality aspects mentioned above are implicitly included.

3.2   Response

A dependency is characterized by the response function that describes the output of a CI as a function of its input(s). The response function depends on the input of products and services and on time.

Input Response.   An input response describes the CI output as a function of the CI products and services used as input. Two types of input response are distinguished:

- Functional behavior describing how the CI output and dependency are related when the dependency supply deteriorates.

- Functional behavior describing how the CI output and dependency are related when the dependency supply recovers.

Note that these input response functions can (but need not) be the same. For example, a gas turbine that generates electrical power normally operates with a certain input gas pressure θ. It may operate in a reduced output mode all the way down to a reduced gas pressure of 0.5θ. The gas turbine, however, will not start with a gas pressure less than 0.8θ. In this case, the electrical power output fails (becomes zero) when the gas pressure drops below 0.5θ. When the gas pressure recovers, the power output resumes only after the gas pressure has risen to 0.8θ.

Time Response.   A time response describes the output of a CI in terms of its temporal behavior after a partial/complete failure. The time response functional behavior has four aspects:

- The time period between the moment the quality of one or more inputs (dependencies) change(s) and the moment this leads to a (quality) change in the CI output.

- The extent to which the CI output changes as a function of time in response to a change in input quality (or qualities).

- The differential aspect of dependencies. This functional behavior describes the effect on the CI output as a consequence of the speed of a (partial) disruption in a dependency. An example of this effect is the stockpiling of a critical commodity like gasoline after a steep price increase.

- The integrating aspect of dependencies. This functional behavior describes the effect on the CI output as a consequence of the effect that a reduction in the level of satisfaction of dependencies causes a continuously increasing lack of product or service output. For example, a field that receives too little water will yield less and less for each day it is under-watered until the crop eventually dies.

3.3   States of Operation

The state of operation of a CI is one of the main factors that influence a dependency. We define four states of operation:

- **Normal State:** This is the state in which the CI operates under normal conditions.

- **Stressed State:** This is the state in which special measures are required to keep CI operations under control.

- **Crisis State:** This is the state in which CI operations are out of control.

- **Recovery State:** This is the state in which CI operations are under control but have not been restored to normal conditions.

Figure 2 presents the CI state transition diagram. In each state, the set of CI products and services on which the CI output depends and the extent to

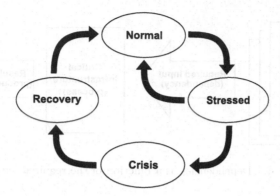

Figure 2. State transition diagram.

which the CI depends on the (input) services and products will, in general, differ. For example, if computer systems are down due to a power outage, there is no longer a critical dependency on telecommunications for the purpose of data transmission. However, if the data can be communicated verbally using a telephone, the critical dependency on telecommunications is increased.

We use hypothetical scenarios in an electrical power grid to clarify the CI states and their transitions. In the power grid, small disturbances occur even in the "normal" state and no special measures have to be taken to ensure control of operations. However, if data communications between the central control room and substations fail, the state of the power grid cannot be monitored and, therefore, the power grid cannot be controlled from the central location. The contingency plan involves dispatching operators to the substations to monitor and control power grid equipment. The operators may use cellular phones to exchange information with the central control room. Because out-of-the-ordinary measures have been put in place to maintain control of operations, the CI is in a "stressed" state.

If the cellular network fails after some time, central monitoring and control of the grid state becomes impossible. The power grid is out of control and is, therefore, in a "crisis" state. After regaining data communications with the substations, the state of the power grid becomes clear at the central control room. However, due to lack of control, the power grid has split into two "islands" and smaller portions of the grid have tripped and, hence, become disconnected from the grid. Note that an island is a power grid partition with specific voltage/frequency characteristics that are different from its neighboring grid(s); this prevents its reconnection with the grid. The operational procedures necessary to recover from this situation are well understood, but they take some time and effort. The power grid is in the "recovery" state until normal operations are restored.

The boundaries between states are often not sharply defined and are open to interpretation. Fortunately, this is not a problem when conducting a dependency analysis, as long as all the states are considered. States can be defined as

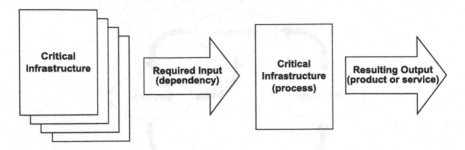

Figure 3. Dependencies as a function of the required output.

needed; it is just that the dependencies that are not considered in one state will be considered as part of some other state. The important issue is to recognize that dependencies can vary according to how states are defined, but all the dependencies in all states of operation must be considered in the analysis.

3.4   Environmental Factors

Certain environmental factors that are outside the scope of a CI can influence dependencies. These factors can worsen or alleviate dependencies, change their response or even create new dependencies. Environmental factors can influence dependencies in the following manner:

- At very low ambient temperatures, the efficiency of a cooling tower increases and a power station may no longer rely on cooling water from a river (input response).

- During rush hour, the effects of a road closure are much more acute than during off-hours (time response).

- In winter, the amount of gas needed for heating is considerably higher than what is needed in summer (quality requirement).

4.   Modeling Dependencies

Having identified the elements of CI dependencies, it is necessary to model the relationships between these elements. Note that the reason for constructing a model is not to generate a mathematical description of dependencies, but to formalize the relationships between the elements that have been identified. Therefore, the model is not intended to be used to analyze operational aspects or to conduct simulations.

As mentioned above, a dependency deals with the relationship between a required input for a CI process and the resulting CI process output in the form of products and/or services. This is the domain of process modeling and we employ its terminology and concepts to construct the CI dependency model as shown in Figure 3.

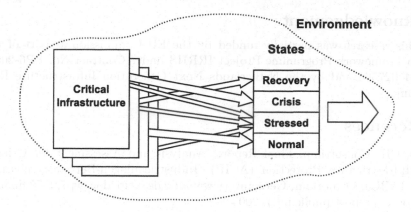

Figure 4. States and environment as part of the dependency model.

The CI output, O, is a function of input and time, i.e., $O = f(I, t)$, where I is the input and t is the time. The time variable describes the time aspects of the inputs, not the changing nature of the dependencies. The dependencies are assumed to be static; their behavior does not change over time.

In general, the CI output is dependent on n inputs and may be expressed as: $O = f(I_{1...n}, t)$. Since each CI input has its own set of qualitative properties, it is represented as a vector of qualitative indicators; thus, the CI output function becomes: $O = f(\bar{I}_{1...n}, t)$. Since the CI output also has a set of qualitative properties, the complete dependency response function can be written as: $\bar{O} = f(\bar{I}_{1...n}, t)$.

The set of dependencies and their qualitative properties are, in general, dependent on the state of the system and environmental factors as shown in Figure 4. Therefore, if a function is defined for every combination of state and environmental factor, the response function of the CI on its dependencies is: $\bar{O} = f_{s,e}(\bar{I}_{1...n}, t)$. This is typically a large set of moderately complex functions that, if developed completely, accurately describes how a CI reacts to changes in its dependencies in all possible situations. Note that the model can also be extended for a CI that produces more than one output by adding a subscript $j = 1..m$ to the output, where m is the number of outputs.

5.   Conclusions

The system-analysis-based dependency model provides a classification of the elements and factors that should be considered to completely describe the behavior of CI dependencies. The dependency model also provides a mechanism for communicating dependencies in a concise and unambiguous manner. Our future research will apply this theoretical framework to a well-documented case study [3]. Also, we will investigate the advantages of combining the dependency model with the service-oriented modeling approach used in the EU IRRIIS Project [2].

Acknowledgements

This research was partially funded by the EU Commission as part of the Sixth Framework Programme Project IRRIIS under Contract No. FP6-2005-IST-4 027568 and by the Netherlands Next Generation Infrastructure Programme.

References

[1] ACIP Consortium, Final Report: Analysis and Assessment for Critical Infrastructure Protection (ACIP), Industrieanlagen-Betriebsgesellschaft (IABG), Ottobrunn, Germany (www.iabg.de/acip/doc/wp7/D75_final_pr ogress_report_public.pdf), 2003.

[2] R. Bloomfield, P. Popov, K. Salako, D. Wright, PIA Preliminary Interdependency Analysis, in Tools and Techniques for Interdependency Analysis (IRRIIS Deliverable D2.2.2) and in Service Oriented Interdependency Analysis (IRRIIS Deliverable D2.2.4), IRRIIS Consortium, Fraunhofer Institute for Intelligent Analysis and Information Systems, Sankt-Augustin, Germany (www.irriis.org/File.aspx?lang=2&oiid=9138&pid=572), 2007.

[3] E. Ciancamerla and M. Minichino, A Mini Telco Blackout Scenario, in Tools and Techniques for Interdependency Analysis (IRRIIS Deliverable D2.2.2), IRRIIS Consortium, Fraunhofer Institute for Intelligent Analysis and Information Systems, Sankt-Augustin, Germany (www.irriis.org /File.aspx?lang=2&oiid=9138&pid=572), 2007.

[4] D. Dudenhoeffer, M. Permann and M. Manic, CIMS: A framework for infrastructure interdependency modeling and analysis, *Proceedings of the Winter Simulation Conference*, pp. 478–485, 2006.

[5] European Commission, Critical Infrastructure Protection in the Fight Against Terrorism, Communication COM (2004) 702 Final, Communication from the Commission to the Council and the European Parliament, Brussels, Belgium, 2004.

[6] European Commission, Proposal for a Directive of the Council on the Identification and Designation of European Critical Infrastructure and the Assessment to Improve its Protection, COM (2006) 787 Final, Communication from the Commission to the Council and the European Parliament, Brussels, Belgium, 2006.

[7] P. Koponen, H. Luiijf, H. Pentikinen, W. Schmitz and T. Uusitale, Report of Scenario, Threat and Vulnerability Refinement, IRRIIS Deliverable D1.2.3, TNO Defence, Security and Safety, The Hague, The Netherlands, 2007.

[8] H. Luiijf, H. Burger, M. Klaver, Q. Boone, C. Poppe and M. van Eck, Critical Infrastructure Protection in the Netherlands: Quick Scan on Critical Products and Services, Ministry of the Interior and Kingdom Relations, The Hague, The Netherlands (cipp.gmu.edu/archive/Netherlands CIreport_0403.pdf), 2003.

[9] D. Mendonca, E. Lee and W. Wallace, Impact of the 2001 World Trade Center attack on critical interdependent infrastructures, *IEEE International Conference on Systems, Man and Cybernetics*, vol. 5, pp. 4053–4058, 2004.

[10] H. Min, W. Beyeler, T. Brown, Y. Son and A. Jones, Toward modeling and simulation of critical national infrastructure interdependencies, *IIE Transactions*, vol. 39(1), pp. 57–71, 2007.

[11] A. Nieuwenhuijs, I. Paarlberg, J. Ribbens and H. Luiijf, Risk Analysis, IRRIIS Deliverable D1.2.2, TNO Defence, Security and Safety, The Hague, The Netherlands, 2007.

[12] A. Nieuwenhuijs and R. Verstoep, Methods for (Inter)Dependency Analysis, EURAM Project Deliverable, TNO Defence, Security and Safety, The Hague, The Netherlands, 2007.

[13] Raad voor de TransportVeiligheid (Dutch National Transport Safety Board), Storing Gasmengstation (Failing Gas Mixing Facility), Report RVTV-CB-2-02.060, The Hague, The Netherlands, 2002.

[14] S. Rinaldi, J. Peerenboom and T. Kelly, Identifying, understanding and analyzing critical infrastructure interdependencies, *IEEE Control Systems*, vol. 21(6), pp. 11–25, 2001.

[15] N. Svendsen and S. Wolthusen, Connectivity models of interdependency in mixed-type critical infrastructure networks, *Information Security Technical Report*, vol. 12(1), pp. 44–55, 2007.

[16] TNO Defence, Security and Safety, TNO's Database on Critical Infrastructure Incidents and Cascading Events (version 117), The Hague, The Netherlands.

Chapter 16

METRICS FOR QUANTIFYING INTERDEPENDENCIES

Emiliano Casalicchio and Emanuele Galli

Abstract   The quantification of interdependencies is a major challenge when attempting to analyze the behavior of critical infrastructures. This paper presents a taxonomy of interdependency quantification metrics based on their information content, decision support and risk analysis capabilities, and computational costs. The paper also discusses a systematic approach for computing metrics and performance indices that measure the effectiveness of strategies designed to enhance critical infrastructure protection and resilience. A case study is used to illustrate the computation of the metrics and performance indices, and their application to the analysis of critical infrastructure interdependencies.

Keywords: Interdependencies, metrics, federated simulation

1.   Introduction

A critical infrastructure is a physical system that, if disrupted, can seriously affect the national security, economy and social welfare of a nation. Examples of critical infrastructures include telecommunications, electric power systems, natural gas and oil, banking and finance, transportation, water supply systems, government and emergency services [1]. Clearly, modern society cannot function if large portions of the critical infrastructure are disrupted or destroyed.

In order to understand the behavior of critical infrastructures, it is necessary to accurately model and quantify their interdependencies [14]. Researchers have proposed several qualitative and quantitative techniques for analyzing interdependencies. Qualitative approaches rely on mathematical formalisms such as Leontief-based models [10], Markov chains [2], Petri nets [8], hierarchical holographic modeling (HHM) [7, 9] and graph theory [15, 16]. Quantitative approaches typically engage discrete simulation or agent-based modeling and simulation (ABMS) [3–6, 14].

Please use the following format when citing this chapter:

Casalicchio, E. and Galli, E., 2008, in IFIP International Federation for Information Processing, Volume 290; *Critical Infrastructure Protection II*, eds. Papa, M., Shenoi, S., (Boston: Springer), pp. 215–227.

While considerable research has focused on interdependency modeling and analysis, very few efforts have examined the issue of quantifying interdependencies. Zimmerman [17] has proposed explicit metrics for quantifying interdependencies. One metric measures the "direction" of infrastructure failures as the ratio between the number of times one type of infrastructure causes damage to another type of infrastructure and the number of times other types of infrastructures cause damage to the first type of infrastructure. Zimmerman and Restrepo [18] have specified a metric that measures the duration of cascading effects; they use this metric to quantify the effects of U.S. power grid outages on other infrastructures.

This paper presents a taxonomy that classifies interdependency metrics on the basis of their information content, decision support and risk analysis capabilities, and computational costs. In addition, it describes systematic approaches for computing metrics using system or model observations, and for calculating performance indices that measure the effectiveness of strategies designed to enhance critical infrastructure protection and resilience.

In general, interdependency metrics may be classified as those that measure the macro characteristics of interdependencies and their impact on system behavior and those quantify the strengths or weaknesses of infrastructures and infrastructure components. Metrics in the first category support decision making at the organizational or strategic level while those in the second category support decision making at the engineering or practical level.

We also use statistical measures, namely the percentile value, cumulative distribution function (CDF) and complementary cumulative distribution function (CCDF). The percentile value and CDF of an observed state variable are used to quantify the degree of satisfaction or goodness of choice. The CCDF of a set of observed outcomes is used to perform survivability analyses.

We employ a case study to illustrate the computation of metrics and performance indices, and their use in analyzing critical infrastructure interdependencies. Two scenarios are examined, outage propagation in infrastructures and victim rescue after a terrorist attack.

2.   Metrics and Performance Indices

We classify metrics for quantifying critical infrastructure interdependencies in terms of decision support capabilities, information content and computational cost. In particular, we identify three categories of metrics: (i) shape metrics that quantify macro or "shape" characteristics of interdependencies such as direction [17] and duration [18] (Figure 1(a)); (ii) core metrics that measure the causes and effects of outages for specific infrastructure components (Figures 1(b) and (c)) and the effectiveness of strategies/mechanisms for improving critical infrastructures protection and resilience; and (iii) sector-specific metrics that measure the states of infrastructures at the global and component levels.

Figure 2 shows how core, shape and sector-specific metrics are positioned in the three dimensional space of decision support capabilities, information

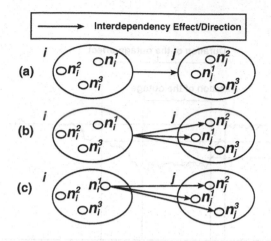

Figure 1. (a) Shape metrics; (b, c) Core metrics.

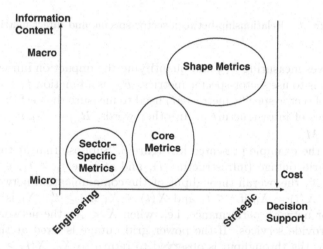

Figure 2. Taxonomy of metrics for quantifying interdependencies.

content and cost. The decision support dimension ranges from the engineering level (low) to the strategic level (high). The information content dimension ranges from the micro level (low) to the macro level (high). The cost dimension ranges from low to high. The first two dimensions are qualitative in nature while cost dimension values depend on the implementation and case study.

2.1 Shape Metrics

Consider the direct metric, relative duration ($R_{i,j}$), which measures the cascading effect of an outage [18]. $R_{i,j} = \frac{T_j}{T_i}$ is defined as the ratio of the duration T_j of an outage in infrastructure j due to an outage in infrastructure i and the duration T_i of the outage in infrastructure i. The computation of a shape

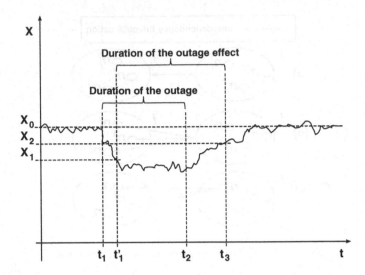

Figure 3.   Relationship between sector-specific and direct metrics.

metric involves measuring $R_{i,j}$ and quantifying the impact on infrastructure j. The solution is to use sector-specific metrics. $R_{i,j}$ is a function $f(\cdot)$ of the time t and the set of sector-specific metrics M_j used to measure the performance levels or capabilities of infrastructure j. In other words, $R_{i,j} = f(t, m_j^1, m_j^2, ..., m_j^p)$ where $m_j^k \in M_j$.

Consider the example presented in Figure 3. Suppose that at time t_1 there is a power grid outage (infrastructure i), and at time $t_1' \geq t_1$, a decrease is observed in X, the overall throughput of the communication network (infrastructure j): $X(t) = X_0$ if $t \leq t_1$ and $X(t) \leq X_1$ if $t \geq t_1'$. X_1 is the critical threshold for network performance, i.e., when $X < X_1$ the network loses the ability to provide services. If the power grid outage is fixed at time t_2 and, after time t_3, the throughput is observed to return to X_0, $X(t) \geq X_2$ at time t_3 and $X(t) \to X_0$ for $t \geq t_3$, we assert that, at time t_3, the cascading effect of the power grid outage has ended. We assume that, when $X(t) \geq X_2$, the communication network can provide services (obviously, $X_1 \leq X_2 \leq X_0$). $R_{i,j}$ is a function $f(t, X)$ of the time and throughput: $R_{g,n} = \frac{t_3 - t_1'}{t_2 - t_1}$ where t_1' is such that $X(t) \leq X_1$ for $t \geq t_1'$ and t_3 is such that $X(t) \geq X_2$ for $t \geq t_3$.

As observed by Zimmerman and Restrepo [18], if $R_{i,j} < 1$, the infrastructure j can react on its own to the outage (e.g., reconfigure its services). Otherwise, if $R_{i,j} > 1$, the infrastructure j is heavily dependent on the outage and it needs some time to restore its services after the outage ends.

An example of an aggregate measure of a shape metric is the total relative duration $R_{i,I}$ of an outage in infrastructure i on a set of infrastructures I. Suppose that the power grid outage impacts the communication network and transportation system, and that the communication network outage impacts credit card transactions. The cascading effect ends when all the infrastructures are restored to their normal operating conditions. Then, the total relative duration of an outage in infrastructure i is given by $R_{i,I} = \max_{j \in I, j \neq i} \{R_{i,j}\}$ where $R_{i,j}$ is a function of sector-specific performance indices of infrastructure j.

2.2   Core Metrics

The direct metric $R_{i,j}$ quantifies a macro characteristic of the interdependencies between infrastructures i and j, but it does not give any information about the infrastructure nodes involved in or affected by the outage propagation. Nor does it provide the impact of the failure of a specific infrastructure or infrastructure component. Core metrics quantify the effects of interdependencies at the level of infrastructure nodes or, more deeply, at the level of node components. Thus, core metrics provide insight into the causes and effects of outages.

Two core metrics can be obtained by refining the shape metric $R_{i,j}$ in order to identify the weakest node in infrastructure j or the most important node in infrastructure i. To identify the weakest node in infrastructure j with respect to an outage in infrastructure i, we define $R_{i,n_j^k} = f(t, M_j^k)$ where n_j^k is the kth node of infrastructure j and M_j^k is the set of metrics used to measure the performance or capabilities of n_j^k. The weakest node is then obtained by evaluating the expression $n_j^l = max_{k \in N_j} \left\{ R_{i,n_j^k} \right\}$ where N_j is the set of nodes comprising infrastructure j.

Similarly, to identify the most important node in infrastructure i that affects infrastructure j, we define $R_{n_i^h, n_j^k} = f(t, M_j^k)$ where n_i^h is the hth node of infrastructure i. The most important node in infrastructure i is determined by evaluating the expression $n_i^l = max_{h \in N_i} \left\{ R_{n_i^h, n_j^k} \right\}$ for each $k \in N_j$.

In general, if a sector-specific metric $m_j^k \in M_j^k$ is used, the weakest node in infrastructure j with respect to an outage in infrastructure i is obtained by evaluating the expression $n_j^l = max_{k \in N_j} \{\Delta m_j^k\}$ where Δm_j^k is the variation of the sector-specific metric considered. Similarly, the most important node in infrastructure i that affects the behavior of infrastructure j is obtained by evaluating the expression $n_i^l = max_{h \in N_i} \{\Delta m_j^k\} \ \forall k \in N_j$. Obviously, depending on the metric considered, the maximization problem can be turned into a minimization problem.

In addition to measuring the loss of performance or capability of an infrastructure, core metrics can be used to measure the effectiveness of strategies for protecting critical infrastructures or enhancing their resilience. For example, core metrics can quantify the effects produced by changing a rescue plan, the consequences of network re-engineering or the effects of a new service reconfiguration strategy. Also, core metrics can be used to specify the probability that a certain percentage of a population will be rescued after an incident, the percentage of fatalities in a population or the duration of rescue operations. These concepts cannot be quantified using direct metrics. Other examples that can

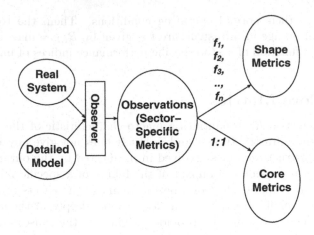

Figure 4.   Computing shape and core metrics from sector-specific metrics.

be quantified by core metrics are the number of damaged infrastructure nodes, the time taken to recover node functionality, the time taken to reconfigure a system or network, and more.

2.3   Computing Shape and Core Metrics

As discussed above, sector-specific metrics are used to compute shape and core metrics. Figure 4 illustrates the relationships between sector-specific metrics, core metrics and shape metrics and the processes for computing shape and core metrics. Parameters that can be used directly as core metrics (i.e., without any transformation) are determined by analyzing a real system or a detailed model of the system (or both). To compute shape metrics, is necessary to identify the relevant sector-specific metrics and the appropriate transformation functions $(f_1, ..., f_n)$ as described in Section 2.1.

2.4   Metric Characteristics

Table 1 summarizes the characteristics of shape metrics, core metrics and sector-specific metrics. In particular, it compares the three types of metrics based on their information content, decision support capabilities and computational cost.

2.5   Statistical Performance Indices

A statistical metric can be used to express the degree of satisfaction with respect to the Xth percentile of a performance index. The Xth percentile of a dataset is defined as the value that is larger than $X\%$ of the data. The Xth percentile of a random variable is obtained by inverting its cumulative distribution function (CDF), which is defined as $F_X(x) = P\{x \leq X\}$. For

Table 1. Summary of interdependency metric characteristics.

Metrics	Information Content	Decision Support	Cost
Shape metrics	Macro level	Support decisions at the organizational and strategic levels	*Low/Medium* Detailed model is not mandatory
Core metrics	Micro level	Support decisions at the engineering and practical levels; Quantify the causes and effects of outages	*Medium/High* Detailed model is mandatory (typically a simulation model)
Sector-specific metrics	Engineering level		
	Input for computing shape and core metrics		

example, the 95th percentile of X is $\tau = F_X^{-1}(0.95)$. Thus, the percentile of interest is easily obtained by plotting the CDF.

For performance indices such as crisis resolution time, rescue time and number of failed nodes it makes sense to measure the degree of satisfaction of a new (counter)measure. On the other hand, for the number of repaired nodes, it is more appropriate to compute X such that $P\{x > X\} = Y$. The value of X is computed using the complementary cumulative distribution function (CCDF). The CCDF, which is commonly used in survivability analysis, is defined as $F_c(x) = 1 - F_X(x) = Pr\{x > X\}$. Upon inverting F_c, we obtain $X = F_c^{-1}(Y)$.

3. Case Study

A report by the U.S. Homeland Security Advisory Council [11] emphasizes that techniques and tools for analyzing critical infrastructure interdependencies and their consequences "are of value only if applied within the context of a clear objective – a desired outcome that is measurable." We use a case study to demonstrate our methodology and, in particular, the application of interdependency metrics.

The case study, which is derived from [4, 5], considers three critical infrastructures: the communication network used for data transmission and voice calls, the power grid and the transportation network of urban roads. Other infrastructures involved in the case study are hospitals and health care centers and the Information System for Civic Emergency Management (IS4CEM), which coordinates recovery in the event of terrorist attacks, catastrophes and infrastructure outages. IS4CEM also provides information about health care center availability, transportation network availability and event evolution.

Two scenarios are examined, outage propagation and victim rescue after a terrorist attack. The outage propagation scenario only considers the main infrastructures (power grid, transportation network and communication network). The scenario demonstrates how shape metrics can quantify the effect of a power grid outage on the behavior of a communication network.

On the other hand, the victim rescue scenario illustrates how core metrics can be used to study the evolution of a crisis in the presence of various types of power grid outages. The scenario assumes several persons have been injured after a terrorist attack. The communication network is used by the injured victims, citizens, authorities, rescue crews and hospitals. Hospitals and rescue crews use the IS4CEM to coordinate rescue operations. The transportation network is used by rescue crews to reach the injured and take them to hospitals; the network is also used by injured victims who drive themselves to hospitals for first aid. The power grid supplies the communication network, IS4CEM, hospitals, rescue crew stations and the transportation network (traffic lights).

4.   Interdependency Analysis

Our simulation experiments using Federated ABMS [5] were designed to demonstrate the ability of core metrics to quantify interdependencies and to verify that the statistical measures used as performance indices are appropriate. Three power grid outage situations were considered for the outage propagation and victim rescue scenarios: no outage, one outage and two outages. The nodes experiencing outages were selected randomly. In the outage propagation scenario, we assume that the time to fix the outage is constant. In the victim rescue scenario, we assume that the outage is permanent for the duration of the simulation.

The scenarios involved three hospitals, ten power grid nodes and ten routers and access points. The victim rescue scenario involved ten rescue team members and 50 injured victims. A total of 50 simulations were conducted for each case for each of the two scenarios; each simulation used a different seed for random number generation.

4.1   Outage Propagation Scenario

We assume that at time $t = 100$ ticks, one or two randomly selected power grid nodes fail. We also assume that no auxiliary power systems are available; therefore, when a power grid node fails, one or more network nodes (routers or access points) go out of service until they receive power. The time taken to repair a power grid node outage is set at 300 ticks.

Figure 5 compares the overall throughput of the communication network $X = \sum_{i \in \mathcal{N}} X_i$ where $\mathcal{N}$ is the set of nodes in the network and X_i is the throughput of node i. As expected, X decreases if one or more routers fail. We assume that the critical threshold for network performance is 8,000 Mbps.

Figure 6 presents the overall throughput at the start ($t = 100$) of a power grid outage (left-hand side) and at the end ($t = 400$) of the outage (right-hand side). As shown in Figure 6 (left), when there is one outage, X degrades at $t = 100$; after three ticks X falls below 8,000 Mbps and stabilizes to around 7,000

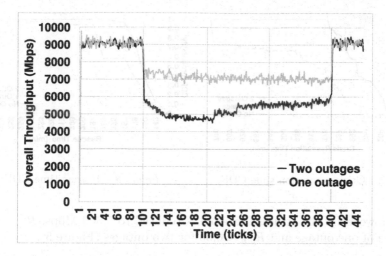

Figure 5. Overall throughput of the communication network.

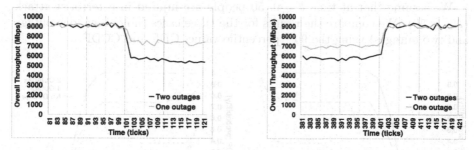

Figure 6. Overall throughput during a power grid outage.

Mbps after 100 additional ticks. When the outage ends at $t = 400$, four ticks pass before normal operating conditions are re-established (Figure 6, right), corresponding to $R_{g,n} \approx 1$. Normal operating conditions are rapidly restored due to the robustness of the routing algorithm and also because delays due to nodes being rebooted or damaged during the abnormal shutdown are not taken into account.

In the case of two outages, a significant degradation in the overall throughput is observed. After three ticks, the overall throughput falls below 6,000 Mbps (Figure 6, left) and after 30 additional ticks, it is below 5,000 Mbps. However, at $t = 214$, the reconfiguration features of the routing algorithm take effect, and at $t = 250$, the overall throughput stabilizes to around 5,500 Mbps (Figure 6, right). Also in this case, $R_{g,n} \approx 1$ and normal operating conditions are re-established a few ticks after the power outages end (Figure 6, right).

The time plot of the sector-specific metric is useful for analysis. When the critical threshold for the throughput is 8,000 Mbps, $R_{g,n} \approx 1$, and the duration of the communication network outage is about the same as that in the power

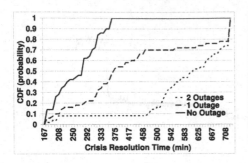

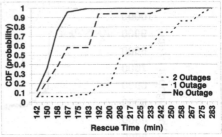

Figure 7. Crisis resolution time CDF.   *Figure 8.* Rescue time CDF.

grid. However, if the critical threshold is reduced to 5,300 Mbps, $R_{g,n} = 0$ in the case of one outage and $R_{g,n} \approx 0.35$ for two outages (Figure 5).

4.2 Victim Rescue Scenario

We assume that at time $t = 0$, 50 people are injured in a terrorist attack ($N_w = 50$). We compare the results for the three cases (no outage, one outage and two outages) using the 90th percentile value, CDF and CCDF.

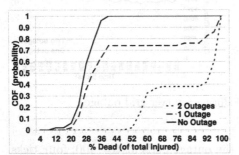

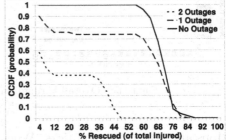

Figure 9. Percentage of dead CDF.   *Figure 10.* Percentage of rescued CCDF.

Figures 7, 8 and 9 show the CDFs of the crisis resolution time (T_c), rescue time (T_r) and percentage of dead ($W_d\%$), respectively. The CDF plots give an excellent indication of system behavior and how the outages increase T_c, T_r and W_d. The CCDF is used to analyze the number of injured victims who are rescued (Figure 10). The CCDF gives the probability that more than $W\%$ of the injured are rescued, i.e., $P\{W_r > W\}$. The value of W such that $P\{W_r > W\} = p$ is obtained by inverting the CCDF.

Table 2 presents the 90th percentile values for T_c, T_r and W_d. Using the CDF and the concept of percentile is easy to compute the probability p_d that $W\%$ of the injured will die and the probabilities p_r and p_c that T_r and T_c, respectively, are less than T seconds, i.e., $p_d = F_d(W)$, $p_r = F_r(T)$ and $p_c = F_c(T)$ where F_d, F_r and F_c are the CDFs of W_d, T_r and T_c, respectively.

Table 2. T_c, T_r and W_d (90th percentile values).

Metric	Outages		
	Zero	One	Two
T_r (sec)	165.83	187.96	269.44
T_c (sec)	350	725	725
W_d (%)	34.66	99	100

Table 3. $W\%$ values such that $P\{W_r > W\} = p$.

$P\{W_r > W\}$	Outages		
	Zero	One	Two
0.90	64%	6%	0%
0.75	66%	22%	0%
0.50	72%	68%	6%

Table 3 shows the $W\%$ values (i.e., more than $W\%$ of the injured are rescued) for various values of $p = P\{W_r > W\}$. These are obtained by fixing a value for p and extracting the corresponding value of W from the CCDF.

5. Conclusions

The interdependency quantification metrics presented in this paper are useful for analyzing and simulating the behavior of critical infrastructures. Shape metrics, with their macro-level information content, support decision makers at the organizational and strategic levels. These metrics can be computed based on engineering-level observation or using high-level system observations that engage simulation or analytic models. In contrast, core metrics measure the causes and effects of outages for specific infrastructure components and the effectiveness of strategies for improving critical infrastructures protection and resilience. They require more computational overhead than shape metrics, but they give decision makers useful information about outages and direct or indirect quantification of interdependencies. Sector-specific metrics measure the states of infrastructures at the global and component levels, and provide input for computing shape and core metrics. Statistical measures, such as the percentile, CDF and CCDF, are also useful for analysis. The case study, involving simulations of outage propagation and victim rescue scenarios, demonstrate the value of the metrics and statistical measures for analyzing critical infrastructure interdependencies.

References

[1] I. Abele-Wigert and M. Dunn, *International CIIP Handbook, Volume 1,* Center for Security Studies, Swiss Federal Institute of Technology, Zurich, Switzerland, 2006.

[2] S. Asavathiratham, B. Lesieutre and G. Verghese, The influence model, *IEEE Control Systems,* vol. 21(6), pp. 52–64, 2001.

[3] E. Bonabeau, Agent-based modeling: Methods and techniques for simulating human systems, *Proceedings of the National Academy of Sciences,* vol. 99(3), pp. 7280–7287, 2002.

[4] V. Cardellini, E. Casalicchio and E. Galli, Agent-based modeling of interdependencies in critical infrastructures through UML, *Proceedings of the Agent-Directed Simulation Symposium of the Spring Simulation Multiconference,* pp. 119–126, 2007.

[5] E. Casalicchio, E. Galli and S. Tucci, Federated agent-based modeling and simulation approach to study interdependencies in IT critical infrastructures, *Proceedings of the Eleventh International Symposium on Distributed Simulation and Real-Time Applications,* pp. 182–189, 2007.

[6] D. Dudenhoeffer, M. Permann and M. Manic, CIMS: A framework for infrastructure interdependency modeling and analysis, *Proceedings of the Winter Simulation Conference,* pp. 478–485, 2006.

[7] B. Ezell, J. Farr and T. Wiese, Infrastructure risk analysis model, *Journal of Infrastructure Systems,* vol. 6(3), pp. 114–117, 2000.

[8] O. Gursesli and A. Desrochers, Modeling infrastructure interdependencies using Petri nets, *Proceedings of the IEEE International Conference on Systems, Man and Cybernetics,* vol. 2, pp. 1506–1512, 2003.

[9] Y. Haimes, *Risk Modeling, Assessment and Management,* Wiley-Interscience, Hoboken, New Jersey, 2004.

[10] Y. Haimes and P. Jiang, Leontief-based model of risk in complex interconnected infrastructures, *Journal of Infrastructure Systems,* vol. 7(1), pp. 1–12, 2001.

[11] Homeland Security Advisory Council, Report of the Critical Infrastructure Task Force, Department of Homeland Security, Washington, DC (www.dhs.gov/xlibrary/assets/HSAC_CITF_Report_v2.pdf), 2006.

[12] K. Hopkinson, X. Wang, R. Giovanini, J. Thorp, K. Birman and D. Coury, EPOCHS: A platform for agent-based electric power and communication simulation built from commercial off-the-shelf components, *IEEE Transactions on Power Systems,* vol. 21(2), pp. 548–558, 2006.

[13] M. North, N. Collier and J. Vos, Experiences creating three implementations of the Repast agent modeling toolkit, *ACM Transactions on Modeling and Computer Simulation,* vol. 16(1), pp. 1–25, 2006.

[14] S. Rinaldi, J. Peerenboom and T. Kelly, Identifying, understanding and analyzing critical infrastructure interdependencies, *IEEE Control Systems*, vol. 21(6), pp. 11–25, 2001.

[15] N. Svendsen and S. Wolthusen, Connectivity models of interdependency in mixed-type critical infrastructure networks, *Information Security Technical Report*, vol. 12(1), pp. 44–55, 2007.

[16] N. Svendsen and S. Wolthusen, Multigraph dependency models for heterogeneous infrastructures, in *Critical Infrastructure Protection*, E. Goetz and S. Shenoi (Eds.), Springer, Boston, Massachusetts, pp. 337–350, 2007.

[17] R. Zimmerman, Decision-making and the vulnerability of interdependent critical infrastructures, *Proceedings of the IEEE International Conference on Systems, Man and Cybernetics*, vol. 5, pp. 4059–4063, 2004.

[18] R. Zimmerman and C. Restrepo, The next step: Quantifying infrastructure interdependencies to improve security, *International Journal of Critical Infrastructures*, vol. 2(2/3), pp. 215–230, 2006.

Chapter 17

AN INTEGRATED APPROACH FOR SIMULATING INTERDEPENDENCIES

Roberto Setola, Sandro Bologna, Emiliano Casalicchio and Vincenzo Masucci

Abstract   The detailed simulation of interdependent critical infrastructures is a hard problem. Major challenges include modeling multiple heterogeneous infrastructures in a single framework and expressing internal dependencies and interdependencies between infrastructures. This paper attempts to address these issues by proposing a simulation framework where several sector-specific simulators (vertical simulators) are integrated into a general simulation environment (horizontal simulator). Specialized software implemented in the vertical simulators models individual infrastructures and their intra-domain dynamics. The horizontal simulator effectively captures inter-domain relationships and merges heterogeneous information from the vertical simulators to facilitate comprehensive infrastructure simulations.

Keywords: Heterogeneous infrastructures, interdependencies, simulation

1.   Introduction

Predicting the behavior of critical infrastructures during crisis or failure conditions is a difficult task. Innovative models and tools are needed to capture and reason about the behavior of critical infrastructures. However, the complexity of the problem severely limits the application of analytic methods. Consequently, simulation methods are increasingly used to investigate the behavior of interdependent infrastructures (see, e.g., [3, 15]).

The primary challenge in critical infrastructure simulation is to model heterogeneous behavior in a single framework. Another major challenge is to model interdependencies between infrastructures and interdependencies between infrastructures and the external environment.

Simulation techniques may be broadly divided into two classes. The first uses domain-specific simulators, each designed for detailed simulations of a single infrastructure. The second engages newer simulation environments where

Please use the following format when citing this chapter:

Setola, R., Bologna, S., Casalicchio, E. and Masucci, V., 2008, in IFIP International Federation for Information Processing, Volume 290; *Critical Infrastructure Protection II*, eds. Papa, M., Shenoi, S., (Boston: Springer), pp. 229–239.

the behavior of different infrastructures is modeled using a single conceptual framework.

We refer to the first class as federated simulators because several "vertical simulators" exchange data. A vertical simulator considers an infrastructure as an autonomous, isolated system; hence, it provides a vertical (partial but detailed) view of the infrastructure. A good example of such a federated simulator is EPOCHS [10], which is designed to analyze interactions between the electric grid and telecommunications networks. Another example is SimCIP, which is being developed under the IRRIIS Project [11].

This class of simulators leverages well-tested simulation packages and data and models accumulated over years of use, which reduces development costs. Moreover, because each simulator is designed for a specific domain, the knowledge elicitation phase is greatly simplified: the simulator and the user engage the same language and vocabulary (i.e., modeling schemas and paradigms). Furthermore, all the intra-domain dependencies are modeled within vertical simulators; the simulation environment only manages the inter-domain dependencies.

Unfortunately, these simulators are unable to capture all the distinct elements that characterize real-world scenarios. In many cases, they describe infrastructure interactions only in terms of functional links (e.g., direct exchanges of goods and services), neglecting other types of interdependencies (e.g., geographical or social links) [16]. Also, because vertical simulators cannot manage information belonging to other domains (except for possibly changing loads and certain model parameters), they are able to reproduce only very elementary interaction mechanisms.

The second class of simulation approaches uses a sufficiently broad and powerful modeling framework to represent multiple heterogeneous infrastructures [1, 5, 8, 14, 17]. We refer to this type of simulator as a "horizontal simulator" because it covers multiple domains. Horizontal simulators engage a variety of concepts, structures and solutions, e.g., complex adaptive systems [16], agent-based modeling [2, 4] and entity-relation approaches [5]. These paradigms capture different aspects of the problem to greater or lesser degrees; therefore, the quality of their results vary according to the specific scenarios being evaluated.

Except for NISAC [17] and a few other government initiatives, horizontal simulators have been tested only on relatively simple scenarios. This is primarily due to modeling issues. It is extremely difficult to acquire detailed information about infrastructure parameters and the dynamical behavior of infrastructures. Part of the problem is that critical infrastructure stakeholders are reluctant to release data that they deem to be sensitive. Also, it is difficult to translate information from infrastructure domains to the abstract formulation adopted by horizontal simulators.

To address the limitations of the two classes of simulation approaches, we propose a simulation framework that integrates multiple vertical simulators in a general horizontal simulation environment. The architecture, which is presented in Figure 1, has three layers: (i) a user layer where different scenarios

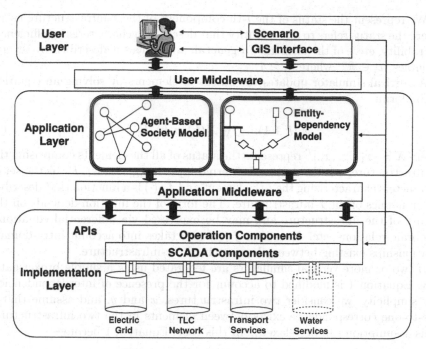

Figure 1. Simulation framework.

are described in terms of component elements, links between elements, event sequences, and simulation tools to be used; (ii) an application layer that manages a collection of horizontal simulators (CISIA [5] and FederatedABMS [4]); and an implementation layer that manages a set of vertical simulators (OM-NeT++ [13], ns2 [9] and e-Agora). Specifically, once a scenario is selected, the user can choose the type of horizontal simulator to be used. Moreover, the user can choose to reproduce everything within the selected simulator or to delegate part of the simulation effort (e.g., intra-domain dynamics) to vertical simulators in the implementation layer.

The simulation framework is being developed under the CRESCO Project [12], which is funded by Italian Ministry of Research to enhance the national capability to study complex systems. However, we must emphasize that this framework is not intended to be a "silver bullet" that comprehensively addresses the critical infrastructure simulation problem. Rather, it is a proof-of-concept scheme that, we hope, will constitute the first step to creating a European Infrastructure Simulation and Analysis Center (EISAC).

2.   CRESCO Architecture

The CRESCO architecture is characterized by the presence of horizontal simulation environments that are used to integrate a set of vertical simulators.

We represent the status of the i-th component of the x-infrastructure as x_i, where the status refers to any quantity that describes a characteristic (efficiency, operability, etc.) of the element. In general, an element is described by several variables, $x_i \in \Re^{n_i}$ where $n_i \geq 1$.

A vertical simulator updates the status of elements by solving an equation of the form:

$$x_i(k+1) = f_X(X(k), u(k), \bar{P}_{x_i}) \tag{1}$$

where $X = [x_1, \ldots, x_n]^T$ represents the status of all the elements comprising the x-infrastructure, u is the vector of external inputs (e.g., loads), $\bar{P}_{x_i}$ is the set of parameters characterizing the i-th element and $f_X(\cdot)$ is a function that describes the dynamics of the x-infrastructure. The form of the function depends on the nature of the infrastructure and may be expressed via differential equations, algebraic relations, etc. Note that $f_X(\cdot)$ also takes into account intra-domain relationships existing between elements in the x-infrastructure.

If two or more vertical simulators are federated using a simple broker gateway, Equation 1 is modified to account for the presence of interdependencies. For simplicity, we consider two infrastructures, x and y, and assume that a one-to-one correspondence exists between elements in the two infrastructures (this assumption can be relaxed). In this case, Equation 1 becomes

$$x_i(k+1) = f_X(X(k), u(k) + \delta(y_i), \gamma(\bar{P}_{x_i}, y_i)) \tag{2}$$

where δ and γ are functions that map the values assumed by the state variable of the y-infrastructure to load variations or parameter changes for the x-infrastructure element. Hence, the federation process corresponds to a fictitious modification of the load u and/or parameters $\bar{P}_{x_i}$, making them dependent on the status assumed by the element of the y-infrastructure that is in direct correspondence with x_i.

As mentioned above, this strategy has several drawbacks. In particular, it only permits the reproduction of simple interdependency phenomena.

The dynamics of an element in a horizontal simulator is described by:

$$\theta_i(k+1) = \Gamma_\theta(\theta_i(k), u(k), M(\Theta)) \tag{3}$$

where $\theta_i \in \Re^{n_i}$ is the state of the i-th element, Θ is the vector of state variables of elements in the simulation scenario, Γ_θ is a function describing the dynamics of each element and $M(\cdot)$ is a function describing the inter- and intra-domain relationships existing between the i-th element and all the other elements without any specific consideration about the nature of the infrastructure. Note that the horizontal simulation techniques proposed in the literature differ substantially in the methodology used to map interdependencies to the $M(\cdot)$ function and in the formalism adopted for their representation.

The main difference between Equations 1 and 3 is that $f_X(\cdot)$ depends explicitly on all the variables of the system while Γ_θ depends only on the state variables of the i-th element; this is because the influence exerted by the other

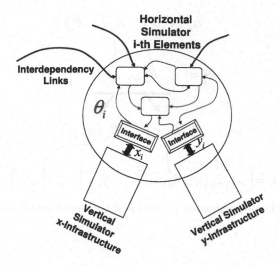

Figure 2.   Global behavior of the i-th element.

elements is mediated by $M(\cdot)$, which codifies the relationships between the different elements. Therefore, Equation 3 provides a less detailed and less coherent representation of intra-domain relationships than Equation 1. However, it is able to describe inter-domain dependencies better because a more general formalism is adopted.

We believe that some of the drawbacks can be overcome by integrating several vertical simulators via a horizontal simulation framework. This strategy leverages the capabilities of the vertical simulators that correctly reproduce the behavior of individual infrastructures and the ability of a horizontal simulator to model a large class of inter-domain relationships.

Figure 2 illustrates how the global behavior of the i-th element is obtained by using Equation 3 to model inter-domain relationships along with information provided by a set of vertical simulators. Specifically, the overall state of the i-th element (θ_i) is obtained by incorporating, within the horizontal simulator model, information about the "partial" view of the element obtained by considering the x- and y-infrastructure models (x_i and y_i, respectively). Moreover, θ_i is used to update the variables of the vertical simulators in order to propagate the consequences of inter-domain phenomena in those environments. Formally, we have:

$$\theta_i(k+1) = \Gamma_\theta(\tilde{\theta}_i(k), u(k) + \delta_\theta u\,(x_i, y_i)\,, \hat{M}(\Theta))$$
$$x_i(k+1) = f_X(\tilde{X}(k), u(k) + \delta u_x(\theta_i), \gamma(\bar{P}_{x_i}, \theta_i)) \qquad (4)$$
$$y_i(k+1) = f_Y(\tilde{Y}(k), u(k) + \delta u_y(\theta_i), \gamma(\bar{P}_{y_i}, \theta_i))$$

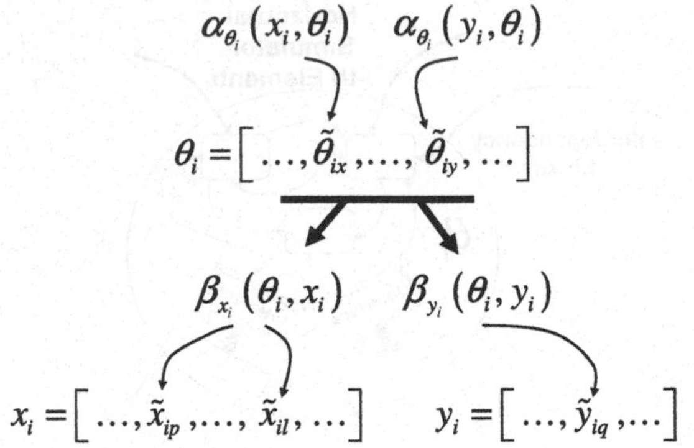

$$\alpha_{\theta_i}\left(x_i,\theta_i\right) \quad \alpha_{\theta_i}\left(y_i,\theta_i\right)$$

$$\theta_i = \left[\,\ldots,\tilde{\theta}_{ix},\ldots,\tilde{\theta}_{iy},\,\ldots\right]$$

$$\beta_{x_i}\left(\theta_i,x_i\right) \quad \beta_{y_i}\left(\theta_i,y_i\right)$$

$$x_i = \left[\,\ldots,\tilde{x}_{ip},\ldots,\tilde{x}_{il},\,\ldots\right] \qquad y_i = \left[\,\ldots,\tilde{y}_{iq},\ldots\right]$$

Figure 3.   Mappings between vertical and horizontal simulator variables.

where $\hat{M}(\cdot)$ is a function that considers only inter-domain relationships and the $\tilde{}$ operator means that the corresponding variable has been updated with regard to its own (i.e., isolated) value based on data provided by other simulators.

Figure 3 shows how the interface components in Figure 1 implement ontology mappings. Note that the functions $\alpha_{\theta_i}(x_i,\theta_i)$ and $\beta_{x_i}(\theta_i,x_i)$ translate vertical simulator quantities into horizontal simulator variables and vice versa.

At each iteration, the horizontal simulator evaluates the overall status of each component in the modeled scenario. This information is translated into quantities recognized by the vertical simulators and input to them. Then, the vertical simulators, using detailed models of each infrastructure, update the network configuration in terms of the actual loads/resources, availability of components, etc. Finally this data, upon being codified appropriately, is sent back to the horizontal simulator, where it is used to refine the status of the element.

Figure 4 presents a simulation scenario. The horizontal simulator has four components: Generation Plant (A), Control Center (B), Urban Area (C) and Distribution Substation (D). Some of these elements have a complex structure, i.e., their behavior is described by considering the results of the union of several heterogeneous aspects. For example, in order to analyze the Generation Plant, it is necessary to consider its electrical behavior (provided by the Electric Grid Simulator) and status of its telecommunications systems (provided by the Telecommunications Network Simulator). However, these are only two "partial views" of the element. To obtain the overall status, it is necessary to integrate them with information related to internal dynamics and the effects induced on the element by inter-domain relationships. This task is performed by the horizontal simulator. Obviously, the overall status of the Generation Plant influences both the Electric Grid and Telecommunications Network. Hence, this status should be made available to the vertical simulators that propagate the effects in their domains.

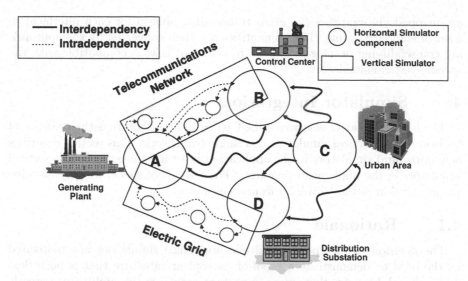

Figure 4. Two vertical simulators integrated in a horizontal simulation environment.

3. Simulation Framework

The CRESCO architecture provides facilities for defining and configuring simulation scenarios, a model for analyzing critical infrastructure interdependencies, and middleware that allows sector-specific models to be integrated in order to simulate the detailed behavior of critical infrastructures. The user layer resides at the top level of the three-layer architecture (Figure 1). It provides an interface for defining and configuring simulation scenarios, entering simulation parameters, and manipulating and visualizing simulation results. Two approaches are considered, CISIA based on the Entity Resource Model [5] and FederatedABMS, which employs an agent-based model [2, 4]. The lowest implementation layer incorporates vertical models of sector-specific infrastructures that are implemented by vertical simulators. These simulators are instantiated at runtime on one or more nodes of the ENEA GRID.

The vertical simulators currently employed in the CRESCO architecture are designed to simulate telecommunications networks, computer systems and the electric power grid. Open-source simulation frameworks that can be modified to work in the CRESCO environment have been adopted to the extent possible. OMNeT++ [13] and ns2 [9] are used for telecommunications network and computer systems modeling while e-AGORA [1], a load flow simulation environment, is used to simulate electricity distribution networks and the power grid.

Application middleware supports interoperability between horizontal and vertical simulators (Figure 1). The middleware coordinates mappings between elements of different simulators. This is facilitated by a common ontology for data and event exchange between different simulation frameworks (despite their disparate representations). The events produced by the horizontal simulators are mapped via wrappers (an event transcoding plug-in for each interface) to a set of standard events. These quantities are then converted by the appropriate transcodifying ontologies module to a format that is compatible with the specific vertical simulator.

4.   Simulator Integration

The most innovative element of the CRESCO architecture is the presence of horizontal and vertical simulators in a single framework. This section describes how horizontal simulators in the application layer are integrated with vertical simulators in the implementation layer. For reasons of space, we only describe the integration of the CISIA horizontal simulator.

4.1   Rationale

The decision to incorporate multiple horizontal simulators was motivated by the need to demonstrate a proof-of-concept architecture that is both flexible and scalable. Another, more important reason is the ability to correctly model various interdependencies and their phenomena. Indeed, as mentioned earlier, existing models do not capture interdependencies, which severely limits the fidelity of their simulations. Also, providing users with multiple tools to investigate scenarios, enables them to conduct better analyses.

FederatedABMS and CISIA adopt similar conceptual representations; this makes the scenarios interchangeable and the results comparable. However, the two horizontal simulators have several different and complementary characteristics. FederatedABMS is an event-driven simulator while CISIA is a discrete-time simulator. FederatedABMS adopts an agent-based formulation; thus, the function $M(\cdot)$ in Equation 3 has the form:

$$M(\Theta) \cong m(k)\Theta. \tag{5}$$

Since relations between agents can be created or destroyed during a simulation, a time-varying incident matrix is employed to codify these relationships.

On the other hand, CISIA is based on the concept of proximity and employs the formulation:

$$M(\Theta) \cong \sum_l M_l(\Theta) \tag{6}$$

where each element $M_l(\cdot)$ in the summation represents a specific mechanism of interrelation. Obviously, neither Equation 5 nor 6 is exhaustive and the implementations of the two simulators impose further limitations. Nevertheless, they provide two interesting and, in certain respects, complementary views of interdependencies. Indeed, the concurrent use of FederatedABMS and CISIA helps users better understand the phenomena produced by interdependencies.

4.2 CISIA Integration

CISIA is a simulation environment designed to analyze complex scenarios involving multiple heterogeneous infrastructures with tight interactions. CISIA's abstract representation decomposes a scenario into macro-components whose behavior is described in terms of their ability to produce goods and services based on the availability of external resources while taking into account the presence (and severity) of failures. Each entity computes its "operative level" (i.e., ability to perform its intended job) and the level of severity associated with different types of failures based on the internal state and external resources; the presence and the severity of internal and external failures are also considered. These quantities are then exchanged among the macro-components to estimate the overall behavior of the system. CISIA's representation employs fuzzy numbers [5, 14] to accommodate uncertainty and capture the linguistic descriptions of system states provided by human experts.

CISIA adopts a resource-service paradigm to facilitate the integration of vertical simulators. Thus, the outputs (x_i and y_i in Equation 4) can be logically managed as external resources. However, it is necessary to translate these quantities to conform with CISIA's more abstract representation. This is accomplished by aggregating data using the appropriate ontology.

The implementation of information flow from CISIA to the vertical simulators is a challenging problem. This is because the software packages were not designed to be integrated with other simulation environments. Moreover, abstract information that characterizes states in CISIA has to be mapped to tangible quantities such as electric power supply parameters. This process involves data decomposition, which introduces a degree of arbitrariness. The process is also complicated by the fact that CISIA codifies data in the form fuzzy numbers. While fuzzy numbers facilitate the fusion of data provided by vertical simulators, they render the inverse process almost intractable. Indeed, in such an instance, it is necessary to convert fuzzy numbers to crisp values, but this leads to information loss.

Another important issue is time synchronization. Since CISIA is a discrete-time simulator, the implementation middleware has to operate as a scheduler to activate the different simulators. Specifically, CISIA performs a simulation for one "time tick" (e.g., one minute in a simulation), then the middleware supplies the vertical simulators with the output of CISIA and activates their execution. When the vertical simulators have completed their calculations, the outputs are sent to CISIA, which starts the simulation for next time tick. Note that when a discrete-time vertical simulator (e.g., ns2) is used, the scenario has to be analyzed in an interrelated manner, which imposes additional constraints on the time tick period.

5. Conclusions

The CRESCO architecture attempts to address the limitations of existing critical infrastructure simulation methods by integrating multiple vertical simulators in a general horizontal simulation environment. The vertical simulators effectively model individual infrastructures and intra-domain dynamics while the horizontal simulators express inter-domain relationships and merge heterogeneous information from different infrastructures. The architecture is intended to be a proof of concept, the first step in creating a comprehensive simulation tool for analyzing multiple critical infrastructures that are tightly coupled and highly interdependent.

Our future research will attempt to develop an ontology that formalizes information flow between vertical simulators and the horizontal simulation environment. The IRRIIS Project [11] has taken a step in this direction by defining an information flow model that supports interdependency analysis; a more formal approach is being investigated by the DIESIS Project [6]. In addition, we will investigate the granularity of domain models used in vertical simulators. These results will assist in integrating information from multiple heterogeneous simulators during large-scale critical infrastructure simulations.

Acknowledgements

The authors wish to acknowledge the technical assistance provided by members of the CRESCO Project: E. Ciancamerla, S. De Porcellinis, S. Di Blasi, G. Di Poppa, E. Galli, A. Jannace, E. Marchei, M. Minichino, S. Podda, S. Ruzzante, A. Tofani and G. Vicoli.

References

[1] C. Balducelli, S. Bologna, L. Lavalle and G. Vicoli, Safeguarding information intensive critical infrastructures against novel types of emerging failures, *Reliability Engineering and System Safety*, vol. 92(9), pp. 1218–1229, 2007.

[2] V. Cardellini, E. Casalicchio and E. Galli, Agent-based modeling of interdependencies in critical infrastructures through UML, *Proceedings of the Agent-Directed Simulation Symposium of the Spring Simulation Multiconference* (www.ce.uniroma2.it/publications/ads2007.pdf), 2007.

[3] E. Casalicchio, P. Donzelli, R. Setola and S. Tucci, Modeling and simulation of interdependent critical infrastructures: The road ahead, in *Communication Networks and Computer Systems: A Tribute to Professor Erol Gelenbe*, J. Barria (Ed.), Imperial College Press, London, United Kingdom, pp. 143–157, 2006.

[4] E. Casalicchio, E. Galli and S. Tucci, Federated agent-based modeling and simulation approach to study interdependencies in IT critical infrastructures, *Proceedings of the Eleventh International Symposium on Distributed Simulation and Real-Time Applications*, pp. 182–189, 2007.

[5] S. De Porcellinis, R. Setola, S. Panzieri and G. Ulivi, Simulation of heterogeneous and interdependent critical infrastructures, *International Journal of Critical Infrastructures*, vol. 4(1/2), pp. 110–128, 2008.

[6] DIESIS Consortium, The DIESIS Project (www.diesis-eu.org).

[7] D. Dubois and H. Prade, *Possibility Theory: An Approach to Computerized Processing of Uncertainty*, Plenum Press, New York, 1998.

[8] D. Dudenhoeffer, M. Permann and M. Manic, CIMS: A framework for infrastructure interdependency modeling and analysis, *Proceedings of the Winter Simulation Conference*, pp. 478–485, 2006.

[9] K. Fall and K. Varadhan, The Network Simulator – ns-2 (nsnam.isi.edu/ns nam/index.php/Main_Page).

[10] K. Hopkinson, R. Giovanini, X. Wang, EPOCHS: Integrated commercial off-the-shelf software for agent-based electric power and communication simulation, *Proceedings of the Winter Simulation Conference*, pp. 1158–1166, 2003.

[11] IRRIIS Consortium, The IRRIIS European Integrated Project, Fraunhofer Institute for Intelligent Analysis and Information Systems, Sankt-Augustin, Germany (www.irriis.org).

[12] Italian National Agency for New Technologies, Energy and the Environment (ENEA), The CRESCO Project, Rome, Italy (www.cresco.enea.it).

[13] OMNeT++ Community Site, OMNeT++ Discrete Event Simulation System (www.omnetpp.org).

[14] S. Panzieri, R. Setola and G. Ulivi, An approach to model complex interdependent infrastructures, presented at the *Sixteenth IFAC World Congress* (www.dia.uniroma3.it/~panzieri/Articoli/WorldIFAC05-CIIP.pdf), 2005.

[15] P. Pederson, D. Dudenhoeffer, S. Hartley and M. Permann, Critical Infrastructure Interdependency Modeling: A Survey of U.S. and International Research, Report No. INL/EXT-06-11464, Critical Infrastructure Protection Division, Idaho National Laboratory, Idaho Falls, Idaho, 2006.

[16] S. Rinaldi, J. Peerenboom and T. Kelly, Identifying, understanding and analyzing critical infrastructure interdependencies, *IEEE Control Systems*, vol. 21(6), pp. 11–25, 2001.

[17] Sandia National Laboratories, National Infrastructure Simulation and Analysis Center, Albuquerque, New Mexico (www.sandia.gov/mission/homeland/programs/critical/nisac.html).

VI

INFRASTRUCTURE MODELING
AND SIMULATION

Chapter 18

SIMULATION OF ADVANCED TRAIN CONTROL SYSTEMS

Paul Craven and Paul Oman

Abstract   This paper describes an Advanced Train Control System (ATCS) simulation environment created using the Network Simulator 2 (ns-2) discrete event network simulation system. The ATCS model is verified using ATCS monitoring software, laboratory results and a comparison with a mathematical model of ATCS communications. The simulation results are useful in understanding ATCS communication characteristics and identifying protocol strengths, weaknesses, vulnerabilities and mitigation techniques. By setting up a suite of ns-2 scripts, an engineer can simulate hundreds of possible scenarios in the space of a few seconds to investigate failure modes and consequences.

Keywords: Railroads, wireless networks, ATCS, ns-2, simulation

1.   Introduction

The transportation sector has been categorized as a critical infrastructure [1]. Any significant disruption in the movement of goods or people threatens the nation's defense as well as its economy [25, 26].

The North American surface transportation network is a complex interacting system designed to provide safety and efficiency, but it is vulnerable to accidents, malicious attacks and natural disasters [28]. Failures at a small number of "choke points" can impact highway, rail, air and maritime transportation throughout the network [21].

Given the importance of surface transportation, it is important to identify and protect the essential components of transportation systems and to ensure resiliency [19]. Simulating failures and analyzing their effects enables engineers to identify critical vulnerabilities, facilitating the construction of reliable, survivable systems [4, 5].

Please use the following format when citing this chapter:

Craven, P. and Oman, P., 2008, in IFIP International Federation for Information Processing, Volume 290; *Critical Infrastructure Protection II*, eds. Papa, M., Shenoi, S., (Boston: Springer), pp. 243–256.

On any given day, the United States surface transportation network moves eight million truckloads of freight across four million miles of roadway using 1.5 million railcars on 170,000 miles of track [21]. Containerization makes the highway and railway freight systems inseparable. Unfortunately, highway and railway communication control systems are vulnerable to malicious and nuisance cyber attacks [3, 7–9]. Railway control communications, in particular, have evolved in an obscure but benign environment where railroad enthusiasts often eavesdrop on control signals to track railcar movements [14].

The U.S. rail system uses communication protocols for tasks ranging from changing track switches to controlling locomotives [6]. Most rail communication protocols do not have simulation environments, requiring engineers to run expensive, time-consuming field experiments to analyze their behavior. For example, the U.S. rail system is currently testing the Positive Train Control (PTC) system designed to prevent train collisions, derailments and injuries to workers [11]. Several pilot projects have been launched, including the North American Joint PTC for the St. Louis-Chicago corridor that sought to implement PTC using the Advanced Train Control System (ATCS) protocol.

The ATCS is widely used in the rail industry for wireless data communications. However, because no simulation models are available for ATCS, its suitability can only be evaluated in physical environments. Unfortunately, time, labor, and safety considerations severely limit the extent of physical testing that can be performed on railroad systems.

Realistic computer simulations of ATCS could enable engineers to test PTC system configurations in the laboratory. The designs could be validated using a pilot project and further simulations could be run on other track segments. Such an approach would have significantly enhanced the results of the North American Joint PTC effort.

Simulation environments also offer effective and safe testbeds for analyzing vulnerabilities. In January 2008, a 14-year-old boy built a wireless device that enabled him to control switches for a tram system in Lodz, Poland [2]. He is suspected of causing four derailments, including one in which twelve people were injured. An ATCS simulation model would have enabled engineers to debug these and other problems in a laboratory environment.

This paper describes a network simulation model of the ATCS for wireless railroad controls. The ATCS is modeled using Network Simulator 2 (ns-2), a popular discrete event simulation system. The simulation model enables engineers to gain a better understanding of ATCS strengths and weaknesses as well as its vulnerabilities and the appropriate mitigation strategies.

2.　ATCS Overview

The ATCS is an open standard for wireless railroad data systems [6]. It is used for controlling signals, switches and monitoring trains over several thousand miles of rail in the United States [22, 30]. The ATCS specifications [1] span several volumes, covering everything from the dimensions of the hardware and electrical connectors to upper-level software protocols.

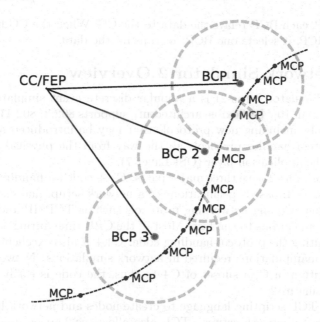

Figure 1. Example ATCS network.

A typical ATCS configuration involves three types of devices (Figure 1). The first is a cluster controller/front end processor (CC/FEP). The FEP coordinates all ATCS traffic and is directly controlled by a railway dispatch center. Several CCs may be connected to a FEP. The FEPs and CCs are usually combined into one unit (CC/FEP). Multiple CC/FEPs can be chained together using a specialized ATCS packet switch.

The second major device is the base communications package (BCP). Each CC coordinates traffic for multiple BCPs. Communications between CC/FEPs and BCPs usually employ wired lines. Typically, CC/FEPs handle around ten BCPs. While a CC/FEP can handle more BCPs, the effect of losing a CC/FEP is minimized by limiting the number of BCPs that connect to it.

The third type of device is a mobile communications package (MCP), which is an interface for equipment in locomotives and wayside devices (e.g., train signals, switches and track sensors). Locomotives use the BCP to send and receive information from wayside devices. Each BCP serves a number of MCPs. Communications between MCPs and BCPs is done wirelessly via full duplex using two separate frequencies. One frequency (typically around 897 MHz) is used for MCP to BCP communications. The other frequency (usually about 935 MHz) is for BCP to MCP communications. Other frequencies may be employed, depending on the licenses obtained by the railroad.

Usually, each MCP is serviced by at least two BCPs; this provides redundancy if there is a problem with a BCP or its communications. Also, MCPs are allowed to move between BCPs. Multiple BCPs usually receive transmissions from an MCP, each BCP relays the data to the CC. When the CC has to send data to an MCP, it selects one BCP to transmit the data.

3.   Network Simulator 2 Overview

Network Simulator 2 (ns-2) is a popular discrete event simulator for networking research [10]. Its flexible architecture supports 802.3, 802.11 and many other protocols, including new protocols that may be introduced as plug-ins. The ns-2 system handles protocols all the way from the physical layer (OSI Layer 1) to the application layer (OSI Layer 7).

Simulations in ns-2 have three major parts: C++ code for handling networking protocols, TCL-based specifications of a network setup, and code for data post-processing. Coding networking protocols such as TCP/IP and HTTP in C++ allows simulations to run fast. Most of the CPU time during a simulation is spent executing the protocol-handling code. C++ is also excellent for coding low-level bit manipulations required in network simulations. Networking code is usually written in C, a subset of C++; thus, the code is easily integrated and tested using ns-2.

Using the TCL scripting language to create nodes and network links allows quick changes to network setups. TCL also allows ns-2 to be used as a full-fledged development platform for simulations. In particular, a user can use TCL to create a suite of simulations to be run with just one command. The ns-2 system uses OTcl [29], an extension to TCL that supports object-oriented development.

Network simulations can generate extremely large log files, which may have to be processed with summarization and analysis tools. Text processing tools such as grep, sed, awk and perl can be used for data summarization. ns-2 incorporates nam, a network animator program that displays animations of network traffic. Programs like gnuplot and Excel can be used to create graphs.

4.   Modeling ATCS

The ATCS simulator is implemented in ns-2 using four main components: scheduler, event interface, handler interface and TCL/C++ language bindings. The scheduler is the heart of the ns-2 system. All the discrete events, which include packet transmissions, are passed to the scheduler along with the times they should be processed. The scheduler then examines each event in order and triggers a "handler" to process the event. Finally, the ATCS simulator binds its C++ code to the TCL scripting language using the same method as the rest of the ns-2 code.

Most of the C++ classes provided in the ATCS simulator are modeled after OSI layers. For example, a C++ class is available for modeling the physical layer, and subclasses are available for wireless and wired modems. Because many ATCS applications are low-level in nature, higher OSI layers (e.g., presentation layer) may be combined with other layers to simplify coding.

Other classes are employed to represent network nodes. These classes follow the "composite pattern" [12]. A class that represents a network node contains multiple OSI layer objects. The node class itself has the same handler interface as the OSI layers.

The next most common class in the ATCS simulator creates the adapter [12] between TCL and C++. The adapter class is static and is responsible for creating and binding a "shadow" object in C++ for each object of that type created in TCL.

While the C++ code models the internals of a working ATCS, specific networks are set up using TCL code. It takes just 25 lines of TCL code to model the communications between the three major types of ATCS nodes: MCP, BCP and CC. Using data files, or even random numbers, makes it easy to put together large simulations involving many nodes.

5. Wireless Medium Modeling

This section describes the wireless medium assumptions and characteristics modeled with the ATCS simulation code written for ns-2.

5.1   Propagation Models

The ATCS runs full-duplex communications with two frequencies, one for outgoing data from the BCP and one for incoming data. The two frequencies are handled independently by the simulator. Propagation can be calculated based on free space loss on a flat plane or by using the Longley-Rice model, which takes elevation into account. By default, the network is assumed to be on a flat plane and the coordinates for each node are in the latitude-longitude format. The received signal strength is calculated using free space loss and the user can account for antenna gain and cable loss.

The Longley-Rice propagation model can be used if the simulation requires terrain effects to be taken into account. This model requires digital elevation models (DEMs) [27] and involves more computational overhead than the free space loss model. The free space loss and Longley-Rice propagation models are discussed in detail later in this paper.

5.2   Transmitter-Receiver Distance

The code for the wireless medium relays copies of each transmitted packet to the radio receivers listening on the corresponding frequency. The time taken for the signal to arrive depends on the distance to the receiver. The distance between the transmitter and receiver is calculated according to their latitudes and longitudes using an adaptation of the Haversine Formula:

$$\Delta lat = lat_2 - lat_1 \tag{1}$$
$$\Delta long = long_2 - long_1 \tag{2}$$

The distance between the transmitter and receiver (in meters) is computed using the following equations:

$$a = sin^2 \left(\frac{\Delta lat}{2}\right) + cos(lat_1)cos(lat_2)sin^2 \left(\frac{\Delta lon}{2}\right) \quad (3)$$

$$b = 2 \cdot atan2(\frac{\sqrt{a}}{\sqrt{1-a}}) \quad (4)$$

$$d = Rb \quad (5)$$

where lat_i is the latitude of point i (radians), $long_i$ is the longitude of point i (radians), $atan2(a, b)$ is the arctangent of a/b, R is the radius of the Earth ($\approx$ 6,371 km), a is the square of half of the straight-line distance, b is the great circle distance (radians), and d is the distance between the transmitter and receiver (km).

Whether the receiver can actually receive and decode the packet depends on how much power the signal has upon arrival. This is where the user has the option to use the free space loss propagation model or the Longley-Rice propagation model.

5.3   Power Loss

The ATCS model estimates the power loss during transmission between two nodes using the free space loss or Longley-Rice propagation models. The models incorporate parameters for antenna gain and signal loss from the cable and connectors.

Free Space Loss Propagation   Free space loss [13] assumes that there are no obstructions between the two nodes and that the signal is not reflected (that would cause it to propagate further). Free space loss has been shown to provide a reasonable approximation for distance-dependent loss [24]. However, the model does not account for losses due to terrain obstructions.

The loss, l, is computed as:

$$l = \left(\frac{4\pi d}{\lambda}\right)^2 \quad (6)$$

where d is the distance between the nodes and λ is the wavelength of the signal.

The source signal spreads out in a sphere whose radius is the distance between the transmitter and the receiver; this gives the $4\pi d$ term in the equation. The longer the wavelength, the larger the antenna and the more signal that is captured; this gives the $\frac{1}{\lambda}$ term in the equation. Also, the signal strength drops off in proportion to the square of both terms. Since the radio channel is specified in terms of its frequency rather than wavelength, substituting for $\lambda = c/f$, yields:

$$l = \left(\frac{4\pi df}{c} \right)^2. \tag{7}$$

Since d is in meters, substituting the value for the speed of light $c \approx 3 \cdot 10^8$ m/s yields:

$$l = \left(\frac{4\pi df}{3 \cdot 10^8} \right)^2. \tag{8}$$

Taking the log_{10} of both sides to obtain values in dB, the equation reduces to:

$$
\begin{aligned}
l_{dB} &= 10 \log_{10} \left(\frac{4\pi df}{3 \cdot 10^8} \right)^2 \tag{9} \\
&= 20 \log_{10} \left(\frac{4\pi}{3 \cdot 10^8} \right) + 20 \log_{10}(f) + 20 \log_{10}(d) \tag{10} \\
&\approx -147.56 + 20 \log_{10}(f) + 20 \log_{10}(d). \tag{11}
\end{aligned}
$$

The ATCS simulation model uses Equation 11 to compute the free space loss.

Longley-Rice Propagation The Longley-Rice propagation model was first published in 1967 [20] and has since undergone several revisions [17]. The latest algorithm and model equations were published by Hufford [15].

The original Longley-Rice algorithm was written in FORTRAN. This algorithm was translated to Microsoft-specific C code by the Institute of Telecommunication Sciences (ITS) [16], and was subsequently modified by Magliacane [18] for use in a Unix environment. Magliacane's code is distributed under the GNU Public License (GPL). It incorporates DEMs, which are available free-of-charge from the United States Geological Survey [27]. A useful feature of the code is that it enables users to create signal propagation maps.

To implement Longley-Rice propagation in the ATCS ns-2 simulator, portions of the ITS code and Magliacane code were adapted and encapsulated in a C++ class, and then modified to interface with TCL and the data structures used by the simulator. This enables the ATCS simulator to use the Longley-Rice model by simply changing the name of the default propagation method, and having the DEMs loaded into the current working directory.

The results of an ATCS simulation can be saved in comma-delimited or packet-dump formats. The comma-delimited format is handled by spreadsheets and text processing tools (e.g., grep, awk and perl). The packet-dump format can be loaded directly into ATCSMon, the ATCS packet-inspection tool.

6. ATCS Simulation Model Validation

It is important to test the ATCS code for ns-2 to ensure that it provides accurate simulations. This section describes three validation procedures used to test the simulation model: (i) running simulation data on an ATCS monitoring tool, (ii) comparing simulation data with laboratory data, and (iii) comparing simulation data with data from a mathematical model.

6.1   ATCSMon-Based Validation

The ATCSMon tool decodes ATCS radio traffic and interprets packets. It is similar to Ethereal, which is used in TCP/IP networks.

In order to test that the ATCS ns-2 simulation produces valid packets, support was added to save packet traces in the ATCSMon format. The simulated packets were compared with real packets to verify that they were similar in content and timing. The ATCSMon visualization feature helped confirm that the simulation data was "realistic."

6.2   Laboratory-Data-Based Validation

This validation study used test data from an ATCS laboratory maintained by Wabtec Corporation. The laboratory setup included several MCPs, one BCP and one FEP/CC; ATCSMon was used to capture data. An identical setup was created virtually using ns-2. The data was identical, except for a CRC code and three bytes used to hold session information. The virtual model was adjusted to handle these data fields.

Packet timing was also compared. In this case, the results were similar, but not exact. Rather than transmitting status data at exactly 60-second intervals, the MCPs would drift a few tenths of a second during each cycle. The difference is significant when large numbers of MCPs are employed. Packet collisions occur when two stations transmit at exactly the same time (every 60 seconds). However, fewer collisions occur when the 60-second cycle drifts a little, This difference is seen more clearly when data from the ns-2 model is compared with ATCS data generated using a mathematical model of ATCS throughput.

6.3   Mathematical-Model-Based Validation

The Sharif-Furman mathematical model of ATCS throughput [23] was used in the study. According to the Sharif-Furman model, the throughput should change smoothly depending on the number of MCP nodes that have traffic. The greater the number of MCPs, the greater the number of packet collisions, which reduces the effective throughput.

We tested this characteristic with multiple simulations of the ATCS ns-2 model. All the MCPs were set the same distance from the BCP, and support for "busy-bit" traffic control was turned off. Simulation runs were performed for networks with five MCPs up to 25 MCPs; each simulation modeled one hour of traffic. The simulations were run, summarized and graphed in one step using TCL scripts. The total computation time required to create twenty hours of simulated ATCS network traffic was less than five seconds.

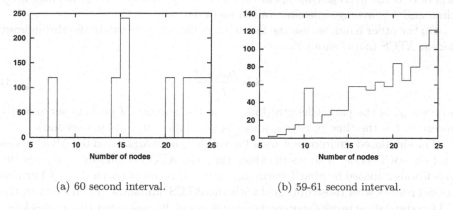

(a) 60 second interval.　　　　　　　(b) 59-61 second interval.

Figure 2. Corrupted packets vs. nodes.

The first group of simulation results did not match the mathematical model. The main reason is that the Sharif-Furman model assumes that packets are scheduled according to a Poisson distribution (i.e., they arrive independently); however, ATCS traffic does not follow a Poisson distribution. Acknowledgement packets are sent upon packet arrival, and status information is usually sent once per minute. This results in a mean number of packets over a time interval that does not equal the variance, violating one of the criteria for a Poisson distribution. Evidence of this can be seen in Figure 2(a), where the number of packet collisions in one hour is plotted against the number of nodes. Instead of a smooth increase in packet collisions, the collisions jump in multiples of 120. Nevertheless, the Sharif-Furman model provides an upper bound for randomly-scheduled ATCS packets.

The simulations show that packet collisions occur when each node transmits status information once a minute and two nodes on the network are set to transmit at exactly the same time. Thus, two packets are marked as corrupted due to each collision. Because the time to retry is somewhat random, the second attempt at sending the packets usually works. However, as discussed earlier, laboratory tests show that most MCPs do not transmit exactly once per minute. Thus, if the simulation is changed to randomize the interval between 59 and 61 seconds, the results are notably different, as shown in Figure 2(b).

Sharif and Furman expressed their results in terms of the throughput that could be expected in a given system and provide a graph of the predicted throughput with 251 byte packets. They used the following equation to compute the throughput:

$$S = \frac{\bar{U}}{\bar{B} + \bar{I}} \tag{12}$$

where $\bar{U}$ is the average time spent on successful packets, $\bar{B}$ is the average busy time and $\bar{I}$ is average idle time (all in seconds).

On the other hand, we use the following equation to calculate the throughput for an ATCS model simulation:

$$S = \frac{l_{bits} \cdot n}{t \cdot r} \tag{13}$$

where l_{bits} is the packet length (bits), n is the number of packets successfully received, t is the time (seconds) and r is the data rate (bits per second).

The simulated environment used for validation incorporated ten MCP nodes and one BCP node. The results show that the ATCS simulator replicates the conditions imposed by Sharif-Furman. Figure 3(a) compares the Sharif-Furman model results with those obtained with the ATCS simulator. Each point in the ATCS simulation results represents an average of 20 runs, each 10 minutes long.

The system load was computed by dividing the bits sent per second divided by the capacity of the data line. In this case, a load of 1.0 implies that ten MCP nodes generate 1,200 bits to transmit every second on a 1200 baud line. Loads greater than 1.0 indicate more data is sent at a faster rate than the baud rate of data transmission. Simulated loads were increased in increments of 0.05 with busy-bits being transmitted. Note that the 251-byte packets used by Sharif-Furman were much larger than the ATCS packets, which were less than 40 bytes.

The Sharif-Furman results show that the predicted throughput is slightly larger than the data offered load for many of the lower load values. In other words, more data was received than was transmitted; but it is not clear from the Sharif-Furman paper what this extra data represents. Consequently, it is difficult to tell the point at which packets start getting dropped for the Sharif-Furman model. This is important because, in most real-time systems, networks must be configured so that dropped packets are very rare. In the case of the ATCS simulation, packets start getting dropped at a load of 0.2 for a packet length of 251 bytes.

In general, the simulation results are slightly lower than the results predicted by the Sharif-Furman model. This is expected because the Sharif-Furman model provides the "ideal" upper bound – due to the fact that packets are generated at random intervals. The ATCS simulation, on the other hand, generates packets at intervals that are mostly periodic in nature, increasing the chance of packet collisions. ATCS packets do not follow the Poisson distribution expected by the Sharif-Furman model; this is reflected in lower throughput for the simulated model.

7.   Modeling Network Loads

The ns-2 ATCS simulator can also be used to model new situations. For example, support for ATCS traffic control can be set to one of three states: (i) BCP busy-bits can be turned off, (ii) BCP transmits only when it has traffic to send, or (iii) BCP always transmits. Figure 3(b) shows the average

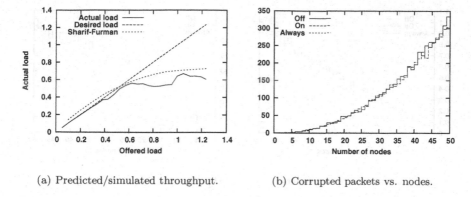

(a) Predicted/simulated throughput.   (b) Corrupted packets vs. nodes.

Figure 3. Simulation results.

number of corrupted packets for simulation runs of one hour with the BCP set to each of the three possible states. For each node count in the graph, twenty simulations were run and the results averaged. Each MCP node transmits a status message over an interval between 59 and 61 seconds. The CC does not send any control messages to the MCPs. The only packets received by the MCPs are acknowledgement packets.

The results in Figure 3(b) show that always transmitting a busy-bit for traffic control significantly impacts the number of corrupt packets. Transmitting the busy-bit only when the BCP needs to transmit data does not significantly impact the number of corrupted packets. However, it should be noted that this is the worst-case scenario because the CC usually sends control messages to the MCPs on a periodic basis and this increases the number of busy-bits sent. The frequency with which control messages are sent depends on the scenario. It is easy to run simulations that model the different scenarios.

Figure 4(a) shows the average times for delivering ATCS packets (over 20 simulation runs). Packets are not counted unless they arrive. the average time increases as more nodes are added to a network. Most packets continue to arrive quickly, but packet collisions and retries drive up the average. Note that transmitting a busy-bit improves the average packet time fairly significantly.

Figure 4(b) shows the average maximum times for deliver packets (over 20 simulation runs). Knowing the expected maximum time for packet delivery is important in real-time applications. Note that this time increases quickly even when only a few nodes added to the system.

8.   Conclusions

The ATCS ns-2 simulation system is a valuable tool for modeling ATCS networks and investigating their behavior in a virtual environment. By setting up a suite of ns-2 scripts, an engineer can simulate hundreds of possible scenarios

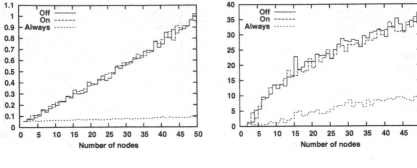

(a) Av. time to deliver packets. (b) Av. max time to deliver packets.

Figure 4. Average packet times.

in the space of a few seconds. The simulation results are useful for understanding ATCS communication characteristics, identifying protocol strengths, weaknesses and vulnerabilities, and developing mitigation techniques. The fidelity of the ATCS simulation model is validated by test results using ATCSMon monitoring software, laboratory data and the Sharif-Furman mathematical model.

References

[1] Association of American Railroads, System Architecture: ATCS Specification 100 (Revision 4.0), Washington, DC (www.atcsmon.com/100 _4_0.htm), 1995.

[2] G. Baker, Schoolboy hacks into city's tram system, *The Daily Telegraph*, January 11, 2008.

[3] M. Benke, On the Survivability of Transportation Systems, M.S. Thesis, Computer Science Department, University of Idaho, Moscow, Idaho, 2005.

[4] M. Benke, A. Abdel-Rahim, P. Oman and B. Johnson, Case study of a survivability analysis of a small intelligent transportation system, *Transportation Research Record: Journal of the Transportation Research Board*, vol. 1944, pp. 98–106, 2006.

[5] S. Butapati, R. Kalidindi, M. Benke, A. Abdel-Rahim, P. Oman and B. Johnson, A case study of critical point identification in the physical and communication layers of a small urban transportation system, *International Journal of Critical Infrastructures*, vol. 2(4), pp. 319–330, 2006.

[6] P. Craven, A brief look at railroad communication vulnerabilities, *Proceedings of the Seventh International IEEE Conference on Intelligent Transportation Systems*, pp. 245–249, 2004.

[7] P. Craven, Security of RCL wireless railway communications, *Proceedings of the IEEE Conference on Control Applications*, pp. 711–715, 2005.

[8] P. Craven and S. Craven, Security of ATCS wireless railway communications, *Proceedings of the ASME/IEEE Joint Rail Conference*, pp. 227–238, 2005.

[9] P. Craven and S. Craven, Security of railway EOT systems, *Proceedings of the ASME/IEEE Joint Rail Conference*, pp. 199–204, 2005.

[10] K. Fall and K. Varadhan, The Network Simulator – ns-2 (nsnam.isi.edu/ns nam/index.php/Main_Page).

[11] Federal Railroad Administration, Positive train control overview, Department of Transportation, Washington, DC (www.fra.dot.gov/us/con tent/1265).

[12] E. Gamma, R. Helm, R. Johnson and J. Vlissides, *Design Patterns: Elements of Reusable Object-Oriented Software*, Addison-Wesley, Boston, Massachusetts, 1995.

[13] D. Green and A. Obaidat, An accurate line of sight propagation performance model for ad-hoc 802.11 wireless LAN (WLAN) devices, *Proceedings of the IEEE International Conference on Communications*, vol. 5, pp. 3424–3428, 2002.

[14] D. Houy, ATCS monitor for Windows (www.atcsmon.com).

[15] G. Hufford, The ITS Irregular Terrain Model (version 1.2.2), Institute for Telecommunication Sciences, National Telecommunications and Information Administration, Boulder, Colorado (flattop.its.bldrdoc.gov/itm /itm_alg.pdf), 1999.

[16] Institute for Telecommunication Sciences, C++ code for Longley-Rice propagation, National Telecommunications and Information Administration, Boulder, Colorado (flattop.its.bldrdoc.gov/itm.html), 2007.

[17] A. Longley and P. Rice, Prediction of Tropospheric Radio Transmission Loss over Irregular Terrain: A Computer Method, ESSA Technical Report ERL 79-ITS 67, Institute for Telecommunication Sciences, National Telecommunications and Information Administration, Boulder, Colorado (www.its.bldrdoc.gov/pub/essa/essa_erl_79-its_67), 1968.

[18] J. Magliacane, Splat! RF signal propagation, loss and terrain analysis tool (www.qsl.net/kd2bd/splat.html).

[19] N. Mead, R. Ellison, R. Linger, T. Longstaff and J. McHugh, Survivable Network Analysis Method, Technical Report CMU/SEI-2000-TR-013, Software Engineering Institute, Carnegie Mellon University, Pittsburgh, Pennsylvania, 2000.

[20] P. Rice, A. Longley, K. Norton and A. Barsis, Transmission Loss Prediction for Tropospheric Communication Circuits, Volumes I and II, Technical Note 101, Institute for Telecommunication Sciences, National Telecommunications and Information Administration, Boulder, Colorado (www.its .bldrdoc.gov/pub/ntia-rpt/tn101), 1967.

[21] L. Ritter, J. Barrett and R. Wilson, *Securing Global Transportation Networks*, McGraw-Hill, New York, 2006.

[22] Securities and Exchange Commission, Norfolk Southern Corporation: Form 10-K (Fiscal year ending December 31, 2003), Washington, DC (www.secinfo.com/dwDMq.11q.htm), 2004.

[23] H. Sharif and E. Furman, Analytical model for ATCS inbound RF channel throughput, *Proceedings of the Forty-First IEEE Vehicular Technology Conference*, pp. 885–892, 1991.

[24] D. Smith, *Digital Transmission Systems*, Kluwer Academic Publishers, Norwell, Massachusetts, 2003.

[25] T. Smith, The impact of highway infrastructure on economic performance, *Public Roads Magazine*, vol. 57(4), pp. 8–14, 1994.

[26] The White House, The National Strategy for the Physical Protection of Critical Infrastructures and Key Assets, Washington, DC (www.whitehouse .gov/pcipb/physical_strategy.pdf), 2003.

[27] United States Geological Survey, 1:250,000-scale digital elevation model (DEM), Reston, Virginia (edcftp.cr.usgs.gov/pub/data).

[28] J. Waite, M. Benke, N. Nguyen, M. Phillips, S. Melton, P. Oman, A. Abdel-Rahim and B. Johnson, A combined approach to ITS vulnerability and survivability analyses, *Proceedings of the Seventh IEEE Conference on Intelligent Transportation Systems*, pp. 262–267, 2004.

[29] D. Wetherall, OTcl (otcl-tclcl.sourceforge.net/otcl).

[30] D. Williams, B. Metzger and G. Richardson, Spec 200 radio code line ducting – Cause and effect, *Proceedings of the American Railway Engineering and Maintenance-of-Way Association Conference*, 2001.

Chapter 19

AN INTEGRATED METHODOLOGY FOR CRITICAL INFRASTRUCTURE MODELING AND SIMULATION

William Tolone, Seok-Won Lee, Wei-Ning Xiang, Joshua Blackwell, Cody Yeager, Andrew Schumpert and Wray Johnson

Abstract   Integral to effective critical infrastructure analysis is the assessment of infrastructure vulnerabilities, which provides insights into potential disruptions that can enhance protection plans and response and recovery operations. Effective critical infrastructures analysis, however, must account for the complex, multi-dimensional characteristics of infrastructures and the dependencies between infrastructures. This paper presents a new methodology for integrated modeling and simulation that supports such analysis. An integrated analysis environment that embodies this new methodology is presented as a proof of concept.

Keywords: Modeling, simulation, geospatial analysis, ontological analysis

1.   Introduction

Critical infrastructures are infrastructures that, if disrupted, can undermine a nation's security, economy, public health and way of life [15]. Recent incidents such as the 2003 blackout in the Northeastern United States and Southeastern Canada and the 2005 hurricanes in Louisiana and Texas demonstrate the catastrophic impacts of critical infrastructure disruptions. While it is unlikely that disruptions can be prevented, effective critical infrastructure analysis can – at the very least – minimize their impact by improving vulnerability assessments, protection planning and strategies for response and recovery.

Critical infrastructure analysis seeks to provide insights into infrastructure behavior and potential disruptions that can increase the efficacy of protection plans and response and recovery operations. The U.S. Government has identified thirteen critical infrastructure sectors (e.g., energy, communications, and banking and finance) [15]. Each sector is a mission-critical, socio-technical system involving complex, multi-dimensional collections of technologies, infor-

Please use the following format when citing this chapter:

Tolone, W., Lee, S.-W., Xiang, W.-N., Blackwell, J., Yeager, C., Schumpert, A. and Johnson, W., 2008, in IFIP International Federation for Information Processing, Volume 290; *Critical Infrastructure Protection II*, eds. Papa, M., Shenoi, S., (Boston: Springer), pp. 257–268.

mation, processes and people. All the sectors are highly interdependent – disruptions in one sector cascade and escalate across the other sectors [12].

In order to account for these characteristics, critical infrastructure analysis must satisfy two important requirements. First, it should emphasize the engineering properties and the behavioral properties of each infrastructure. Engineering properties describe the technical characteristics of an infrastructure in terms of the underlying physics-based properties of the inanimate objects that constrain infrastructure operation. Behavioral properties describe the relational properties that emerge from business processes, decision points, human interventions, information availability, reliability and consistency, in addition to the engineering properties of the infrastructure.

Second, critical infrastructure analysis must be conducted *in situ*, i.e., in context. Suchman [13] argues that context gives meaning to action – separating actions from the context in which they are performed causes the meanings or implications of the actions to be lost. Examining infrastructures in isolation ignores the complex dependencies that exist between infrastructures and the contextual factors that constrain infrastructure behavior. This results in vulnerability assessments that are at best incomplete and at worst invalid.

These two requirements must constitute the foundation for any comprehensive, holistic and systemic analysis of critical infrastructures, especially modeling and simulation activities that support infrastructure protection. This paper presents a new methodology for infrastructure modeling and simulation that addresses the two requirements. The methodology is realized within an integrated environment that supports effective critical infrastructure analysis.

2.   Related Work

Modeling and simulation are important activities that facilitate the exploration and analysis of complex phenomena, especially those encountered in critical infrastructure systems. In fact, for many phenomena, modeling and simulation may be the only viable means for exploration and analysis. This is particularly true for phenomena that are characterized by organic collections of events involving open systems — systems that may include social, economic, technical, civic, environmental, informational and geographic contexts. Effective modeling and simulation of these phenomena often require a system-of-systems approach that recognizes the various dimensions of the phenomena and the relationships between the dimensions.

A comprehensive survey of critical infrastructure modeling and simulation solutions can be found in [10]. Several solutions decompose analysis to the exploration of individual infrastructures. Many useful single infrastructure solutions exist (see, e.g., [4, 11]). However, decomposition methods fail to recognize the importance of the behavioral properties of infrastructures and the complex dependencies existing between infrastructures. Furthermore, these solutions are difficult to generalize due to the unique characteristics of each infrastructure.

Other solutions focus on infrastructure interdependencies (see, e.g., [3, 6]). These solutions attempt to recognize the *in situ* requirement and model the

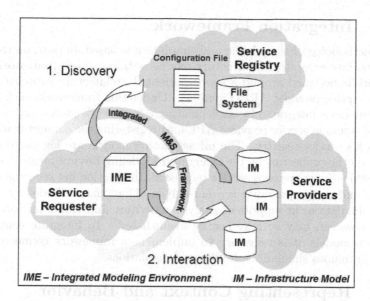

Figure 1. Integrated modeling and simulation framework.

complex behavior that emerges from the interdependencies. However, these solutions do not adequately incorporate the unique behaviors of the underlying infrastructures. While interdependencies can lead to cascading and escalating effects [12], these effects arise specifically from the interplay of the interdependencies and the individual behavior of infrastructures. When the behavior of individual infrastructure is ignored, the fidelity of the model is greatly reduced.

Still other solutions attempt to construct comprehensive models of critical infrastructures (see, e.g., [2, 5, 9, 12, 14]). However, detailed comprehensive models are difficult to construct due to the unique characteristics of each infrastructure. As a result, these models emphasize higher levels of analysis at the cost of detailed analysis.

Recently, there have been efforts to develop hybrid solutions for critical infrastructure modeling and simulation (see, e.g., [1, 16]). Pederson and colleagues [10] describe these efforts as adopting a "coupled modeling" approach. Under this approach, individual infrastructure models are integrated in a generalized manner with models of infrastructure dependencies to enable system-of-systems analysis, which couples the fidelity of individual infrastructure models with the requirement for *in situ* analysis. Our modeling and simulation solution leverages this coupled approach.

3.   Modeling and Simulation Methodology

This section describes the modeling and simulation methodology, which builds on our previous work in the area [16]. The methodology leverages existing infrastructure models and a representation of context and behavior.

3.1   Integration Framework

The methodology for modeling and simulation is based, in part, on the ability to integrate separate infrastructure models within a single framework. The framework is designed around a service-oriented architecture supported by a common service provider API (Figure 1). Under this framework, each infrastructure model is integrated by implementing a framework connector, which realizes the common service provider API, and registering the connector with the framework's service registry. The infrastructure models are leveraged during analysis via the connectors by the Integrated Modeling Environment (described below), which functions as a service requester. Interaction between the service requester and service providers is event-driven. Thus, the methodology enables discrete simulations in support of analysis activities. Individual infrastructure models, however, may or may not be event-based. To integrate continuous simulation models, it is necessary to implement a framework connector that adapts continuous simulations to discrete simulations.

3.2   Representing Context and Behavior

Because context gives meaning to action [13], examining the behavior of critical infrastructures in isolation and outside of space and time leads to a loss in the meaning or implication of infrastructure behavior. John Locke's definition of "knowledge" inspires our representation of context and the meaning it embodies. Locke [8] describes knowledge as the ability to distinguish concepts or ideas. In other words, knowledge emerges from relationships among concepts. Our representation leverages this definition and draws on ontology principles and the notion of a relation to provide a representation of context and behavior. Our methodology uses relations to support the specification of contextual and behavioral properties along three dimensions: function, time and space. These dimensions situate infrastructure features and their collective behavior by answering how, when and where features are related. In this context, an infrastructure feature is any modeled component of an infrastructure.

Functional Relations Under our methodology, each infrastructure feature may be associated functionally with other infrastructure features. We define functional relations according to a specified commodity and relational rule, and by leveraging a provider/subscriber paradigm. Commodities are tangible or intangible goods or services that may be generated, transported or consumed by infrastructure features. Relational rules further restrict the relation by constraining the set of origin features that may provide a commodity to a destination feature. Most relational rules constrain this behavior according to provider/subscriber proximity.

A functional relation is represented by the tuple, (*origin* × *commodity* × *destination* × *relational_rule*), which states that the infrastructure feature *origin* provides the *commodity* to infrastructure feature *destination* according to the *relational_rule*. Given that the collective critical infrastructure of a region may contain tens of thousands of features, it is not feasible to specify every functional relation. Therefore, we allow functional relations to be specified at a type/subtype level and an instance level using selection sets. A selection set is a specification that resolves to a set of features according to a specified criterion. For example, functional relations can be specified that state that infrastructure features of type *origin_type* provide a *commodity* to infrastructure features of type *destination_type* according to the *relational_rule*.

Temporal Relations Under our methodology, each infrastructure feature may be associated with temporal latencies for enabling or disabling the feature. A temporal relation is represented by the tuple, (*feature* × *commodity* × *effect* × *duration*), which states that when an infrastructure *feature* loses or gains access to a *commodity*, the *effect* (i.e., disable or enable) is delayed by a *duration*. For example, if an infrastructure feature losses access to the essential commodity electricity, the disabling effect of losing the commodity is delayed until the specified latency has passed; this latency may model a limited alternative commodity source (e.g., battery backup). Similarly, once an infrastructure feature gains access to its essential commodities, the enabling effect is delayed until the specified latency has passed; this latency can model the startup time required to enable the feature. If access to an essential commodity is restored before the disablement latency has expired, then the disable event is discarded. Similar to functional relations, temporal relations for infrastructure features may be specified at the type/subtype or instance levels.

Spatial Relations Finally, our methodology recognizes that infrastructure features, as physical objects, are spatially tangible. Therefore, each infrastructure feature may be associated with a location in space. Its location and spatial relationships with other infrastructure features are represented by geographic coordinates and also, as in many geographic information systems, by topological relationships [7]. A spatial relation is represented by the tuple, (*feature* × *location*), which states that infrastructure *feature* is located at *location* in geographic space. Spatial relations of infrastructure features are used in numerous ways, including for proximity analysis according to relational rules (e.g., nearest provider in a given radius), spatial correlations (e.g., map overlays) and geo-visualizations.

Infrastructure Context and Behavior Ontology Integrating functional, temporal and spatial relations leads to an ontology for modeling infrastructure context and behavior (Figure 2). An ontology models the well-defined dimensions of a domain in terms of objects, attributes and relations. It also enables the construction of a common understanding through a common language and representation for analytical discourse. In our ontology, functional and temporal relations are represented by the objects in grey. Spatial relations are modeled by the "Space" association between the "Feature" object and the "Location" object.

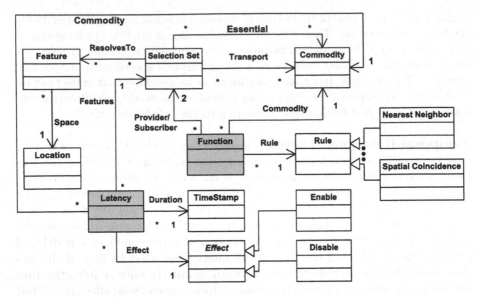

Figure 2. Infrastructure context and behavior ontology.

4.   Integrated Methodology

Our new methodology leverages the integration framework and the context and behavior ontology. It involves five steps.

1. **Infrastructure Model Identification and Development:** Infrastructure models are realized by using third party products (e.g., [4, 11]) or by instantiating generic infrastructure models that are built into the integration framework (e.g., utility, transport and channel networks).
2. **Connector Development:** Each infrastructure model must instantiate a connector for the model to participate in the integration framework. The framework provides a simple connector API for connector development.
3. **Infrastructure Model Importation:** The modeling environment, as a service requester, requires from each infrastructure model a representation of the infrastructure features for the model for the features to participate in the context and behavior ontology.
4. **Integrated Model Development:** Functional, temporal and spatial relations are specified (ontology instantiation); relationships are instantiated based on these specifications.
5. **Integrated Modeling and Simulation:** Models are explored, simulations are executed and analyzed, models are validated and analysis products are constructed.

These five steps are not necessarily performed in a sequential manner. Each step remains ongoing as analysis questions change, infrastructure models evolve (due to data acquisition, verification and validation), and the integrated model

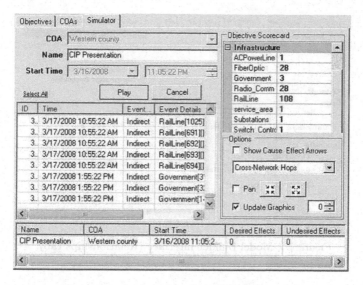

Figure 3.   Analyst interface (Simulator tab).

evolves (due to model evolution, verification and validation). Thus, analysis is an organic activity that is seamlessly integrated with infrastructure model development, integrated model development, and verification and validation.

5.   Integrated Modeling Environment

The Integrated Modeling Environment (IME) facilitates system-of-systems analysis by enabling the horizontal fusion of infrastructure models. System-of-systems analysis seeks to explore and understand the collective behaviors of integrated systems. In the context of critical infrastructure protection, system-of-systems analysis may require the integration of separate models of, for example, the electric power, telecommunications, natural gas distribution and transportation infrastructures in a geographic region. Analysts may use the IME to conduct integrated, multi-model analyses using simulations to explore and understand the collective behaviors of the integrated models.

The primary interface for the analyst includes a multi-tab palette and a geo-visualization of a given region. The Analyst interface palette is presented in Figure 3. Included in this palette are three tabs. The first tab, "Objectives," enables analysts to specify desired and undesired effects aggregated under a named objective. An effect represents the disabling of a domain model element (infrastructure feature). Objectives may be specified from a red-team or blue-team perspective.

The second tab allows analysts to specify sequences of scheduled events (courses of action), where each event represents the enabling or disabling of an infrastructure feature at a specific time during the simulation.

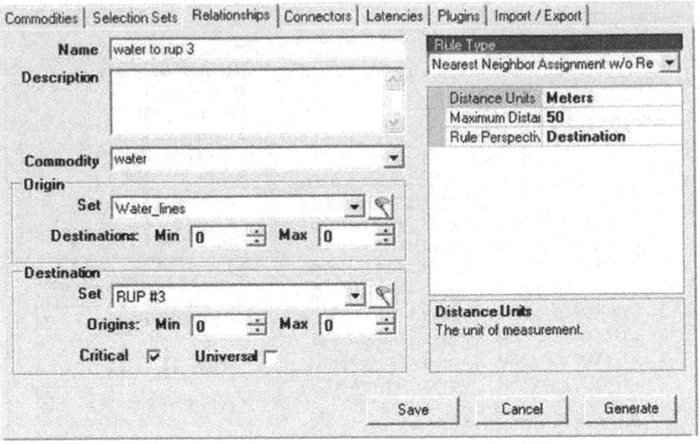

Figure 4.   Model Builder interface (Relationships tab).

The third tab, "Simulator," is visible in Figure 3. This tab allows analysts to select a course of action, specify a start time and initiate a simulation. As the simulation executes, the analyst sees on the left-hand side of this tab an event stream capturing infrastructure feature enable and disable events. Features are enabled/disabled as a function of individual infrastructure model behavior and as a function of the relations specified in the infrastructure context and behavior ontology. Each simulation event includes a timestamp. The right-hand side of the simulator tab contains a scorecard that aggregates simulation event stream data along various dimensions (e.g., time, infrastructure and feature type). Saved simulations are listed at the bottom of the tab. As the simulation executes, analysts can observe the effects in the geo-visualization. Dynamic changes in feature symbology reflect domain model state changes (i.e., enabling and disabling of features).

To conduct meaningful analysis, however, the context and behavior ontology must be specified. This activity is supported by a separate Model Builder interface palette. The palette includes, among other tabs, interfaces for specifying commodities, relationships, latencies and connectors. The "Relationships" tab (Figure 4) enables model builders to specify and manage the functional relations for domain models. The "Latencies" tab provides model builders with a means to manage the temporal relations that specify infrastructure feature enabling and disabling latencies. Finally, the "Connectors" tab provides model builders with a means to manage the participating infrastructure models. Several infrastructure models have been integrated into the IME via the connector framework (e.g., [4, 11]). In addition, the IME, by default, provides the aforementioned built-in models (utility, transport and channel networks).

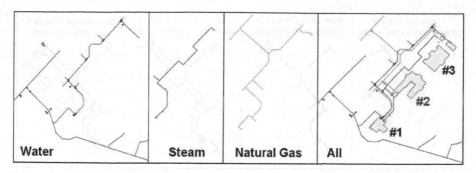

Figure 5. Example infrastructure models.

6.   Critical Infrastructure Analysis

This section presents an example application of our integration methodology. The example involves a small geographic region with several buildings and three critical infrastructures (natural gas, steam and water). Figure 5 presents each infrastructure and a layered view of all three infrastructures.

Table 1. Temporal relations.

Selection Set	Commodity	Effect	Duration
Steam Source	Steam	Disable	1.00:00:00 (d.h:m:s)

To support integrated modeling and simulation across the infrastructures, it is necessary to geo-code relevant infrastructure features to establish spatial context. Next, the commodities that are essential to operating the infrastructures are identified (steam, gas and water). The temporal latencies for infrastructure features are then specified to establish the temporal context. Table 1 lists the single temporal latency specification used in the example.

Table 2. Functional relations.

Origin	Commodity	Destination	Rule
Water Line	Water	Building #1	Nearest Neighbor
Building #1	Steam	Steam Source	Nearest Neighbor
Steam Line	Steam	Buildings #2 and #3	Nearest Neighbor
Gas Line	Gas	Building #1	Nearest Neighbor

Finally, the functional relations among the infrastructure features are specified. Table 2 presents the three functional relations used in the example.

During analysis, the Analyst interface (Figure 3) is used to specify objectives and courses of action, and to execute and explore simulations. In the exam-

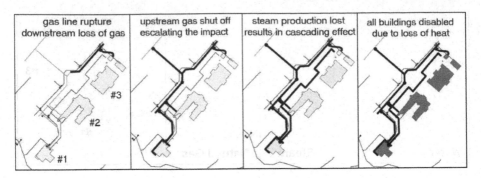

| gas line rupture downstream loss of gas | upstream gas shut off escalating the impact | steam production lost results in cascading effect | all buildings disabled due to loss of heat |

Figure 6. Example simulation (disabled features in bold).

ple, the objective is to maintain the operation of Buildings #2 and #3 (i.e., the analyst specifies an objective with the undesired effects of disabling these buildings). The course of action is initiated by a gas line fracture due to ongoing construction. Subsequent to the fracture, downstream gas is lost (Panel 1 in Figure 6). To contain the leak, a gas valve is closed one hour into the simulation as scheduled in the course of action. This results in the loss of the gas commodity to Building #1 (Panel 2). The loss of gas to Building #1 halts the production of steam (Panel 3). After twenty-four hours, Buildings #2 and #3 cannot function because they have no heat (Panel 4). The integrated modeling and simulation behavior demonstrated by the simulation is realized by the behaviors of the individual infrastructure models and the temporal, spatial and functional relations in the IME context and behavior ontology.

The simulations may be explored further, replayed and saved for subsequent analysis. Analysts may use the scorecard interface to examine the order of impact of simulation events and the plausible impact to each critical infrastructure. In addition, analysts can examine the event trace to understand and/or validate the event chain that lead to (un)desired effects. During the analysis, the ontology may be refined, e.g., by adding/deleting/modifying commodities, functional relations and/or temporal latencies, to explore "what-if" scenarios.

7.   Conclusions

The new methodology for critical infrastructure modeling and simulation emphasizes the engineering and behavioral properties of individual infrastructures and enables analyses to be conducted in functional, spatial and temporal context. The methodology effectively captures the complex, multi-dimensional characteristics of individual infrastructures and the dependencies between infrastructures, helping provide insights into potential disruptions that can increase the efficacy of protection plans and response and recovery operations.

The methodology, as realized in the IME, is being actively used to explore and analyze critical infrastructures for large-scale geographic regions (> 100,000 square km). An integrated model also has been developed for an urban region (> 500 square miles with a population exceeding 800,000); the critical infrastructures in the integrated model include electric power, natural gas distribution, water distribution, telecommunications and transportation. Other applications include a corporate IT infrastructure model for a Fortune 100 company that integrates models for hardware, software, business applications, business processes and business units; and an urban neighborhood model covering roughly 1,000 contiguous acres that serves a population of more than 20,000.

Evaluation of the methodology is a priority [17, 18]. Verification and validation are enabled by the methodology's adherence to the principle of transparency. All analysis enabled by the ontology is completely transparent to analysts; event traces can be explored and questioned by subject matter experts. The result is an ongoing interleaving of analysis with verification and validation, which improves the underlying ontology and the resulting analysis.

Current research is focusing on augmenting the methodology and its underlying framework to accommodate non-deterministic models and infrastructure degradation. In addition, efforts are underway to enhance the expressiveness of the IME ontology and the IME visualization facility, especially the ability to view multiple infrastructure models along their functional, spatial and temporal dimensions.

References

[1] E. Casalicchio, E. Galli and S. Tucci, Federated agent-based modeling and simulation approach to study interdependencies in IT critical infrastructures, *Proceedings of the Eleventh IEEE International Symposium on Distributed Simulation and Real-Time Applications*, pp. 182–189, 2007.

[2] A. Chaturvedi, A society of simulation approach to dynamic integration of simulations, *Proceedings of the Winter Simulation Conference*, pp. 2125–2131, 2006.

[3] D. Dudenhoeffer, M. Permann and M. Manic, CIMS: A framework for infrastructure interdependency modeling and analysis, *Proceedings of the Winter Simulation Conference*, pp. 478–485, 2006.

[4] ESRI, ArcGIS Network Analyst, Redlands, California (www.esri.com/soft ware/arcgis/extensions/networkanalyst/index.html).

[5] F. Flentge and U. Beyer, The ISE metamodel for critical infrastructures, in *Critical Infrastructure Protection*, E. Goetz and S. Shenoi (Eds.), Springer, Boston, Massachusetts, pp 323–336, 2007.

[6] O. Gursesli and A. Desrochers, Modeling infrastructure interdependencies using Petri nets, *Proceedings of the IEEE International Conference on Systems, Man and Cybernetics*, vol. 2, pp. 1506–1512, 2003.

[7] C. Lo and A. Yeung, *Concepts and Techniques of Geographic Information Systems*, Prentice Hall, Upper Saddle River, New Jersey, 2007.

[8] J. Locke, *An Essay Concerning Human Understanding* (books.google.com /books?id=cjYIAAAAQAAJ), 1690.

[9] J. Marti, J. Hollman, C. Ventura and J. Jatskevich, Design for survival: Real-time infrastructures coordination, presented at the *International Workshop on Complex Network and Infrastructure Protection*, 2006.

[10] P. Pederson, D. Dudenhoeffer, S. Hartley and M. Permann, Critical Infrastructure Interdependency Modeling: A Survey of U.S. and International Research, Report No. INL/EXT-06-11464, Critical Infrastructure Protection Division, Idaho National Laboratory, Idaho Falls, Idaho, 2006.

[11] PowerWorld Corporation, PowerWorld Simulator, Champaign, Illinois (www.powerworld.com/products/simulator.asp).

[12] S. Rinaldi, J. Peerenboom and T. Kelly, Identifying, understanding and analyzing critical infrastructure interdependencies, *IEEE Control Systems*, vol. 21(6), pp. 11–25, 2001.

[13] L. Suchman, *Plans and Situated Actions: The Problem of Human-Machine Communication*, Cambridge University Press, Cambridge, United Kingdom, 1987.

[14] N. Svendsen and S. Wolthusen, Multigraph dependency models for heterogeneous critical infrastructures, in *Critical Infrastructure Protection*, E. Goetz and S. Shenoi (Eds.), Springer, Boston, Massachusetts, pp 337–350, 2007.

[15] The White House, National Strategy for Homeland Security, Washington, DC (www.whitehouse.gov/homeland/book/nat_strat_hls.pdf), 2002.

[16] W. Tolone, D. Wilson, A. Raja, W. Xiang, H. Hao, S. Phelps and W. Johnson, Critical infrastructure integration modeling and simulation, *Proceedings of the Second Symposium on Intelligence and Security Informatics (LNCS 3073)*, Springer, Berlin-Heidelberg, Germany, pp. 214–225, 2004.

[17] A. Weeks, An Assessment of Validation Methods for Critical Infrastructure Protection Modeling and Simulation, M.A. Thesis, Department of Geography and Earth Sciences, University of North Carolina at Charlotte, Charlotte, North Carolina, 2006.

[18] A. Weeks, A. Schumpert, S. Lee, W. Tolone and W. Xiang, A new approach to verification and validation in CIP modeling and simulation, presented at the *Twenty-Sixth International ESRI User Conference*, 2006.

Chapter 20

USING 3D MODELS AND DISCRETE SIMULATIONS IN INFRASTRUCTURE SECURITY APPLICATIONS

Pierluigi Assogna, Glauco Bertocchi, Alberto Paoluzzi,
Michele Vicentino, Giorgio Scorzelli and Roberto Zollo

Abstract   Next generation systems for critical infrastructure protection must support capabilities such as behavior analysis, situation modeling and data mining integrated within sophisticated virtual or augmented reality interfaces. This paper describes the design goals and implementation of a platform for critical infrastructure security applications. The platform is designed to support semi-automated 3D modeling of infrastructures, 3D integration of sensor networks, situation modeling and visual simulation via 3D animation, and advanced situation analysis. Such a system would enable operators to recognize preliminary indications of crisis situations and promptly activate the appropriate countermeasures. It would also assist them in optimizing normal operations and conducting simulations for emergency planning and crisis management.

Keywords: Geometric modeling, simulation, infrastructure security

1.   Introduction

Visual presentations can offer excellent situation awareness for security applications. An advanced platform, providing a 3D geometric model of the system to be protected and facilities for event discovery, tracking and situation evaluation, is an ideal candidate. It could serve as point of reference for integrating vision, sensor, tracking and security systems designed for infrastructure protection. It would provide a reliable basis for high-level situation awareness and support coordinated and optimized decision making.

Critical transport infrastructures that straddle national borders, such as tunnels, bridges, railways hubs and airports, require a novel security approach. Their ability to address threats and react to crises relies on the strong coordination of operational activities. This is because security threats may arise

Please use the following format when citing this chapter:

Assogna, P., Bertocchi, G., Paoluzzi, A., Vicentino, M., Scorzelli, G. and Zollo, R., 2008, in IFIP International Federation for Information Processing, Volume 290; *Critical Infrastructure Protection II*, eds. Papa, M., Shenoi, S., (Boston: Springer), pp. 269–278.

not only from malicious attacks but also from natural events (storms, floods, earthquakes) and unexpected events (traffic congestion, accidents). Security should always be maintained and the systems should be able to deal with all the facets of the problem. For this reason, an advanced security system must be able to infer the consequences of events based on the information received and the inferences should be reliable even when some of the information is missing.

Virtual or augmented reality interfaces [14, 21] can be very useful. Consider, for example, a building on fire or a railroad during a storm, where video feeds are not available. An advanced security system could use virtual/augmented reality to reproduce the situation and support optimal decision making through modeling and simulation. However, existing security systems are typically clever assemblies of sensor subsystems with limited capabilities for assisting personnel during normal operations and crises. Moreover, they are not designed to be used when responsibility is shared between different organizations as in the case of transnational critical infrastructures.

This paper describes the development goals and implementation directions of a new platform for infrastructure security applications. The platform is intended to provide: (i) (mostly) automatic 3D modeling of infrastructures; (ii) 3D integration of sensor networks, including video surveillance; (iii) situation modeling though hierarchical event graphs annotated with actor models and behavior; (iv) visual simulation via 3D animation; (v) situation analysis based on the divergence of sensor feedback from evolving simulations; and (vi) weak signals of risky situations deduced by comparing the results of situation analysis with a knowledge base of past events and scenarios. This paper also discusses the use of geometric modeling and concurrent programming tools that support sophisticated modeling, simulation and analysis functionality.

2.   Awareness Paradigm

Current security systems are useful for providing alerts and alarms based on signals from sensor networks. However, they do not offer the high-level functionality needed to accomplish complex tasks such as: (i) identifying unusual and potentially dangerous or difficult circumstances, (ii) recognizing the weak signals of risky situations, (iii) promptly activating countermeasures, and (iv) assisting personnel in the optimized management of crises. An awareness platform with this functionality can be created by integrating:

- 3D geometric models of an infrastructure that are used as the basis for all information collected about the infrastructure.
- An interoperable knowledge framework that captures information about the infrastructure along with its behavior, events, users, resources, etc., which can be used as a basis for statistical and situational models.
- Pre-existing heterogeneous sensor and security systems.
- Virtual or augmented reality interfaces and advanced gaming techniques.

A critical infrastructure surveillance system cannot limit itself to a representation of what is happening; it should also provide tools for analyzing the patterns, rhythms and interplays of events, and for anticipating future impact. This enables automatic as well as human responses to be more effective and proactive. Software agents provide a useful abstraction for a security platform: the agents perform all the major activities (e.g., sensing the environment, acting on devices and alerting security personnel). In particular, we imagine a "holonic," multi-level organization of agents that maintain and use an awareness base represented by the integration of models and sensing, surveillance and control functions. Note that a "holon" [10] is a component of a system that can work autonomously even if detached from it, and that works well in cooperation with other holons. According to this vision, the security platform could represent the intelligence of the controlled infrastructure, almost like a living organism endowed with self-consciousness [10].

A security platform should enforce modeling capabilities to the maximal extent; this is because all the support provided would be grounded on model-based simulations. Permanent situation awareness would be achieved using techniques that model an infrastructure, simulate its normal behavior, acquire and track normal and abnormal events, understand the weak signals that indicate a crisis and react to them in an optimal manner. The ability to simulate events, actions and reactions would enable the security platform to maintain the critical infrastructure in a safe state. Operations personnel could interact with the platform, adding experience and judgment that cannot be coded or simulated.

To implement such a platform, we are employing a novel approach for symbolic situation modeling. The approach uses (machine- and human-readable) executable and combinable storyboards [2]. The implementation engages the Erlang concurrent programming language [1] integrated within an advanced 3D modeling environment based on the geometric language PLaSM [15] and augmented with gaming engines.

3.   Spatial Modeling

Howarth [9] has shown that spatial models play a key role when interpreting a dynamic, uncertain world for surveillance applications. We surveyed a number of works dealing with spatial models and their use in security applications. Based on this research, we selected the cellular decomposition of space as a foundation for supporting visual surveillance applications. We use the geometric language PlaSM to handle geometric information. Figure 1 presents the virtual model of a warehouse district produced using a few pages of PLaSM code. The runtime evaluation of submodels of buildings or portions of buildings produces the 3D scenes.

The design language PLaSM is a geometry-oriented extension of FL, a functional language developed by Backus' group at IBM [4]. Building on the paradigm proposed by Backus in his Turing Award Lecture [3], FL introduces an algebra over programs that provides several interesting features. In particular, existing programs are combined very elegantly to create new programs. Programs that are equivalent to and simpler than the original programs can be

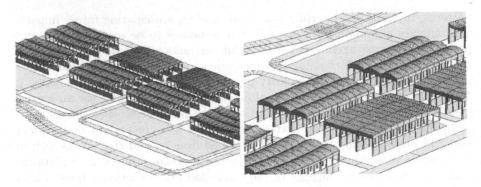

Figure 1. Virtual model of a commercial district.

created at design time or compilation time. Significant benefits in programming style and efficiency are achieved through the use of program prototyping.

Primitive objects in FL include characters, numbers, truth values and polyhedral complexes. A polyhedron is a quasi-disjoint union of polytopes (bounded convex sets). Expressions are either primitive objects, functions, applications or sequences. According to the FL semantics, arbitrary PLaSM scripts can be written using only three programming constructs:

- **Application:** The application `f:x` of function `f` to the value `x` of an input parameter (element of the function domain) produces an output value in the function codomain.

- **Composition:** The composition of functions `(f~g~h):x ≡ (f~g):` `(h:x) ≡ f:(g:(h:x))` produces the pipelined execution of their reversed sequence (Figure 2).

- **Construction:** The construction of a vector function `[f,g,h]` produces the parallel execution of its component functions `[f, g, h]:x ≡ <f:x,` `g:x, h:x>` (Figure 2).

4.   Model Generation

We capitalize on a novel parallel framework [6] for high-performance solid and geometric modeling that compiles the generating expression of a model into a dataflow network of concurrent threads, and splits the model into fragments that are distributed to computational nodes and generated independently. Progressive BSP trees are used for adaptive and parallelizable streaming dataflow evaluation of geometric expressions, and associated with polyhedral cells of hierarchical polyhedral complex (HPC) data structures used by the PLaSM language.

The security platform design makes strong use of spatial models produced by the cellular decomposition of structures (buildings, tracks, lanes, tunnels, bridges, etc.) from 2D plans. Figure 3(a) shows a 2D map of the Palatino Hill

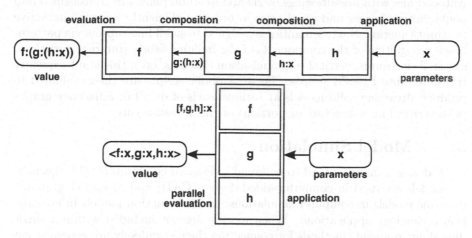

Figure 2. Main paradigms of the PLaSM language.

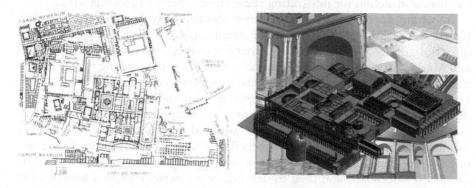

Figure 3. (a) Palatino Hill (2D map); (b) *Domus Augustana* (3D PLaSM image).

in Rome. Figure 3(b) presents the 3D PLaSM reconstruction of the emperor's palace (*Domus Augustana*), a site endowed with the strongest security system known in ancient times. Note the enhanced level of awareness provided by the 3D model compared with the 2D model.

We are currently working on the automatic generation of PLaSM models from line drawings in the Autocad format [2]. A geometric representation of an infrastructure or portion of an infrastructure, progressively generated at increasing levels of detail, will be produced at runtime by a streaming dataflow process.

The generation of models of complex buildings from plans is a difficult and largely unsolved inverse problem [11]. The difficulty of reconstructing 3D buildings from architectural plans is confirmed by the rarity of scientific literature on the topic (see, e.g., [9, 11]). However, a fast semi-automatic solution has been proposed by Paoluzzi and Scorzelli [17]. Their procedure is as follows. First,

Autocad files with line-drawings of 2D architectural plans are transformed into double interval trees and quad trees in order to efficiently answer interactive proximity queries. Next, semantics is assigned to small line subsets via pattern-based recognition of the components of the building fabric (internal partitions, external enclosures, vertical communication elements, etc); this is subsequently translated into PLaSM scripts. These symbolic scripts are then evaluated to produce streaming solid models at various levels of detail or adjacency graphs of the critical infrastructure or portions of the infrastructure.

5.   Model Simulation

Modeling techniques tend to be found in isolated communities [18]: geometric models are used in computer-aided design (CAD) and computer graphics; dynamic models in computer simulations; and information models in information technology applications. When models are not included within a single digital environment, methods for connecting them seamlessly are generally not established. One of the major challenges we faced in our research was to identify the best abstraction for integrating these three different modeling areas.

According to [13], discrete concurrent systems may be modeled and simulated using three paradigms: event graphs and PERT (event scheduling), bipartite graphs and Petri Nets (activity scanning), and finite-state systems and Markov chains (process interaction). Network programming techniques [5] may be used to animate complex simulations. Here, the behavior of each actor is described by a path in an activity network that codifies the storyboard as a directed acyclic graph and describes causal and temporal relationships between events. Each storyboard arc may be associated with a spline in the configuration space of the actor, which models fine behavior permitted by its degrees of freedom. This model is hierarchical, since each arc may be substituted by its (local) storyboard and used to decompose a macro event to a finer level of detail. Also, the parameters of the probability distributions of stochastic variables of interest (e.g., the most likely time or the lead/lag time of an event) may be computed. The depth of the event hierarchy may vary locally depending on the complexity of events and the degree of realism of a simulation [16].

Petri nets [20] may be used to mathematically describe the evolution of a concurrent system. This approach uses networks with two types of nodes (places and transitions) and arcs where several types of tokens may move within the network. The state of the modeled system is given by the distribution of tokens in places. The annotations of fine behavior are described by splines in configuration space, defined by discrete sets of points consisting of at least two known configurations (in the case of linear behavior). Petri nets may be hierarchical and timed. The hierarchical communicating and concurrent state machine (HCSM) framework may be used to plan the behavior of reactive synthetic agents in interactive simulation environments [7]. The HCSM framework is well suited to modeling the reactions of autonomous agents and directing them to produce the desired simulations.

6. Architectural Issues

The main architectural goal is to integrate advanced modeling, simulation, virtual or augmented reality, and gaming and tracking techniques in a centralized framework. The intent is to provide a platform where the tasks involved in securing a critical infrastructure can be evaluated and optimized, and where security personnel are provided with high-level decision-making tools, including interoperable tools for situation modeling and simulation.

6.1 Concurrent Programming

The implementation employs PLaSM for geometric programming and Erlang for simulation. Erlang [1] is a concurrent functional programming language and runtime system, which is characterized by strict evaluation, single assignment and dynamic typing. Strict, or eager evaluation, means that expressions are evaluated as soon as they are bound to variables and the values are subsequently recalled without evaluation. The language is purely functional, without the mutable state that is induced by multiple assignments. Thus, the code is easy to understand and facilitates correctness proofs. Dynamic typing means that type checking is performed at runtime.

Erlang adopts a mathematical model of computation that uses "actors" as universal primitives for concurrent computing [8]. The actor model has been used both as a theoretical framework for concurrency as well as the basis for several practical concurrent systems. An actor can make local decisions, create other actors, send and receive messages, and determine how to respond to messages. Data structures, functions, semaphores, monitors, ports, descriptions, logical formulas, numbers, identifiers, demons, processes, contexts and databases are all special cases of actors, whose behavior is described by message sending.

6.2 Event Processing

The platform is designed to use complex event processing (CEP) techniques implemented using Erlang. CEP integration will employ a state-of-the-art architecture for stream event processing in complex computer systems [12, 19]. Different events, combined with different behavior and environments, will elicit adequate responses from the platform so that, even when unattended, it can perform actions to avoid or minimize unwanted scenarios. Optimal control will be achieved, of course, by combining automatic responses with the experience and judgment of experts.

This approach to security awareness, providing sensor fusion as well as event discovery, registration and interpretation, will make strong use of spatial models. As discussed earlier, these models are produced as cellular decompositions of structures generated from PLaSM representations created semiautomatically from 2D line drawings.

The platform will employ advanced techniques for interactive visualization of, and user interaction with, real-time and recorded surveillance data. Research results in the areas of visual perception, 3D interactive computer graphics, virtual reality and gaming will be incorporated. State-of-the-art techniques for 3D navigation and spatial montage of streaming sensor data will be implemented to produce a task-specific interface optimized for situational awareness.

6.3   Management Support

The platform will provide support for workforce management, especially in the case of crises that require significant manual intervention. The tasks to be supported will range from routine camera surveillance by operators to *ad hoc* crisis management by decision makers. Different types of users will be able to access and interact with relevant information provided by the underlying databases and (generated) knowledge.

Flexible, task-specific user interfaces will support the collection, retrieval and presentation of information. A set of guidelines and components for implementing highly effective, task-specific user interfaces will be developed. These interfaces will enable automated (software-agent-based) actions as well as human actions directed from an operations control center. In particular, the interfaces will provide semantically-rich support based on the "newspaper," "agenda," "map," "telephone" and "television" metaphors.

7.   Conclusions

Securing critical infrastructures requires sophisticated systems that provide capabilities such as behavior analysis, situation modeling and data mining integrated within virtual or augmented reality interfaces. Our advanced situational awareness system is designed to support semi-automated 3D modeling of infrastructures, 3D integration of sensor networks, situation modeling and visual simulation via 3D animation, and advanced situation analysis. In addition to offering sophisticated functionality, the system is designed to be highly scalable to handle large, complex infrastructures. Our paradigmatic reference for awareness, simulation and control of normal and abnormal situations is applicable to operation planning, security enforcement, crisis management and training. It can also be used within product lifecycle management platforms in aerospace, automotive and manufacturing industries, where geometric information is central to collaborative activities ranging from production to marketing.

References

[1] J. Armstrong, *Programming Erlang: Software for a Concurrent World*, Pragmatic Bookshelf, Raleigh, North Carolina, 2007.

[2] P. Assogna, G. Bertocchi, A. Paoluzzi, G. Scorzelli and R. Zollo, From 2D plans to 3D building models for security modeling of critical infrastructures, to appear in *International Journal of Shape Modeling*, 2008.

[3] J. Backus, Can programming be liberated from the von Neumann style? A functional style and its algebra of programs, *Communications of the ACM*, vol. 21(8), pp. 613–641, 1978.

[4] J. Backus, J. Williams and E. Wimmers, An introduction to the programming language FL, in *Research Topics in Functional Programming*, D. Turner (Ed.), Addison-Wesley Longman, Boston, Massachusetts, pp. 219–247, 1990.

[5] C. Bajaj, C. Baldazzi, S. Cutchin, A. Paoluzzi, V. Pascucci and M. Vicentino, A programming approach for complex animations (Part I: Methodology), *Computer-Aided Design*, vol. 31(11), pp. 695–710, 1999.

[6] C. Bajaj, A. Paoluzzi and G. Scorzelli, Progressive conversion from B-rep to BSP for streaming geometric modeling, *Computer-Aided Design and Applications*, vol. 3(5), pp. 577–586, 2006.

[7] J. Cremer, J. Kearney and Y. Papelis, HCSM: A framework for behavior and scenario control in virtual environments, *ACM Transactions on Modeling and Computer Simulation*, vol. 5(3), pp. 242–267, 1995.

[8] C. Hewitt, P. Bishop, I. Greif, B. Smith, T. Matson and R. Steiger, Actor induction and meta-evaluation, *Proceedings of the First Annual ACM SIGACT-SIGPLAN Symposium on Principles of Programming Languages*, pp. 153–168, 1973.

[9] R. Howarth, Spatial models for wide-area visual surveillance: Computational approaches and spatial building-blocks, *Artificial Intelligence Review*, vol. 23(2), pp. 97–155, 2005.

[10] A. Koestler, *The Ghost in the Machine*, Arkana, London, United Kingdom, 1967.

[11] R. Lewis and C. Sequin, Generation of 3D building models from 2D architectural plans, *Computer-Aided Design*, vol. 30(10), pp. 765–779, 1998.

[12] D. Luckham and B. Frasca, Complex Event Processing in Distributed Systems, Technical Report CSL-TR-98-754, Computer Systems Laboratory, Stanford University, Palo Alto, California, 1998.

[13] J. Miller, G. Baramidze, A. Sheth and P. Fishwick, Investigating ontologies for simulation modeling, *Proceedings of the Thirty-Seventh Annual Symposium on Simulation*, pp. 55–63, 2004.

[14] R. Ott, M. Gutierrez, D. Thalmann and F. Vexo, Advanced virtual reality technologies for surveillance and security applications, *Proceedings of the ACM International Conference on Virtual Reality Continuum and its Applications*, pp. 163–170, 2006.

[15] A. Paoluzzi, *Geometric Programming for Computer-Aided Design*, John Wiley and Sons, Chichester, United Kingdom, 2003.

[16] A. Paoluzzi and A. D'Ambrogio, A programming approach for complex animations (Part II: Reconstruction of a real disaster), *Computer-Aided Design*, vol. 31(11), pp. 711–732, 1999.

[17] A. Paoluzzi and G. Scorzelli, Pattern-driven mapping from architectural plans to solid models of buildings, presented at the *Israel-Italy Bi-National Conference on Shape Modeling and Reasoning for Industrial and Biomedical Applications*, 2007.

[18] M. Park and P. Fishwick, Integrating dynamic and geometry model components through ontology-based inference, *Simulation*, vol. 81(12), pp. 795–813, 2005.

[19] L. Perrochon, W. Mann, S. Kasriel and D. Luckham, Event mining with event processing networks, *Proceedings of the Third Pacific-Asia Conference on Knowledge Discovery and Data Mining*, pp. 474–478, 1999.

[20] J. Peterson, Petri nets, *ACM Computing Surveys*, vol. 9(3), pp. 223–252, 1977.

[21] I. Sebe, J. Hu, S. You and U. Neumann, 3D video surveillance with augmented virtual environments, *Proceedings of the First ACM SIGMM International Workshop on Video Surveillance*, pp. 107–112, 2003.